SOUND FORGE 6
POWER!

Scott R. Garrigus

Sound Forge 6 Power!

Copyright ©2002 Muska & Lipman Publishing, a division of Course Technology

Credits: Senior Editor, Mark Garvey; Production Editor, Rodney A. Wilson; Copyeditor, Karen Annett; Technical Editors, Caleb Pourchot, Sonic Foundry; Cover Design and Interior Design and Layout, Chad Planner, Pop Design Works; Indexer, Kevin Broccoli, Broccoli Information Management.

Publisher: Andy Shafran

MUSKA&LIPMAN

Library of Congress Catalog Number 2002112021

ISBN 1-929685-64-5

5 4 3 2 1

Muska & Lipman Publishing
2645 Erie Avenue, Suite 41
Cincinnati, Ohio 45208
www.muskalipman.com
publisher@muskalipman.com

About the Author

www.garrigus.com

Scott R. Garrigus has been involved with music and computers since he was 12 years old. After graduating from high school, he went on to earn a B.A. in music performance with an emphasis in sound recording technology at UMass, Lowell. In 1993, he released his first instrumental album on cassette, entitled Pieces Of Imagination. In 1995, he began his professional writing career when his first article appeared in Electronic Musician magazine. In 2000, he authored his first book, *Cakewalk Power!* This was the first book to deal exclusively with the Cakewalk Pro Audio, Guitar Studio, and Home Studio software applications. In 2001, his second book, *Sound Forge Power!*, which was the first book to deal exclusively with Sonic Foundry's Sound Forge audio editing software, was published. Also in 2001, his third book, *Sonar Power!*, which was the first book to deal exclusively with Cakewalk's Sonar software, was published. Today, Garrigus continues to contribute articles to Electronic Musician, in addition to a number of other print and online publications. He also publishes his own music technology e-zine, called DigiFreq (**www.digifreq.com**), which provides free news, reviews, tips, and techniques for music technology users.

Dedications

To Mom, Dad, Babci, Dziadzi, Grandma, Grandpa, Mark, and Steve. Thanks for all your love and support. And to Ron, Claire, Ellie, Vinny, and Ron Jr. for being there and making me feel like a part of your family. Also, to my cat, Figaro, who recently turned 16 years old.

Acknowledgements

Thanks to all my music technology friends who take the time to visit my Web site and to read my ramblings in the DigiFreq newsletter each month. The DigiFreq family is now over 9,000 strong!

Thanks to all the Sound Forge users who's dedication and support helped to make this book possible.

Thanks to all my friends over at Sonic Foundry (Dave Chaimson, Caleb Pourchot, Rob Uhrina, and others).

Thanks also to the Muska & Lipman publishing team.

And as ever, thank you, God for everything.

Contents

7 Editing Basics 123

8 Exploring the Processing Functions 141

Introduction

This is the first book on the market that deals exclusively with Sonic Foundry's Sound Forge 6. You can find plenty of generic books about using computers to create and record music that may provide a small amount of information about Sound Forge 6, but none of them provide complete coverage of the product. Of course, Sound Forge 6 comes with an excellent manual in electronic format on its CD-ROM, but like most other manuals, it is meant only as a feature guide.

Instead of just describing the features of the program and how they work, I'm going to dig deep down into the software and show you exactly how to use the product with step-by-step examples and exercises that will help make your audio editing sessions run more smoothly. I explain all of the features available, and I do it in a manner you can understand and use, right away. Sound Forge Studio users will be interested to know that all the functions found in that program can be found in Sound Forge 6 as well. Therefore, this book is of use to you, too.

So why should you listen to me? Well, I've been using Sound Forge for many years. I've already written one Sound Forge-related book before this one—Sound Forge Power! I've also written about Sound Forge and other Sonic Foundry products in numerous review articles for magazines, such as Electronic Musician, Keyboard, and Recording. In addition, I've been working with the people at Sonic Foundry for quite some time now, learning all there is to know about Sound Forge 6, as well as testing the product during the beta process. And the people at Sonic Foundry have helped me develop much of the information in this book, making sure that everything is "officially" technically accurate. How's that for a seal of approval? Suffice it to say, I know my way around the product, and now I want to share that knowledge with you.

I'm going to assume that Sound Forge 6 is installed on your computer and that you know how to start the program. In addition, you should have at least skimmed through the manual that comes with the software and have all your external audio and MIDI gear set up already. I'm also going to assume that you know how to use your mouse for clicking, dragging, double-clicking, right-clicking, and so on. You should also know how to work with basic Windows features, such as Windows Explorer and the Control Panel. And you should have access to the World Wide Web, or perhaps a friend who does. Otherwise, all you need is a strong interest in learning how to get the most out of Sound Forge 6. Just leave the rest up to me, and I promise that you'll be working with Sound Forge 6 like you never have before. You might even have some fun with it, too.

How This Book is Organized

You'll find that although I've tried to avoid overlapping content between this book and the manual that comes with Sound Forge, in some instances, this overlap just can't be avoided. I wanted to be sure to help you understand all the important features of the program, and doing so means including some basic explanations to begin with. For the most part, though, the information included in this book is more "how-to" rather than "this feature does so-and-so."

Chapter 1, "MIDI and Digital Audio Basics," and Chapter 2, "Getting Started with Sound Forge," provide an introduction to computer music and the software. These chapters explain the importance of registration and how to find help, as well as the major features and more obscure parts of the software and how they work together. You also find a brief description of the differences between Sound Forge 6 and Sound Forge Studio.

Chapter 3, "Customizing Sound Forge," shows you how to make Sound Forge work the way you want it to. This chapter explains program preferences and workspace customization, as well as how to find the optimal settings for MIDI and audio functionality.

In Chapter 4, "Working with Audio Files," you learn how to work with audio files. This chapter includes step-by-step instructions for opening, closing, and saving existing audio files. You also learn how to create new audio files and the ideal formats to use.

Chapter 5, "Getting Around in Sound Forge," and Chapter 6, "Recording and Playback," describe how to navigate within Sound Forge and how to record and play back your audio files. You'll find instructions on how to record and play audio, and you learn about synchronizing Sound Forge via SMPTE. I explain the importance of the Current Position Cursor and show you how to use the Transport menu, Go To, and Markers, as well as the Zoom features. After you read these chapters, you'll be "steering" Sound Forge like a pro.

In Chapter 7, "Editing Basics," and Chapter 8, "Exploring the Processing Functions," you're ready to dive into editing. First, I explain the basics to you, including the Data Window, Edit menu, and Edit tool. Then, you can investigate the processing tools in more detail.

Chapter 9, "Exploring Effects," explains one of my favorite parts of Sound Forge: Effects. The things you can do with these tools are amazing. I cover all of the Effects functions, and show you how to use them the proper way. I even share some cool presets I've developed, so you can use them in your own audio editing sessions.

Chapter 10, "Additional Audio Tools," takes a look at all of the "extras" that come with Sound Forge. These include functions such as audio spectrum analysis, audio data statistics, and even some basic sound synthesis. Many of these functions come in handy in a variety of situations.

For those of you interested in creating audio for multimedia and the Internet, Chapter 11, "Producing for Multimedia and the Web," shows you how to use Sound Forge to add audio to video and also how to export your audio files in the various formats developed specifically for distribution on the Internet, including RealAudio, Windows Media, and MP3.

Finally, Chapter 12, "Using Sound Forge with MIDI," and Chapter 13, "Sound Forge and Sampling," jump into some of the more complicated features that Sound Forge offers. These features include triggering audio files via MIDI, using the Virtual MIDI Router, and how to create and edit your own sample loops.

My hope is that, by reading this book, you will learn how to master Sound Forge 6. And, along the way, if you have a little fun while you're at it, that's all the better.

Conventions Used in This Book

As you begin to read, you'll see that most of the information in this book is solid and useful. It contains very little fluff. I won't bore you with unrelated anecdotes or repetitious data. But to help guide you through all this material, I'll use several different conventions that highlight specific types of information that you should keep an eye out for.

TIP

Tips are extra information that you should know related to the current topic being discussed and, in some cases, include personal experiences and/or specific techniques not covered elsewhere.

CAUTION

Cautions highlight actions or commands that can make irreversible changes to your files or potentially cause problems in the future. Read them carefully because they may contain important information that can make the difference between keeping your files, software, and hardware safe, and you from losing a huge amount of work.

NOTE

Of course, sometimes you might like to know, but don't necessarily need to know, certain points about the current topic. Notes provide additional material to help you avoid problems or shed light on a feature or technology, and they also offer related advice.

1

MIDI and Digital Audio Basics

If you're anything like me, you want to get started right away learning all about Sound Forge. But if you don't understand the basic concepts and terms associated with computer music, you might have a hard time working your way through this book. So, just to give you a quick overview of the most significant aspects of music technology, this chapter will do the following:

▶ Define MIDI and explain how it works

▶ Define digital audio and explain how it works

▶ Explain the difference between MIDI and digital audio

Of course, this one chapter can't replace an entire book about the subject. If you want to learn more about MIDI and digital audio, plenty of extended resources are available. For example, there is an e-book called the Desktop Music Handbook available for free reading on the Web. You can find it at http://www.cakewalk.com/Tips/Desktop.htm.

What Is MIDI?

MIDI (which stands for Musical Instrument Digital Interface) is a special kind of computer language that lets electronic musical instruments (such as synthesizer keyboards) "talk" to computers. It works like this: Suppose you use a synthesizer keyboard as your musical instrument. Every key on the keyboard of your synthesizer has a corresponding electronic switch. When you press a key, its corresponding switch is activated and sends a signal to the computer chip inside your keyboard. The chip then sends the signal to the MIDI interface in your keyboard, which translates the signal into MIDI messages and sends those messages to the MIDI interface in your computer system.

NOTE

A MIDI interface is a device that is plugged into your computer allowing it to understand the MIDI language. Basically, you can think of the interface as a translator. When your electronic musical instrument sends out MIDI messages to your computer, the MIDI interface takes those messages and converts them into signals that your computer can understand.

The MIDI messages contain information telling your computer that a key was pressed (called a Note On message), which key it was (the name of the note represented by a number), along with how hard you pressed the key (called the MIDI velocity). For example, if you press Middle C on your keyboard, a Note On message is sent to your computer telling it that you pressed a key. Another message containing the number 60 is sent telling the computer that you pressed Middle C. And a final message is sent containing a number from 1 to 127 (1 being very soft and 127 being very loud), which tells your computer how hard you pressed the key.

Different MIDI messages represent all the performance controls on your keyboard. In addition to each key, MIDI messages represent the modulation wheel, pitch bend wheel, and other features. Your computer can store all the MIDI messages that are sent to it as you play your keyboard. The timing of your performance (how long it takes you to press one key after another and how long you hold down each key) can be stored as well. Your computer can then send those MIDI messages back to your keyboard with the same timing, so that it seems like you are playing the music, but without touching the keys. The basic concept goes like this: You play a piece of music on your keyboard. Your performance is stored as instructions in your computer. Then, those instructions are sent back to your keyboard from the computer, and you hear the piece of music played back exactly the same way you performed it, mistakes and all (see Figure 1.1).

Figure 1.1
This diagram shows how MIDI messages are recorded and played back with a computer

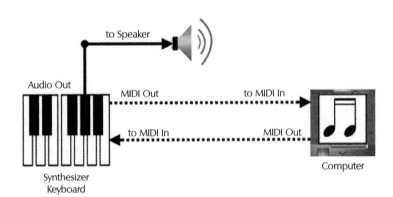

What Is Digital Audio?

Digital audio is the representation of sound as numbers. Recording sound as digital audio is similar to recording sound using a tape recorder, but slightly different. Let's say you have a microphone connected to your computer system. When you make a sound (such as singing a tune, playing a musical instrument, or even simply clapping your hands), the microphone "hears" it and converts the sound into an electronic signal. The microphone then sends the signal to the sound card in your computer, which translates the signal into numbers. These numbers are called samples.

NOTE

A sound card is a device that is plugged into your computer allowing it to understand the electronic signals of any audio device. Basically, you can think of the sound card as a translator. When an audio device (such as a microphone, electronic musical instrument, CD player, or anything else that can output an audio signal) sends out signals to your computer, the sound card takes those signals and converts them into numbers that your computer can understand.

The samples contain information telling your computer how the recorded signal sounded at certain instants in time. The more samples used to represent the signal, the better the quality of the recorded sound. For example, to make a digital audio recording that has the same quality as audio on a CD, the computer needs to receive 44,100 samples for every second of sound that's recorded. The number of samples received per second is called the sampling rate.

The size of each individual sample also makes a difference in the quality of the recorded sound. This size is called the bit depth. The more bits used to represent a sample, the better the sound quality. For example, to make a digital audio recording with the same quality as audio on a CD, each sample has to be 16 bits in size.

NOTE

Computers use binary numerals to represent numbers. These binary numerals are called bits, and each bit can represent one of two numbers: 1 or 0. By combining more than one bit, computers can represent larger numbers. For instance, any number from 0 to 255 can be represented with 8 bits. With 16 bits, the range becomes 0 to 65,535.

Your computer can store all the samples that are sent to it. The timing of each sample is stored as well. Your computer can then send those samples back to the sound card with the same timing so that what you hear sounds exactly the same as what was recorded. The basic concept goes like this: Your sound card records an electronic signal from an audio device (such as a microphone or CD player). The sound card converts the signal into numbers called samples, which are stored in your computer. Then, those samples are sent back to the sound card, which converts them back into an electronic signal. The signal is sent to your speakers (or other audio device), and you hear the sound exactly as it was recorded (see Figure 1.2).

Figure 1.2
This diagram shows how audio is converted into numbers so that it can be recorded and played back with a computer

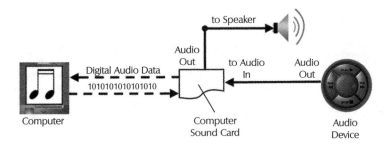

So, What's Really the Difference?

After reading the explanations of MIDI and digital audio, you might still be wondering what the difference is between them. Both processes involve signals being sent to the computer to be recorded and then the computer sending those signals back out to be played, right? Well, the point that you must keep in mind is that, when you're recording MIDI data, you're not recording actual sound. You are recording only performance instructions. This concept is similar to a musician reading sheet music, with the sheet music representing MIDI data and the musician representing a computer. The musician (or computer) reads the sheet music (or MIDI data) and then stores it in memory. The musician then plays the music back via a musical instrument. Now, what if the musician uses a different instrument to play back the music? The musical performance remains the same, but the sound changes. The same thing happens with MIDI data. A synthesizer keyboard can make all kinds of different sounds, but playing the same MIDI data back with the keyboard yields the exact same performance, no matter what.

When you're recording digital audio, you are recording actual sound. If you record a musical performance as digital audio, you cannot change the sound of that performance, as described earlier. And because of these differences, MIDI and digital audio have their advantages and disadvantages. Because MIDI is recorded as performance data and not actual sound, you can manipulate it much more easily than you can manipulate digital audio. For example, you can easily fix mistakes in your performance by simply changing the pitch of a note. And MIDI data can be translated into standard musical notation. Digital audio can't. On the other hand, MIDI can't be used to record anything that requires actual audio, such as sound effects or vocals. With digital audio, you can record any kind of sound whatsoever. And you can always be sure that your recording will sound exactly the same every time you play it back. With MIDI, you can't be sure of that because, although the MIDI data remains the same, the playback device or sound can be changed.

I hope that this description clears up some of the confusion you may have about MIDI and digital audio. You need to be familiar with a number of other related terms, but I will cover them in different areas of the book as I go along. For now, as long as you understand the difference between MIDI and digital audio, I can begin talking about the real reason you bought this book—how to use Sound Forge.

2

Getting Started with Sound Forge

Now that you have a basic understanding of the technology involved with MIDI and digital audio, I think you'll find it easier to grasp the functionality provided by Sound Forge. Ready to get started? This chapter will do the following:

▶ Tell you how to obtain the latest product updates

▶ Give you a quick overview of Sound Forge's features

▶ Briefly cover the new features in Sound Forge 6

▶ Describe a basic studio environment

▶ Let you know where to look for help, if problems arise

What Version of Sound Forge Do You Have?

Even though you're using Sound Forge 6, it still may not be the latest version. Sonic Foundry is constantly fixing and improving the software. Any problems that you may experience might easily be remedied with an update. To find out exactly what version you're using, start Sound Forge, and click Help > About Sound Forge. A dialog box similar to Figure 2.1 appears, displaying your exact version number. You should then check to see whether a more recent update is available.

Figure 2.1
The About Sonic Foundry Sound Forge dialog box shows the program's current version number

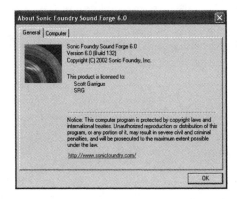

Get the Latest Product Update

Although automatically receiving new product updates would be nice, most companies (except maybe Microsoft) can't afford to send out CDs to all their users every time they create updates. That's one of the reasons the Internet has become such a wonderful tool. Sometimes, the answer to your problem is just a download away. Sonic Foundry provides a support area on its Web site where you can get the latest updates for Sound Forge. Just follow these steps to get the updates:

1. Log on to the Internet, start Sound Forge, and choose Help > Sonic Foundry On The Web > Latest Sound Forge Updates. This opens your Web browser and takes you to Sonic Foundry's Downloads page, as shown in Figure 2.2.

Figure 2.2
You can download updates from the Sonic Foundry Downloads page

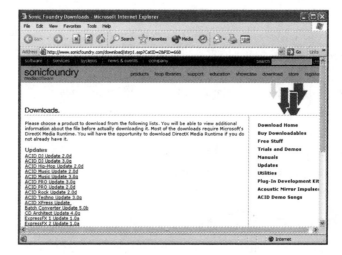

2. From the list of available updates, select the product in which you're interested.

3. Click the appropriate download link. Type in your name and e-mail address on the next page that appears. This takes you to the final page, from which you can download the update.

4. Create a temporary folder on your Windows desktop, and download the update file to that folder.

5. Run the file, and your software is upgraded. That's all there is to upgrading.

NOTE

Think you've found a bug? Just because a software product is released to the public doesn't mean it's perfect. Improvements are always being made. That's why updates become available. If you have a problem with Sound Forge on a regular basis, and you can reproduce that problem by performing the same steps each time, you may have found a bug in the software. Before you go spreading any rumors, first tell a friend about it, and see whether he or she can reproduce the problem on his or her computer system. If so, then you should drop an e-mail to Sonic Foundry by filling out the form on the following Web page: http://www.sonicfoundry.com/support/supportmail.asp, and let the people there know about the problem. The staff may already be aware of the bug and be working on a fix for it. But then again, they may not, and although your diligence won't make you famous, you'll feel good to know that you may have saved your fellow Sound Forge users a lot of frustration.

A Quick Tour of Sound Forge

Because Sound Forge is such a powerful application, you can use it for a variety of different tasks. They include audio editing and mastering, developing sound effects and sample loops, producing compact discs, creating audio for the World Wide Web, and even postproduction for films and videos. Sound Forge provides a number of features to support all these endeavors, and more. And when used in conjunction with your favorite digital audio sequencing software, Sound Forge provides you with all the power you need to produce recordings just like the professional sound studios do. However you decide to use Sound Forge, you'll find plenty of flexibility and functionality in the tools provided.

Audio Files

Because Sound Forge is an audio editing application, it doesn't provide a proprietary file format in which to store data. The reason for this is because audio data can be stored in a variety of file formats. The two most popular are WAV (on the Windows platform) and AIFF (on the Macintosh platform). These formats are so popular that they have pretty much become standard, but there are many other file formats floating around out there that provide different advantages and characteristics as compared to WAV and AIFF. Some of these include MP3, Windows Media, and RealAudio. In all, Sound Forge is able to load and save over thirteen different formats, and that's not including the ACM formats. I talk more about file formats in Chapter 4.

Workspace

To allow you to work with audio files, Sound Forge provides the Workspace. This is the main area of the program that holds the Data Windows (which I'll talk about in a moment) for each of the open audio files. Sound Forge allows you to have more than one audio file open at once (see Figure 2.3).

CHAPTER 2

Figure 2.3
The Workspace is the
main area used to work
with audio files in
Sound Forge

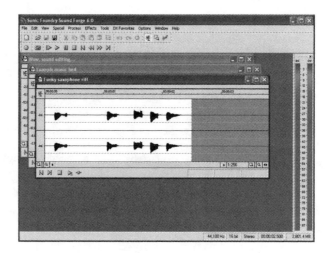

You can save and load the layout of the Workspace in special Workspace files, which provide a quick and easy way for you to set up Sound Forge for each of your different projects. I talk more about the Workspace in Chapter 3.

Workspaces only save the files that are open, not the layout of other windows like the meters.

Data Window

When you open an audio file in Sound Forge, its data is displayed in a Data Window. If you open more than one file at a time, each file is shown in its own Data Window. While working with an audio file, you see the sound waves representing the data in that file; see an example in Figure 2.4.

Figure 2.4
Each audio file opened
in Sound Forge is
displayed in a Data
Window

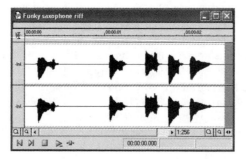

Not only does a Data Window allow you to see the audio data in a file, but you can also edit and process the data. In addition, you can add effects. I talk a lot more about Data Windows and how to use them throughout the book.

Menus

All of the editing, processing, and effects features that Sound Forge provides can be accessed from its drop-down menus. The ones that you will probably use the most are the Special, Process, Effects, and Tools menus (see Figure 2.5).

And the new DX Favorites, maybe.

Figure 2.5
All of the features in Sound Forge can be accessed via drop-down menus

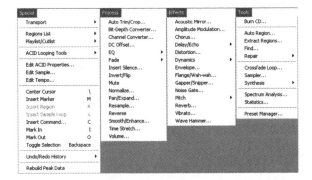

Each menu represents a different group of features. The Special menu represents most of the navigation, recording, and playback features. The Process menu represents the audio processing features, such as equalization and amplitude manipulation. The Effects menu represents the effects features (as its name implies). And the Tools menu provides additional features that don't fall into the aforementioned categories, such as Spectrum Analysis. I talk more about all of the audio processing features in Chapters 8, 9, and 10.

Record Dialog Box

In addition to loading and saving existing audio files, you can also use Sound Forge to create and record new files. For recording audio, Sound Forge provides the Record dialog box (see Figure 2.6).

Figure 2.6
You can record new audio files in Sound Forge using the Record dialog box

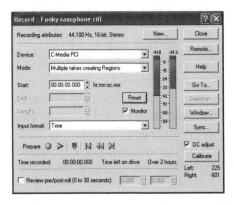

CHAPTER 2

Sound Forge allows you to record audio using bit depths of up to 64, and a variety of sampling rates from 8 Hz to 192 KHz. The Record dialog box provides its own set of input meters, and it even provides MTC/SMPTE synchronization. I talk more about recording audio with Sound Forge in Chapter 6.

Spectrum Analysis

One of the more advanced features provided by Sound Forge is Spectrum Analysis. Even though the Spectrum Analysis feature may seem complicated, it really isn't that difficult to use. It's definitely worth taking the extra effort to learn how it works. In basic terms, the Spectrum Analysis feature allows you to examine your audio data via special graphs that display the amplitude and frequency content found in the data. This allows you to process your data and actually "see" the effect of the processing. This feature has quite a bit of power, so I talk a lot more about it in Chapter 10.

What's New in Sound Forge 6?

Sound Forge 6 introduces a number of changes and new features, many of which were suggested by users. These features include the following:

▶ Nondestructive Editing and Multitask Background Processing. You can now copy, cut, delete, and paste audio data nondestructively. Changes to your audio file are now only performed when you save the file. In addition, while one audio file is being processed in the background, you can work on another file without having to wait for the processing to finish. I explain more in Chapter 7.

▶ Updated Audio Plug-In Chainer. You can now select, edit, and process your audio data while keeping the Audio Plug-In Chainer open. This provides much more flexibility than the previous version. I go into detail in Chapter 9.

▶ Plug-In Manager. You can use the Manager to manage and organize the DirectX plug-ins installed on your system. The Manager provides a new window that gives you a Windows Explorer-style view of your DirectX audio plug-ins and plug-in chains. I tell you more about this in Chapter 9.

▶ DX Favorites Menu. You can now group and access all of your favorite DirectX plug-ins in one place. I show you how to use this feature in Chapter 9.

▶ New Customization Features. You can now take advantage of the new tabbed docking windows, customizable toolbars, and a new Play Device toolbar. I talk more about these features in Chapter 3.

▶ Additional File Support. Sound Forge 6 can now handle files larger than 4 GB and load or save QuickTime, MPEG-1 and 2, and Windows Media video files. See Chapter 4 for more information.

▶ Updated Preset Manager. You can now back up, transfer, and delete user-defined presets for Sound Forge, ACID, and Vegas all from the same Preset Manager application. I show you how in Chapter 8.

▶ Enhanced Zoom Functions. You can now zoom in on your audio data using a ratio of 24:1 (24 pixels = 1 sample) for very precise editing, and you can save custom zoom settings for quick and easy observation of your audio data. I show you how in Chapter 7.

▶ Improved Video Features. You can use a number of new video features that help you work with video files in Sound Forge. Some of these include new video file properties, frame numbering options, rendering preferences, and new Video Preview window options. More details can be found in Chapters 4 and 11.

A Basic Studio Setup

Over the years, I've built up quite an arsenal of tools that currently reside in my home studio. But you don't need a ton of gizmos and gadgets to produce great music. If I were to scale down my setup to include only the basics, I'd be left with everything needed to compose and record my tunes.

Computer

Other than Sound Forge and additional music software, a basic studio revolves around one main component, your PC. If you already have a PC, be sure to check it against Sonic Foundry's system requirements for Sound Forge.

NOTE
Sonic Foundry's system requirements for Sound Forge are as follows:

System requirements:

200 MHz Processor

Windows-compatible sound card

CD-ROM drive (for installation only)

Supported CD-R drive (for CD burning only)

24-bit color display

32 MB RAM

25 MB hard disk space for program installation

Microsoft Windows 98SE, Me, 2000, or XP

DirectX 8.0 or later (included on CD-ROM)

Internet Explorer 4.0 or later (Version 5.0 included on CD-ROM)

If your system matches (or exceeds) the system requirements, then you should be all set to run Sound Forge. If not, then you should seriously consider either upgrading or purchasing a brand-new system. If you decide to go with a new system, you might want to think about building it yourself or picking out the components and having it built for you. It's not that a generic Gateway or Dell PC won't do, but they are not really optimized for audio work, which is the main reason I decided to put my own system together. I cheated a little, though, and had a company called Aberdeen, Inc. (www.aberdeeninc.com) build the base system for me. The components I selected for my current system are as follows:

- ▶ ABIT BE6-II Pentium III ATX motherboard
- ▶ Intel Pentium III processor 700 MHz w/256 K L2
- ▶ Pentium III heatsink with cooling fan
- ▶ 384 MEG SDRAM 168-pin DIMM PC100 memory
- ▶ Promise Ultra66 PCI IDE Controller
- ▶ Teac 3.5 1.44 MB floppy drive
- ▶ 2 WD Expert WD205BA hard drives 20.5 GB 9ms 7200rpm Ultra/66
- ▶ Addtronics Super Tower ATX 8x5.25 / 3x3.5 300W ATX
- ▶ Creative Encore 6X PC-DVD drive
- ▶ Ricoh MP7060A CD-RW drive
- ▶ Diamond Stealth III S540 video card

Of course, by today's standards, my PC is a bit outdated, but you don't need a top-of-the-line system to get good performance. This computer serves me very well, and when it comes time to get a new one, I'll continue to use this system for other tasks like dedicated software synth playback, and so on. But, if you have the money, by all means get the most powerful system you can afford. You won't be sorry.

TIP

One of the reasons I'm able to still get away with using an outdated system is because I have optimized it for audio work. There are a number of things you can do to your PC that make it run more efficiently for the purpose of making music. These include adjustments to the system itself as well as to the Windows OS. If you want more information about how to optimize your audio PC, check out my feature article in Issue 14 of DigiFreq. You can download the issue for free at:

http://www.digifreq.com/digifreq/issues.asp

Sound Card

There are many things to consider when choosing a particular card. You should look for a PCI-based sound card (one that is installed inside of your computer) rather than a USB-based sound card. USB audio interfaces don't really provide enough bandwidth to transfer audio data fast enough for sufficient use. A PCI sound card works much better. However, with the new USB 2.0 spec, that shouldn't present a problem once manufacturers update their products in the near future. You should also be aware of the connection types that sound cards supply. The typical sound card provides a number of different audio inputs and outputs including line level, microphone level, and speaker. Line level inputs and outputs are used to transfer sound from cassette decks, radios, electronic keyboards, or any other standard audio device. Microphones generate a very small audio level by themselves, so they need a special input of their own, which is connected to an internal preamplifier on the sound card. Speakers also need their own special connector with a built-in amplifier to produce a decent amount of volume. Some high-end sound cards also offer digital inputs and outputs. These special connectors let you attach the sound card directly to compatible devices, such as some CD players and DAT (digital audio tape) decks. Using these connections gives you the best possible sound, because audio signals stay in the digital domain and don't need to be converted into analog signals. You should also be aware that connectors come in a variety of forms. Low-cost cards usually provide the same 1/8-inch" jacks used for headphones on boom boxes. For better quality, there are 1/4-inch", RCA, or XLR jacks. Connections can also be balanced or unbalanced. Balanced connections provide shielding to protect the audio signal against RFI (radio frequency interference). Unbalanced connections don't provide any type of protection.

If you want to be able to record more than one audio track at once, you need a card with multiple audio connections. Most average sound cards internally mix all of their audio sources down to one stereo signal, but other, higher-end (more expensive) cards let you record each device separately on its own discrete stereo channel. This capability is much more desirable in a music recording studio, but not everyone needs it. A good quality audio signal is something that everybody desires. During recording, the sampling rate (which I talked about in Chapter 1) plays a big part in the quality of the audio signal. Suffice it to say, the higher the sampling rate that a sound card can handle, the better the sound quality. The sampling rate of a CD is 44.1 kHz (44,100 samples per second) and all sound cards on the market support this. Professional cards can hit 48 kHz or higher. Bit resolution (also discussed in Chapter 1) is a factor in determining digital sound quality as well. The more bits you have to represent your signal, the better it sounds. The CD standard is 16 bits, which is supported by all sound cards. Some cards (again, mostly high-end) go up to 20, 22, or even 24 bits.

Two other measurements you need to look out for are signal-to-noise ratio and frequency response. As with the other measurements, the higher the better. Because all electronic devices produce some amount of noise, the signal-to-noise ratio of a sound card tells you how much higher the signal strength is compared to the amount of internal noise made by the sound card. The bigger the number, the quieter the card. A good signal-to-noise measurement is about 90 dB or higher. Frequency response is actually a range of numbers, which is based on the capabilities of human hearing. The frequency response of human hearing is approximately 20 Hz to 20 kHz. A good sound card encompasses at least that range, maybe even more.

What do I use? I decided to go with the Mona from Echo Audio. The Mona provides a wide variety of professional features, and the sound quality is great. My main reasons for choosing it, however, were good software drivers, built-in preamps, and multiple connections. If you get a card with built-in preamps, you can eliminate the need for yet another component in the signal chain, which can potentially add noise. And if you get a card with multiple connections, you can usually do away with having to use a mixing board, which can also be a source of additional noise. I love being able to just plug my microphone and instruments directly into my sound card, knowing that I'm getting the cleanest signal possible. The Mona does come with a hefty price tag; however, you can find lower-priced cards with fewer but similar features. I usually recommend checking out the products available from Echo Audio (www.echoaudio.com) and M-Audio (www.midiman.com).

CHAPTER 2

MIDI Interface

If you have any external MIDI devices (like a MIDI keyboard), then you need a MIDI interface for your computer. I've already explained MIDI interfaces back in Chapter 1, but I didn't really go into what you should know when looking to buy one. If you have a simple setup with only one MIDI keyboard, then you can easily get away with a simple single- or double-port MIDI interface. The best way to go here is to get a USB-based interface. This means it is easy to install (just plug it in) and it won't take up an IRQ or PCI slot inside your computer. Also be sure that the interface has Windows 2000- or Windows XP-compatible drivers (depending on what OS you are using). Bad drivers can cause problems. Other than that, the only major differences between interfaces are the number of ports they provide. If you have a lot of external MIDI devices, it's best to connect each device to its own dedicated MIDI port. I'm currently using a Midiman MidiSport 2x2 USB interface under Windows XP. It works great and does just what I need it to. I usually recommend checking out the products available from Midiman (www.midiman.com) when people ask me about MIDI interfaces.

Microphone

If you plan on doing any acoustic recording (vocals, acoustic guitar, etc.), you need a good microphone. There are literally hundreds of mics on the market and entire books have been written on the subject, so I won't go into great detail here. Basically, the microphone you choose depends on the application. For me, I needed a good vocal mic but not something that was going to put me in the poor house. Although I would love to get a Neumann U87 (one of the best), there's no way I can afford one. So luckily, Shure came to my rescue with their KSM27. It's a great vocal mic that isn't too expensive. You can find more information about it at: http://www.shure.com/microphones/models/ksm27.asp?PN=Selection%20Guides. I like that it can also be used for other applications in a pinch. But what's right for me may not be right for you, so I've rounded up a number of online resources that allow you to educate yourself on the subject of microphones:

- ▶ A Beginners Guide to Microphones - http://www.recordingwebsite.com/articles/microphones.html
- ▶ Microphone University - http://www.dpamicrophones.com/uni.htm
- ▶ Shure Performance and Recording Microphone Selection Guide - http://www.shure.com/selectionguides/sel-perfrecmics.html
- ▶ The Microphone FAQ - http://www.harmony-central.com/Other/mic-faq.txt
- ▶ Microphone Manufacturers List - http://www.harmony-central.com/Recording/manufact.html#mic

Speakers

Of course, you also need to be able to hear the music that you're recording, so you need a good set of speakers (or monitors as they're called in the professional audio world). Like microphones, there are literally hundreds of different monitors on the market. For home studio purposes, you probably want to get yourself a good pair of active, nearfield monitors. They're called active because they come with a built-in amplifier, which saves you the trouble of having to buy an external amp and trying to match it up to your monitors. And they're called nearfield because you listen to them at a fairly close distance (about four feet). This lets you set up your home studio in just about any space you can find because you don't have to acoustically treat the room, at least not professionally.

There are a wide variety of monitors available, but I'm currently having fun with the V4's from KRK Systems. These are a great pair of active, nearfield monitors that really deliver great sound. I also love that they've been designed for small workstation areas, and they're shielded, which means you can sit them close to your computer screen without problems. Of course, as with microphones, what I like may not be what you like, so I've compiled a number of online resources that will help you learn about and choose the right monitors for you:

> ▶ Ten Powered Nearfields Reviewed - http://www.prorec.com/prorec/articles.nsf/files/0B7FAE7ED3205D3C86256AE10 0044F41

> ▶ Audio FAQ (Speakers) - http://www.tm.tue.nl/vakgr/ok/vos/audio-faq/faq-09.htm

> ▶ eCoustics.com Speaker Articles - http://www.ecoustics.com/Home/Home_Audio/Speakers/Speaker_Articles/

> ▶ Speakers Manufacturer List - http://www.harmony-central.com/Recording/manufact.html#speak

Find Help When You Need It

Sonic Foundry provides a number of ways for you to find help when you're having a problem with Sound Forge. The two most obvious places to look are the manual and the Sound Forge Help file. At the first signs of trouble, you should go through the included troubleshooting information. If you can't find an answer to your problem there, then you can pay a visit to the Sonic Foundry Web site.

The Support page of the Sonic Foundry Web site (http://www.sonicfoundry.com/support/) contains a lot of helpful information, including a Knowledge Base and tutorials that provide details on a number of topics. You should check them first. If you still can't find a solution to your problem, the next place to look is in the Sonic Foundry forums (http://www.sonicfoundry.com/forums/). In the forums, you can trade tips, advice, and information with other Sound Forge users. And many times, you'll find that someone has had the same problem you're having, and he or she has already found a solution. Also, be sure to check out Appendix D, "Sound Forge Resources on the Web," later in this book for even more helpful information.

TIP

In addition, be sure to sign up for a free subscription to my DigiFreq music technology newsletter. DigiFreq is a monthly e-mail newsletter that helps you learn more about music technology. It provides free news, reviews, tips, and techniques for music technology users. By applying for your own free subscription, you can learn all about the latest music product releases, read straight forward reviews, explore related Web resources, and have the chance to win free products from brand-name manufacturers. To get your own free subscription, go to: http://www.digifreq.com/digifreq/.

Of course, you can also contact Sonic Foundry Technical Support directly. You can either e-mail your questions to support@sonicfoundry.com, or you can call 608-204-7704 (USA). Currently, the hours are Monday through Friday, from 9 a.m. to 11:30 a.m. and 12:30 p.m. to 5 p.m. Central Standard Time.

3

Customizing Sound Forge

Although we all may be Sound Forge users, it doesn't mean we like to work with the product in the same exact way. I have my way of doing things, and you probably have your own way. Luckily, Sound Forge provides a number of settings so that you can make the program conform to your own way of working. In this chapter, you'll learn to:

▶ Associate different types of audio files with Sound Forge

▶ Customize the program's Workspace, including colors, toolbars, window layouts, and other general settings

▶ Set up the MIDI parameters

▶ Set up the audio parameters

General Options

Sound Forge provides a number of general options that affect the overall operation of the software. These include the logo splash-screen, program close confirmation, and the textured background. They may not sound very significant, but it's these little things that can affect your efficiency while using the software.

Splash-Screen

One of the first things you'll probably want to change about the behavior of Sound Forge is the automatic display of the logo splash-screen, which pops open every time you run the software. I mean, how many times do you need to be reminded of what version you have? Turning this feature off gets you up and running with Sound Forge a little quicker. To do so, just follow these steps:

1. Choose Options > Preferences to open the Preferences dialog box, and click the General tab as shown in Figure 3.1.

Figure 3.1
You can set a number of
general options in
Sound Forge's
Preferences dialog box

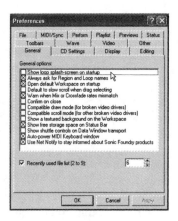

2.   In the list of options, double-click Show Logo Splash-Screen On Startup to
     deactivate that feature.

3.   Click OK.

Now, whenever you run Sound Forge, you won't have to put up with the annoyance of the
splash-screen.

NOTE
In the Preferences dialog box, you may have noticed a number of other
parameters that allow you to change the behavior of Sound Forge. I cover
more of them in this chapter and throughout the book.

Program Close Confirmation

If you're prone to errant mouse clicks, you may want to set up Sound Forge so that it asks you to
confirm your decision before you exit the software. In most cases, you won't need this option.
Even with this option deactivated, Sound Forge still warns you if you haven't saved your data
before you can exit the program. So, in essence, you really don't need the program close
confirmation option, and it's deactivated by default. But if you'd rather have that extra measure
of protection, you can activate this feature by simply selecting Options > Preferences to open the
Preferences dialog box, and clicking the General tab. Then, in the list of options, double-click
Confirm On Close to activate that feature, and click OK. From now on, Sound Forge always
warns you before closing down.

Textured Background

The Workspace area (which I talk about shortly) in Sound Forge is usually shown with a blank,
gray background color. If you'd rather see the Workspace background shown as a textured

graphic that matches the color of the rest of the application, you can do so by choosing Options > Preferences to open the Preferences dialog box, and click the General tab. Then, in the list of options, double-click Show A Textured Background On The Workspace. This option doesn't affect Sound Forge's performance, but I usually keep it deactivated anyway.

File Associations

Sound Forge provides support for many different types of audio files. They include WAV files, AIF files, MP3 files, and so on. (Don't worry, I go into more detail about each of the different file types in Chapter 4.) By default, none of the file types are associated with Sound Forge during installation. This means that if you double-click on an audio file within Windows Explorer, the file is opened or played using a software application other than Sound Forge.

If you want to automatically open certain audio file types within Sound Forge by double-clicking on them, you can easily associate the file types using Sound Forge's Sound File Associations feature. Just do the following:

1. In Sound Forge, choose Options > Preferences.

2. In the Preferences dialog box, click the File tab.

3. Click Associate Sound File Extensions to open the Sound File Associations dialog box (see Figure 3.2).

Figure 3.2
You can associate file types in Sound Forge's Sound File Associations dialog box

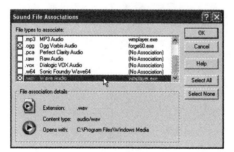

4. The File Types To Associate section lists all the file types that can be associated with Sound Forge. The first column shows the three-letter file extension. The second column shows the name of the file type. The third column shows the name of the program to which each file type is currently associated. To associate a file type with Sound Forge, just double-click it to place an X next to it.

5. To associate all the files in the list with Sound Forge, click the Select All button. Click the Select None button to do the opposite.

6. When you're finished selecting the file types, click OK.

7. Sound Forge tells you that "This may overwrite file associations used by other applications," and then asks if you're sure you want to continue. Click Yes.

8. Click OK to close the Preferences dialog box.

CHAPTER 3

From now on, whenever you double-click one of the associated file types in Windows Explorer, it automatically opens in Sound Forge.

The Workspace

Not only can you change the general behavior and file handling features of Sound Forge, but you can also change the way Sound Forge looks and the way it responds to your commands. By customizing the Sound Forge Workspace, you can increase your efficiency with the program and make it more comfortable to work with. Some of the adjustments you can make are to the colors, toolbars, Data Window layouts, and keyboard shortcuts.

Colors

Sound Forge allows you to change the colors of many of the graphic elements within the program. I haven't found much use for making color changes, though. The default colors that the program ships with work just fine for me. However, you might find a different set of colors more pleasant to work with, or maybe you can see some colors better than others. Changing the colors Sound Forge uses is simple; just follow these steps:

1. In Sound Forge, choose Options > Preferences.

2. In the Preferences dialog box, select the Display tab (see Figure 3.3).

Figure 3.3
In the Preferences dialog box under the Display tab, you can change the appearance of Sound Forge to your liking

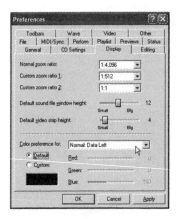

3. In the bottom half of the dialog box is a drop-down list labeled Color Preference For, which shows all of the screen elements you can change. To change the color of an element, select it from the list.

4. Select how you want that screen element to look by choosing the Custom option.

5. To create your own custom color for the screen element, change the values of the Red, Green, and Blue parameters by dragging the sliders. The mixture of the three values is what produces the final color, which is shown in the small rectangle in the lower-left corner of the dialog box.

6. Repeat Steps 3 through 5 for each screen element you want to change.

7. When you've completed your changes, click OK.

Your color changes take effect as soon as you close the Preferences dialog box. If you ever want to return to the default color values, just repeat the previous steps; however, for each element, instead of selecting the Custom option, select the Default option.

Toolbars

To increase your productivity, Sound Forge provides a number of toolbars for quick access to many of its major functions. So, instead of having to click through a series of menus, you can simply click a single toolbar button. Toolbars are available for standard file access functions, recording and playback controls, and so on.

Sound Forge allows you to change the position of its toolbars, as well as whether they are visible. Why wouldn't you want to have all the toolbars on the screen all the time? Because they can clutter up the Workspace and get in the way while you're working on a project.

Change Their Position

Just as with most toolbars in other Windows programs, you can dock these toolbars to the top, bottom, or even the sides of the Workspace. And if you drop a toolbar anywhere within the Workspace, it becomes a little floating window (see Figure 3.4).

Figure 3.4
Toolbars can be docked to the top, bottom, or sides of the Sound Forge Workspace; they can also reside anywhere else within the Workspace as small floating windows

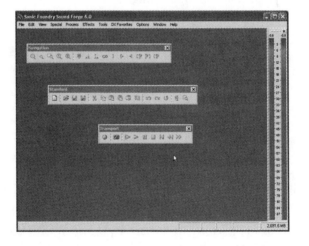

Change Their Visibility

To change the visibility of the toolbars, you need to access the Toolbars tab in the Preferences dialog box or just choose View > Toolbars and the dialog box appears (see Figure 3.5).

Figure 3.5
Choose View > Toolbars
to change the visibility
of Sound Forge's
toolbars

By placing or removing the X next to each selection in the box, you control whether the associated toolbar is visible. For example, if you remove the X in the box next to the Standard selection, the Standard File Functions toolbar disappears.

Change Their Configuration

In addition to docking and changing the visibility of the toolbars, you can also change their configuration. What I mean by this is you can change what buttons appear on each of the toolbars, thus customizing them to your own liking.

NOTE

Unfortunately, there is still one shortcoming to Sound Forge's toolbars: You can't create your own specialized toolbars in addition to the ones already provided. You are stuck with having to customize an existing toolbar. So, for example, you can't create a brand-new toolbar and name it My Special Editing Tools.

Customizing an existing toolbar is very easy. To show you how to do this, I'll walk you through an example. I'll describe how I created a special toolbar that I use to prepare audio files for the Internet. (I'll talk more about preparing audio files for the Internet in Chapter 11.)

1. Because most of the toolbars are already crowded with existing buttons (although they can be removed), I like to use one of the toolbars that is fairly empty when creating a special toolbar of my own. For this example, I'll use the Levels toolbar. Choose View > Toolbars to display the Preferences > Toolbars dialog box.

2. Double-click the Levels option and click Apply to make the Levels toolbar appear.

3. Click the Customize button to open the Customize Toolbar dialog box (see Figure 3.6). The Current Tools section of the box shows all of the buttons currently assigned to the selected toolbar. In this case, the Levels toolbar is empty. The

Available Tools section shows all of the buttons that can be assigned to the selected toolbar.

Figure 3.6
Use the Customize Toolbar dialog box to configure an existing toolbar to your liking

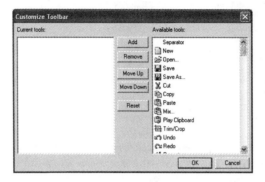

4. To assign a button to a toolbar, select a button/function from the Available Tools list and then click Add. For this example, add the DC Offset button/function first (see Figure 3.7).

Figure 3.7
Use the Available Tools list to assign a button/function to the selected toolbar

5. If you want to delete a button from the selected toolbar, select the button in the Current Tools section and click Remove.

6. To change the position of a button on the toolbar, select the button in the Current Tools section and use Move Up and Move Down to move the button up or down within the list.

7. You can also set a toolbar back to its default configuration by clicking Reset.

8. For this example, add three more buttons to the toolbar as follows: Paragraphic EQ, Graphic Dynamics, and Normalize.

9. Use Move Up and/or Move Down so that the buttons appear in the following order in the list: DC Offset, Paragraphic EQ, Graphic Dynamics, and Normalize (see Figure 3.8).

CHAPTER 3

Figure 3.8
Add some additional
buttons to the sample
toolbar

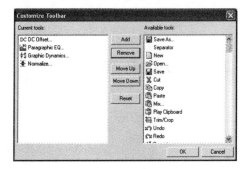

10. In addition to buttons, you can add Separators if you want to group different buttons together. To add a Separator, choose Separator from the Available Tools list and click Add. Move the Separator to the bottom of the Current Tools list.

11. Add one more button: Save As. Move it to the bottom of the Current Tools list.

12. Click OK to close the Customize Toolbar dialog box.

13. Click OK to close the Preferences > Toolbars dialog box.

When complete, the Levels toolbar will have four buttons, a separator, and one more button in addition to the two level readouts it already contained (see Figure 3.9).

Figure 3.9
The Levels toolbar has
been customized for our
own needs

Now you can use this toolbar to easily access all the functions needed to prepare your audio for the Internet (see Chapter 11 for more information).

Data Window Layouts

Because Sound Forge allows you to have more than one audio file open at once, you need to deal with multiple Data Windows, which were described in Chapter 2, and are explained more thoroughly in later chapters. When you want to close Sound Forge, the size, position, and file name of the Data Windows currently open are saved automatically. This capability is nice because the next time you open the program, you can pick up exactly where you left off.

TIP
If you do not want Sound Forge to automatically open with the same configuration as your previous session, you can turn this feature off. Choose Options > Preferences > General and double-click the Open Default Workspace On Startup option to deactivate it. Click OK.

As you get more experienced with Sound Forge, you'll probably find that having the Data Windows set up in certain configurations helps your editing sessions go more smoothly. For instance, let's say you're working with four different audio files. You might like to have them positioned so that each Data Window takes up one-quarter of the Workspace (see Figure 3.10).

Figure 3.10
The size, position, and file name of all currently open Data Windows are automatically saved when you close Sound Forge

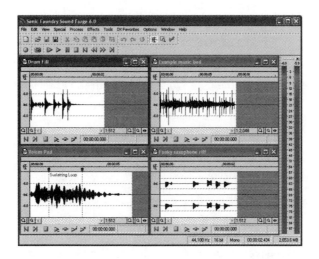

What if you come up with a few favorite configurations that you like to use during different stages of the same project? That's where Workspace files come in. Using Workspace files, you can save the size, position, and file name of all the currently open Data Windows. Then, you can later load the saved Workspace files for quick and easy organization. You can do so by using the Workspace > Open and Workspace > Save As features.

Save and Load a Workspace

You save and load a Workspace file like this:

1. Open the audio files that you want to work with.

2. Arrange the Data Windows in the Workspace in the positions and sizes that you want them to be saved.

3. Choose File > Workspace > Save As to open the Save Workspace dialog box (see Figure 3.11).

Figure 3.11
You can save Workspace
files by using the Save
Workspace dialog box

4. Type a name for the new Workspace file in the File Name parameter.

TIP

I've found that giving a descriptive name to each Workspace file helps me
when I want to load them. For example, I include the names of each open
audio file in the name of the Workspace file, along with a hint as to their
positions. If I have four files open, with each one taking up one-quarter of the
Workspace, I name the Workspace file "Drums-Bass-Guitar-Piano-
QuarterScreen.sfw."

5. Click the Save button to save your new Workspace file.

6. To load your new (or previously saved) file, simply choose File > Workspace >
    Open to open the Open Workspace dialog box.

7. Select a file from the list, and click the Open button. The Workspace file is
    loaded, and the configuration of the Data Windows is changed accordingly.

Window Docking and Stacking

In addition to the Data Window configurations, you can also set how other windows in Sound
Forge are configured. This pertains to all the windows listed under the View menu (Regions
List, Playlist/Cutlist, Keyboard, Video Preview, Time Display, Play Meters, Undo/Redo History,
Plug-In Manager, and the Audio Plug-In Chainer). What I mean by configured is that these
windows can be docked or stacked to provide a less cluttered working environment in Sound
Forge.

Docking a window works the same as docking a toolbar. Let's walk through an example so you
can see how it works:

1. Choose View > Plug-In Manager (or press Alt + 8 on your computer keyboard) to
    open the Plug-In Manager window.

2. If you drag the window to the left or right side of the Sound Forge Workspace, it
    changes in appearance and docks to that side (see Figure 3.12).

Figure 3.12
Windows can be docked
to the left or right side
of the Sound Forge
Workspace

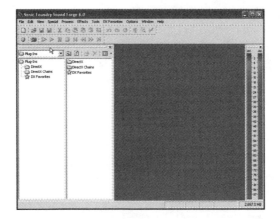

3. If you drag the window to the top or bottom of the Sound Forge Workspace, it changes in appearance and docks to that location (see Figure 3.13).

Figure 3.13
Windows can also be
docked to the top or
bottom of the Sound
Forge Workspace

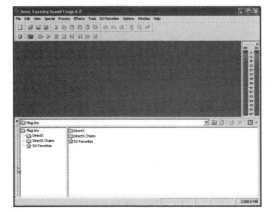

4. To undock a window, click the bar located on the top or side of the docked window and drag it to an open place in the Sound Forge Workspace.

TIP
If you are dragging a window around the Sound Forge Workspace, and you don't want it to be docked, hold down the Ctrl key on your computer keyboard as you drag the window.

CHAPTER 3

Stacking windows is also quite easy and it works by docking more than one window in the same place. Let me show you an example:

1. Choose View > Regions List (or press Alt + 1 on your computer keyboard) to open the Regions window.

2. Dock the Regions window to the bottom of the Sound Forge Workspace.

3. Choose View > Undo/Redo History (or press Alt + 7 on your computer keyboard) to open the Undo/Redo History window.

4. Dock the Undo/Redo History window in the same place as the Regions window. Notice that both windows are now stacked on top of each other and there are tabs on the bottom of the windows (see Figure 3.14).

Figure 3.14
Dock windows in the same location to stack them

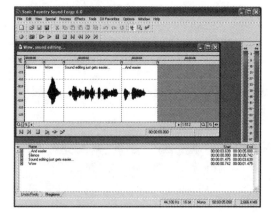

5. To access the window you want to use, click the appropriate tab to bring that window to the front.

6. You can also dock more windows in the same location without stacking them. Choose View > Playlist/Cutlist (or press Alt + 2 on your computer keyboard) to open the Playlist/Cutlist window.

7. Dock the Playlist/Cutlist window to the bottom of the Sound Forge Workspace, but drag it toward the bottom right of the Workspace instead of the bottom left. Notice that now you have two stacked windows on the bottom left and one docked window on the bottom right (see Figure 3.15).

Figure 3.15
You can have both docked and stacked windows located next to each other

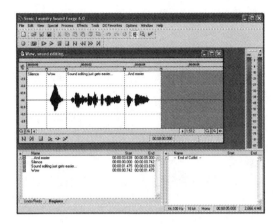

In addition, notice that the Play Meters are also still docked to the right side of the Sound Forge Workspace, but their vertical size has changed to make room for the docked windows on the bottom of the Workspace. This is how I usually have my windows configured when working with Sound Forge because it provides easy access to the Undo/Redo History, and I can easily drag and drop Regions from the Regions window to the Playlist/Cutlist window. I talk more about all of the aforementioned windows later in the book.

Keyboard Shortcuts

As with most Windows software, Sound Forge provides keyboard shortcuts for most of its functions. Like toolbars, they give you quick access to the program's features. Instead of having to click through a series of menus, you can simply press a key combination on your computer's keyboard. Many of these key combinations are displayed next to their assigned menu functions, like in the File menu (see Figure 3.16).

Figure 3.16
The keyboard shortcut for opening a file in Sound Forge is Ctrl + O

For a full list of all the keyboard shortcuts that work within Sound Forge, choose Help > Keyboard Shortcuts. Unfortunately, you can't change any of the default keyboard shortcuts, and you can't assign your own, either. There is, however, a partial solution to this problem; a feature called MIDI Triggers.

MIDI Triggers

The MIDI Triggers feature allows you to assign MIDI note and controller messages to a number of the functions within Sound Forge.

NOTE

There are seven types of MIDI messages, each providing different kinds of functionality within the MIDI language. These categories include Notes, Key Aftertouch, Channel Aftertouch, Controllers, Program Changes, Pitch Bend, and System Exclusive.

The Notes category pertains to MIDI Note On and MIDI Note Off messages. When you press a key on your MIDI keyboard, a MIDI Note On message is sent. When you release the key, a MIDI Note Off message is sent.

On some MIDI keyboards, in addition to pressing the keys, you can press and hold them down to apply varying degrees of pressure. This pressure is called aftertouch. Depending on how the synthesizer is programmed, aftertouch lets you control how loud it is or even how it sounds. Aftertouch comes in both key and channel varieties. Key aftertouch allows you to have different pressure levels for each individual key on the keyboard. Channel aftertouch restricts you to a single pressure level over the entire range of the keyboard.

A wide range of controller MIDI messages is available. Basically, these messages give you control over different aspects of your MIDI synthesizer or device. Some controller messages let you control volume, whereas others let you control the position of a synthesizer sound in the stereo field. However, far too many are available to discuss them all here.

Program changes (also called Patch Changes) let you select from the many different sounds available in a MIDI synthesizer. For example, a Program Change #1 MIDI message might activate a piano sound in your synthesizer, and Program Change #10 might activate a glockenspiel sound.

Pitch Bend messages allow you to temporarily alter the tuning of your MIDI instrument. Many MIDI keyboards have a lever or a wheel that lets you control pitch bend. Moving this wheel makes the instrument send out Pitch Bend (also called Pitch Wheel) messages.

System Exclusive messages pertain to special MIDI data that is (as the name implies) exclusive to the instrument sending and receiving it. For instance, the manufacturer of a MIDI synthesizer might include special functions in the product that can't be controlled via standard MIDI messages. By using System Exclusive messages, the manufacturer gives you access to these special functions but still keeps the product compatible with the MIDI language.

For more in-depth information about MIDI and the different types of messages available, check out the free Desktop Music Handbook at:

http://www.cakewalk.com/Tips/Desktop.htm

What this means is that you can use some of the controls on your MIDI keyboard or device as pseudo-keyboard shortcuts. For example, you can assign the Special >Transport > Play function in Sound Forge to the Middle C key on your keyboard. Then, when you press Middle C, Sound Forge plays the audio data in the Data Window that is currently active.

TIP

If your studio is set up so that your computer isn't located next to your MIDI keyboard or controller, using MIDI Triggers is a great way to still have access to Sound Forge. For example, if you want to be able to start and stop playback of audio in Sound Forge via your MIDI keyboard, you can just assign one MIDI Trigger to the Special > Transport > Play function and another MIDI Trigger to the Special > Transport > Stop function.

You can easily create your own MIDI Triggers via the MIDI Triggers dialog box. Here's how:

1. Choose Options > MIDI Triggers to open the MIDI Triggers dialog box (see Figure 3.17).

Figure 3.17
You can create MIDI Triggers in the MIDI Triggers dialog box

2. In the Event list, select the Sound Forge function for which you want to create a MIDI Trigger.

3. In the Trigger section, choose either the Note or Controller option to assign a MIDI note or MIDI controller as the MIDI Trigger, respectively.

4. If you select the Note option, be sure to also select a value for the channel parameter, which assigns a specific MIDI channel for the MIDI Trigger. And then select a value for the note parameter, which designates the MIDI note to be used for the MIDI Trigger.

5. If you select the Controller option, you need to assign a value for the channel parameter as well. And then select a value for the controller parameter, which designates the MIDI controller to be used for the MIDI Trigger. Finally, select a value for the value parameter, which designates the value of the MIDI controller to be used for the MIDI Trigger.

TIP

Instead of entering values for the note and controller parameters via your computer keyboard, you can also use your MIDI keyboard to do the same thing. Simply activate the Enable MIDI Input Sync/Trigger option. Then, activate a key or controller on your MIDI keyboard. The values for the parameters are set automatically.

6. After you've set up all your MIDI Triggers, save the current configuration by clicking the Save As button, and typing a name in the Save Preset dialog box. Then, click OK.

TIP

You can save as many different MIDI Trigger configurations as you want. This comes in handy if you want to create one set of MIDI Triggers for use with one MIDI device, and another set of MIDI Triggers for use with a different MIDI device, and so on.

7. When you're done, click the OK button.

After you've created (or changed) a set of MIDI Triggers, notice that activating certain controls on your MIDI device triggers their assigned functions within Sound Forge.

TIP

If you create MIDI Triggers, activating their associated notes or controllers on your MIDI device activates their assigned functions in Sound Forge. You really don't want this to happen while you're performing, so you need a quick way to turn MIDI Triggers on and off. In the Event list in the MIDI Triggers dialog box, there is a function labeled Enable/Disable Triggers. You can assign a MIDI Trigger to this function to be a sort of "on/off switch." This allows you to turn MIDI Triggers on and off without having to access the MIDI Triggers dialog box every time.

TIP

You may have picked up on the fact that I mentioned MIDI Triggers as only a partial solution to keyboard shortcuts. And, after using the MIDI Triggers dialog box, you probably already know why. Basically, Sound Forge only allows you to create MIDI Triggers for a select number of its functions rather than for all of them. The only solution I've found to work around this little problem is to purchase a separate software application called QuicKeys.

QuicKeys is PC automation software. It allows you to record your computer keyboard keystrokes and mouse clicks. You can then assign to those recordings any keyboard shortcut combinations that you want. You can even create your own custom toolbars for use within any of your PC applications. It's a very powerful program, and I find it indispensable. For more information about the product, go to: www.quickeys.com. You can also read my review of QuicKeys at:

http://www.newtechreview.com/newtechreview/reviews.asp

MIDI Settings

Sound Forge is a digital audio editing application, so you wouldn't think there would be any need for it to provide MIDI functionality. But because Sound Forge provides audio recording and playback features, the good people at Sonic Foundry have also included synchronization features within the program. This means that you can use Sound Forge in conjunction with other software (such as your MIDI sequencer) and other devices (such as external tape recorders). I talk more about synchronization and using Sound Forge with other software and devices in Chapter 6 and Chapter 12. In the meantime, you need to tell Sound Forge which MIDI input and output ports on your MIDI interface that you want to use.

NOTE

As I explained in Chapter 1, a MIDI interface is a device that is plugged into your computer that allows it to understand the MIDI language. Every MIDI interface has at least two connections on it called MIDI ports. One is the MIDI In port, which is used to receive MIDI data. The other is the MIDI Out port, which is used to send MIDI data. Some of the more sophisticated MIDI interfaces on the market have multiple pairs of MIDI ports. For instance, I use a Music Quest 8Port/SE, which has eight MIDI In and Out ports. Having all of these ports allows me to connect more than one MIDI instrument to my computer.

CHAPTER 3

Setting Up Your MIDI Ports

To see what MIDI ports Sound Forge is currently using and to designate which ports you want to use, perform the following steps:

1. Choose Options > Preferences to open the Preferences dialog box. Then click the MIDI/Sync tab (see Figure 3.18).

Figure 3.18
Under the MIDI/Sync tab in the Preferences dialog box, you can set the MIDI input and output ports to be used by Sound Forge

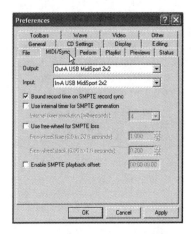

2. From the Output drop-down list, select the MIDI output port that you want to use. This parameter designates which output port Sound Forge will use to send MIDI data.
3. From the Input drop-down list, select the MIDI input port that you want to use. This parameter designates which input port Sound Forge will use to receive MIDI data.

NOTE

You'll notice an extra option in both the Input and Output drop-down lists called MIDI Mapper. Selecting this option tells Sound Forge to use the MIDI settings designated by the Windows MIDI Mapper. By utilizing the settings under the MIDI tab of the Multimedia Properties dialog box in Windows, you can have Windows direct the MIDI messages on individual MIDI channels to different MIDI devices. For example, if you have two different MIDI devices hooked up to your computer, you can have Windows send any MIDI data coming in on channels one through ten to the first device, and any MIDI data coming in on channels eleven through sixteen to the second device. But for the purposes of using MIDI with Sound Forge, you don't really want to use the MIDI Mapper option.

4. Click OK.

Sound Forge is now set to use the MIDI ports you designated to send and receive MIDI data.

Audio Settings

Because Sound Forge's main purpose is to deal with digital audio data, there are quite a few more settings available for audio than there are for MIDI. Most of these settings relate to obtaining the best recording and playback performance from Sound Forge. But there are a few other settings that allow you to adjust additional aspects of Sound Forge's behavior pertaining to audio, such as telling the program where to store audio data and which sound card ports to use for recording and playback.

During installation, Sound Forge attempts to make some educated guesses as to what the audio settings should be, and although these settings work just fine, you might find that you still need to make a few adjustments. However, adjusting these settings can be tricky, and, unfortunately, there are no set rules. There are, however, some general guidelines you can follow.

Temporary Storage Folder

When you open an existing audio file (or create a new one) in Sound Forge, the program creates a temporary file that is used to hold the audio data while you perform your editing tasks. Sound Forge also creates a number of other temporary files if you use its Undo/Redo and Clipboard functions (which I talk about in Chapter 7). To keep things somewhat organized, Sound Forge uses a single folder on your hard drive to store all of these temporary files. Initially, this folder is set to a default location, but Sound Forge allows you to change this setting if you want.

Why would you want to change the location of the temporary storage folder? Well, Sound Forge uses your hard drive extensively when you are performing your recording, playback, and editing tasks. Essentially, this means that the faster your hard drive works, the faster Sound Forge works. So, if you happen to use a separate (and more powerful) hard drive exclusively for your audio data, then you should definitely place your temporary storage folder for Sound Forge there, too. In addition, in some instances (which I talk about in Chapter 4), Sound Forge can save files faster if its temporary storage folder is kept in the same location as all your other audio data. To change the location of the temporary storage folder, follow these steps:

1. Create a new temporary storage folder by using Windows Explorer to create a new folder as you normally would on the hard drive of your choice. For this example, let's say that you have two hard drives, one named "C:" and another named "D:". The "D:" drive is where you store all your audio data, so you should create your new folder there. You could name it something like: "D:\Sound Forge Temp Files\".

2. In Sound Forge, choose Options > Preferences to open the Preferences dialog box. Then, click the Perform tab (see Figure 3.19).

Figure 3.19
The Perform tab in the
Preferences dialog box
lets you change the
temporary storage folder
setting

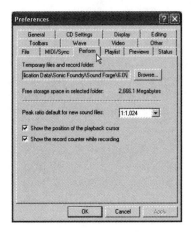

3. Click the Browse button to open the Browse For Folder dialog box (see Figure
    3.20).

Figure 3.20
The Browse For Folder
dialog box allows you to
designate the location of
the temporary storage
folder

4. Select the hard drive on which your new temporary storage folder is located
    from the list.
5. Select your new temporary storage folder in the list.
6. Click OK twice to close both dialog boxes.

From now on, when you open an existing file or create a new file, Sound Forge stores the
temporary data in the new temporary storage folder that you specified.

Record and Playback Settings

Just as you had to tell Sound Forge which input and output ports to use for MIDI, you also have
to tell it which sound card input and output you want to use for playback and recording of
audio. Because Sound Forge doesn't provide multitrack recording, you only need to assign one
input for recording and one output for playback. Here are the steps to do so:

1. Choose Options > Preferences to open the Preferences dialog box. Then click the
    Wave tab (see Figure 3.21).

Figure 3.21
Under the Wave tab of
the Preferences dialog
box, you can assign the
sound card input and
output you want Sound
Forge to use for
recording and playback
of audio

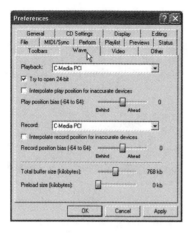

2. From the Playback drop-down list, select the sound card output you want to use.

3. From the Record drop-down list, select the sound card input you want to use.

NOTE

In addition to your sound card inputs and outputs, you'll also notice an extra
option in both the Playback and Record drop-down lists called the Microsoft
Sound Mapper. Selecting this option tells Sound Forge to use the sound card
settings designated by the Microsoft Sound Mapper. By utilizing the settings
under the Audio tab of the Multimedia Properties dialog box in Windows, you
can have Windows automatically control which sound card input(s) and
output(s) are used for audio data.

In addition, the Microsoft Sound Mapper provides extra capabilities, such as
audio data compression and translation. I talk more about audio data
compression in Chapter 4. Audio data translation occurs when you try to play
a sound file that has a bit depth or sampling rate that's not supported by your
sound card. In a case like this, the Microsoft Sound Mapper can automatically
translate the data so that Sound Forge can still play the audio data using your
sound card. Unfortunately, depending on the power of your computer, this
real-time processing can put a lot of strain on your system, so it's usually best
to have Sound Forge send audio data directly to your sound card input(s) and
output(s) rather than using the Microsoft Sound Mapper. Just make sure the
format of your audio data is supported by your sound card and you won't
need to use the Microsoft Sound Mapper unless you're dealing with
compression (which, as I mentioned, I talk about later).

4. Click OK.

CHAPTER 3

TIP

If you have a sound card that provides multiple outputs, there may be times when you want to use a different output for playback in Sound Forge. Instead of having to go through all the motions of opening the Performance dialog box and making adjustments, you can use the Play Device toolbar to change your audio output on the fly. To open the toolbar, choose View > Toolbars and double-click the Play Device option in the list. You only have to do this once. From then on, you can keep the toolbar open. Then, if you want to change the audio output quickly, just choose a new output from the Play Device toolbar drop-down list.

Interpolate and Position Bias

While setting up the sound card input and output, you may have noticed a couple of other parameters associated with the Playback and Recording drop-down lists under the Wave tab of the Properties dialog box. These are the Interpolate and Position Bias settings.

During recording and playback, Sound Forge provides a counter that shows you (in terms of a certain measurement, such as time) at what point in the current audio file that data is being recorded or played. Usually, the driver software of your sound card provides this counter value, but, unfortunately, many sound card drivers don't report their counter values accurately. This means that during recording, your time counters will be off, or during playback, your Markers (which I talk about in Chapter 5) will be positioned within your data incorrectly.

To remedy this problem, Sound Forge provides the Interpolate and Position Bias parameters. The Interpolate feature allows Sound Forge to provide the counter value during recording and playback rather than making the program rely on possibly inaccurate sound card drivers. By default, both the Playback and Record Interpolate features are deactivated. If you want to activate them, do the following:

1. Choose Options > Preferences to open the Preferences dialog box.
2. Click the Wave tab.
3. Place a check mark next to the Interpolate Play Position For Inaccurate Devices option to activate the Playback Interpolate feature.
4. Place a check mark next to the Interpolate Record Position For Inaccurate Devices option to activate the Record Interpolate feature.
5. Click OK.

The Position Bias feature allows you to specify an offset that Sound Forge should add to the counter value in order to compensate for an inaccurate sound card driver value. By default, both the Playback and Record Position Bias features are set to zero, which means they have no effect. But if you find that you are having problems with the counter value either lagging behind or counting ahead of the actual sound during playback or recording, you may be able to correct the problem by assigning values to the Position Bias parameters. Just do the following:

1. Choose Options > Preferences to open the Preferences dialog box.
2. Click the Wave tab.

3. Adjust the slider or the arrow buttons to increase or decrease the value for the Play Position Bias setting.

4. Adjust the slider or the arrow buttons to increase or decrease the value for the Record Position Bias setting.

NOTE

Most sound cards that exhibit an inaccurate counter value problem provide a value that counts ahead of the actual sound. So, you want to enter a positive value for the Position Bias settings. Typical values are 4, 8, 16, and 32, which correspond to the typical inaccuracies of many sound card drivers. Try out these values and keep adjusting the Position Bias settings until you get an accurate counter reading.

5. Click OK.

RAM Buffer

Sound Forge uses a part of your computer's RAM (memory) to provide a small playback and recording buffer. This buffer helps to optimize the program's playback and recording performance by eliminating skips and gaps in the audio data. If you find that you're getting bad recording or playback performance, you may want to try increasing the buffer value. Most often, though, the default value of 768 kb works just fine. To adjust the buffer size, do the following:

1. Choose Options > Preferences to open the Preferences dialog box.

2. Click the Wave tab.

3. At the bottom of the dialog box, adjust the slider to change the value for the Total Buffer Size setting.

NOTE

By increasing the buffer size, you may find that Sound Forge exhibits a slight delay when you start playback. This is due to the fact that it must first load data into the buffer before it begins to play. But this is a small price to pay for better performance. Just keep increasing the value until you no longer hear skips and gaps in your data.

4. Click OK.

Preload

Sound Forge also provides another parameter to help playback performance. The Preload parameter lets you determine how much data is sent to your sound card driver before playback begins. This can help eliminate any skips or gaps that occur during playback. By default, this parameter is set to zero, meaning it is deactivated. Unless you are having problems, you should leave the Preload parameter off. But in case you need to, here's how to adjust it:

1. Choose Options > Preferences to open the Preferences dialog box.

2. Select the Wave tab.

3. At the bottom of the dialog box, adjust the slider to change the value for the Preload Size setting.

TIP

By increasing the Preload Size, you may find that Sound Forge exhibits a slight delay when you start playback. This is due to the fact that it must first send data to the sound card driver before it begins to play. But this is small price to pay for better performance. Just keep increasing the value until you no longer hear skips and gaps in your data.

CAUTION

Some sound cards do not support this option. You'll find out very quickly if you hear noise or dropouts in your audio when you first try to play it back after you have adjusted the Preload Size parameter. If this happens, you should set the Preload Size to zero and leave it alone. You'll have to use the previously mentioned RAM buffer feature to try to eliminate performance problems instead.

4. Click OK.

Other Performance Optimizations

In addition to the previously mentioned parameter settings, there are a few other adjustments you can make to help Sound Forge perform more smoothly. More than likely, you won't have to make these adjustments because they don't consume much computer processing power, but if you experience glitches in playback or recording, these tweaks may help.

Turn Off the Playback Position Counter and Record Counter

During playback, Sound Forge displays a playback position counter in the bottom area of the Data Window, and during recording, Sound Forge displays a time counter in the Record dialog box. If you find you are having performance problems, you may want to deactivate these features. Here's how:

1. Choose Options > Preferences to open the Preferences dialog box. Then click the Perform tab.

2. To deactivate the playback position counter, remove the check mark next to the Show The Position Of The Playback Cursor option.

3. To deactivate the record time counter, remove the check mark next to the Show The Record Counter While Recording option.

4. Click OK.

Turn Off the Meters

During playback, Sound Forge displays audio amplitude (volume) levels in the Play Meters window (which is docked on the right side of the Sound Forge Workspace by default). To help with playback performance, you can turn the meters off by closing the window. To do so, choose View > Play Meters (or press Alt + 6 on your computer keyboard).

During recording, Sound Forge displays audio amplitude levels via the Record Meters in the Record dialog box. To help with recording performance, you can turn the meters off by removing the check mark next to the Monitor option in the Record dialog box (I talk more about the Record dialog box in Chapter 6).

TIP

There are a number of other things you can do to your PC that will make it run more efficiently for the purpose of making music. These include adjustments to the system itself as well as to the Windows OS. If you want more information about how to optimize your audio PC, check out my feature article in Issue 14 of DigiFreq. You can download the issue for free at:

http://www.digifreq.com/digifreq/issues.asp

4

Working with Audio Files

Because audio data can be stored in a variety of file formats, Sound Forge has to support many different types of audio files. You can't really perform any tasks in Sound Forge without first creating a new audio file or opening an existing one. So, in this chapter's discussion of audio files, you'll learn to:

▶ Explain the different audio file formats

▶ Open an existing audio file

▶ Create a new audio file

▶ Save an audio file

Understanding Audio File Formats

Just as different physical methods of storing audio were developed over time for different applications and reasons (vinyl records, tape, compact disc, and now DVD, etc.), different computerized methods for storing audio data have been developed as well. These methods come in the form of audio file formats. An audio file format is simply a specification stating the structure of how audio data in a file should be stored. For example, one audio file format may specify that the bits and bytes of audio data should be ordered in a certain manner, and another format may specify that the data be ordered in an entirely different manner. Of course, this is a very simplified explanation, but what it boils down to is that the same audio data can be stored in a variety of different ways.

Why do you need more than one audio file format? Because you may want to use your audio data for different tasks, such as playback on a CD, music or sound effects in a video game, a film or video soundtrack, or even for downloading over the Internet. Each task may require that your audio data be saved in a different way. For example, audio for a CD must be stored using a bit depth of 16 and a 44.1 KHz sampling rate. But for downloading over the Internet, you use a different bit depth and sampling rate because at 16 bit, 44.1 KHz, every minute of stereo audio consumes about 10 MB of disk space! That's a lot of data to push over a lowly phone line.

In addition to providing different bit depths and sampling rates, some audio file formats also offer data compression. This means that by saving to certain file formats, you can shrink the size of your audio files for use in low-bandwidth situations, as mentioned earlier with the Internet. Sometimes, the compression doesn't affect the quality of your audio, but most of the time it does. With compression, you have to find a good compromise between the quality of your audio data and the size of the file you want to end up with. There are many different compression schemes available, and I talk about those shortly.

Different audio file formats also exist because of the many different computer platforms that have been created over the years, such as the Amiga, Macintosh, NeXT, and the Windows PC. To provide you with as much flexibility as possible, Sound Forge allows you to open and save a large number of the existing audio file formats. Some of these, you might never use, but just in case, it's good to know that you can if the need arises. Let's go over each of the audio file formats that Sound Forge supports.

Dialogic VOX (.VOX)

This is an optimized audio file format that is mainly used for telephony applications. The Dialogic VOX format allows you to save 16-bit audio data and compress it down to 4-bit audio data, which gives you a 4:1 compression ratio. This means that you can save files that are very large in size and compress them down significantly. Of course, the quality of the audio is affected, and the format only supports monophonic data. Dialogic VOX audio files have a .VOX file extension, and they use ADPCM as their compression method.

NOTE

PCM (Pulse Code Modulation) is a coding method used to represent uncompressed audio data. It is the most common method of audio data configuration, and is used in many of the available audio file formats. ADPCM (Adaptive Delta Pulse Code Modulation) is a coding method used to represent compressed audio data. There is a standard ADPCM method, which is approved by the International Multimedia Association (IMA). There are also a wide number of variants available that have been developed by companies such as Microsoft. The different variants produce different results in terms of quality and file size.

Intervoice (.IVC)

Like the Dialogic VOX format, the Intervoice format is for use in telephony applications. It only supports 8-bit, monophonic audio data, but it provides a number of different compression schemes. These schemes include both A-Law and u-Law. Intervoice files have a .IVC file extension.

NOTE

A-Law is an audio compression scheme optimized for compressing voice audio data, and is commonly used for telecommunications applications in the United States. The A-Law compression scheme allows for the encoding of 16-bit PCM audio into 8-bit PCM audio. The scheme is very similar to u-Law, except that each scheme uses different coding and decoding methods.

u-Law (or mu-Law, pronounced "mew-law") is also a compression scheme optimized for compressing voice audio data, but instead is commonly used for telecommunications applications in Europe. As with A-Law, u-Law allows for the encoding of 16-bit PCM audio into 8-bit PCM audio.

Audio Interchange File Format AIFF (.AIF/.SND)

This is the standard file format for saving audio data on the Macintosh. If you ever need to transfer audio files between the PC and the Mac, this is the format you should use. The format supports 8-bit and 16-bit monophonic and stereo audio data. Files in this format may or may not also contain a Mac-Binary header. If a file of this type doesn't contain a Mac-Binary header, it probably has .AIF for a file extension. If a file of this type does contain a Mac-Binary header, Sound Forge opens it but identifies the file as a Macintosh Resource instead. In this case, the file probably has .SND for a file extension.

NOTE

Files on the Macintosh are stored with what is called a Mac-Binary header. This is a small section of information stored in the beginning of a file that identifies the type of file to the Mac OS (operating system) and other applications. This is how the Mac can tell whether a file contains text, graphic, or audio data, and so on. If you want to learn more about how files work on the Mac, check out all the technical information available at http://www.apple.com/.

MP3 Audio (.MP3/.MPG/.MPEG)

More than likely, you've heard of the MP3 audio file format. It's all the rage (literally) these days with people on the Internet. News about the format has even made it into the mainstream media because the format is being used to post illegal copies of music all over the Web. Why is the format so popular? Because it allows you to compress your audio data with about a ratio of 12:1, and the quality of the audio is very close to CD quality. Sound Forge provides support for opening MP3 files and saving to MP3. Unfortunately, the save feature requires an extra purchase. Even though MP3 functionality is included with Sound Forge, it only allows 20 uses unless you unlock it with a purchased serial number code. There are no restrictions when it comes to opening MP3 files, though.

NOTE

For more information about the MP3 format, check out the HowStuffWorks site at: http://www.howstuffworks.com/mp3.htm.

Ogg Vorbis (.OGG)

In addition to MP3, you may have heard of the Ogg Vorbis audio file format. It's a fairly new type of file format that does pretty much the same thing as MP3, but some say it provides better quality and smaller file sizes. To find out all you ever wanted to know about this format, go to: http://www.vorbis.com/.

NeXT/Sun (.AU/.SND)

Like the Macintosh AIFF, the NeXT/Sun audio file format is also a standard format, but it's for the NeXT and Sun Sparc station computer systems rather than the Mac or PC. This format supports many types of audio data, including 8-bit and 16-bit, monophonic and stereo. It also provides support for a variety of compression schemes, but Sound Forge only supports the most common (u-Law) compression for this format. If you download a lot of audio files from the Internet, you'll file many of them with the .AU file extension. Most of these files are 16-bit audio that have been compressed to 8-bit u-Law data for transferring over the Net or for use in Java applications.

RealMedia (.RM)

If you spend any time surfing the Internet, you've more than likely heard of this file format. The RealMedia file format allows you to create streaming audio and video files for transmission over the Internet. It supplies sophisticated proprietary compression features for making it possible to transmit audio and video data over the Internet (even through a lowly telephone connection) in real time. This means that you can start listening to or viewing the data as it downloads rather than having to wait for the whole file to be stored on your computer's hard drive. The RealMedia format was created by RealNetworks. If you want to find out more about this format, surf on over to http://www.real.com/.

Sound Designer 1 (.DIG/.SD)

Yet another product-specific format, the Sound Designer 1 audio file format is for use with the Sound Designer 1 software application on the Macintosh. And it only supports 16-bit monophonic audio. The files have either a .DIG or an .SD extension.

Video for Windows (.AVI), QuickTime (.MOV), MPEG-1 & 2 (.MPG)

Believe it or not, in addition to audio data, Sound Forge allows you to load and save video data in the form of AVI, MOV, and MPG files. You can't edit the video data, but you can edit the audio data stored within a video file. AVI, QuickTime, and MPEG are special digital video file formats specifically designed for working with video on computers. Each format uses its own unique compression scheme to achieve video quality as good as possible in a file size as small as possible. AVI (Audio Video Interleaved) is a Windows-based format, which means that any computer running Windows can play AVI files. QuickTime is a Mac-based format, which means that any Macintosh computer can play QuickTime files. With special players software, a computer running Windows can also play QuickTime files. MPEG (Motion Picture Expert Group) is a more advanced format that sometimes requires special hardware for playback. Sound Forge can both load and save all of these file types, but the MPEG formats require an additional purchase.

Microsoft Wave (.WAV)

Like MP3, Wave is another very popular audio file format that you've probably heard about. Wave is a Windows-based format, which means that any computer running Windows can play Wave files. The format supports a lot of different types of audio data, including 8-bit and 16-bit, monophonic and stereo audio. The Wave format also provides support for a huge number of different compression schemes, including many of the different ADPCM variants via the Microsoft ACM (Audio Compression Manager). The ACM is a part of Windows that works transparently, providing access to any compression schemes that are installed on your computer. Windows ships with a number of different schemes, and you probably also have a number of others from audio product manufacturers. If you're working with Windows, then you probably use the Wave format for about 90 percent of your audio work. Most sound and music software on the Windows platform supports this format. Wave files have a .WAV file extension.

Windows Media Audio/Video (.WMA/.WMV)

Similar to RealMedia, Windows Media Audio/Video is a special audio/video file format that allows you to create streaming audio/video files for transmission over the Internet. The format is a Windows-based format, which means that any computer running Windows (with the Windows Media Player installed) can play Windows Media files. Like RealMedia, Windows Media Audio supplies sophisticated proprietary compression features for making it possible to transmit audio/video data over the Internet in real time. And also similar to RealMedia, the compression does affect the quality of your audio/video data. Windows Media files have .WMA (audio) and .WMV (video) extensions. If you want to find out more about this format, surf on over to http://www.microsoft.com/windowsmedia/.

RAW File (.RAW/*.*)

RAW audio format files (as the name states) contain plain PCM audio data. The data is not saved in a specific format (like those mentioned earlier). When you save a RAW file, the audio data is saved in a "plain brown wrapper," so to speak. It's pure audio data. And when you go to load a RAW file in Sound Forge, you must specify certain parameters for the data to be loaded.

Perfect Clarity Audio (.PCA)

In addition to all of the aforementioned audio file formats, Sonic Foundry also provides its own format called Perfect Clarity Audio. Similar to MP3, Perfect Clarity Audio uses compression to create small file sizes, but unlike MP3, the quality of the audio is not affected. Perfect Clarity Audio is known as a lossless audio file format, which means there is no loss of quality when audio is saved to this format even though the file size is smaller than if you had saved the same audio data to the WAV file format. This is a nice way to store audio data in a limited amount of space without having to worry about affecting the quality, but keep in mind that only Sonic Foundry products support this format. So, you still need to store your data in another format if you want it to be accessible from within other audio applications.

CHAPTER 4

TIP
If you want to dig even deeper and find more in-depth information about these (and other) audio file formats, be sure to check out the Audio File Format FAQ (Frequently Asked Questions). You can find it on the Internet at:

http://home.sprynet.com/~cbagwell/audio.html.

Opening Audio/Video Files

There are a number of ways to open an existing file in Sound Forge. The quickest way is to use the bottom portion of the File menu (see Figure 4.1). Sound Forge lists your previously opened audio files here.

Figure 4.1
Your previously opened audio files are listed in the bottom portion of Sound Forge's File menu

To open one of these files, just choose File and then click the file you want to open (or press Alt + F + the number of the file in the list). Sound Forge keeps track of the last two to nine files you've worked with. When you open one more than the maximum number of allowed listed files, the file on the bottom of the list is bumped off—not killed or deleted, just removed from the list. You can set the maximum number of previously opened files to be listed using the Preferences dialog box. Just choose Options > Preferences and click the General tab. At the bottom of the dialog box, make sure there is a check mark next to the Recently Used File List option. Then, simply enter a number from 2 to 9 to set the maximum number of files to be included on the list.

You can also open an existing file by using Sound Forge's Open function. To do so, follow these steps:

1. Choose File > Open to display the Open dialog box (see Figure 4.2). Notice that this dialog box provides a bit more functionality than the standard Windows Open dialog box.

Figure 4.2
You can also open
existing files in Sound
Forge using the Open
dialog box

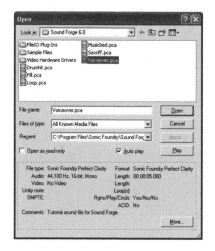

2. Locate the folder in which the file resides using the Look In drop-down list. Or, for a list of recently accessed folders, use the Recent drop-down list.

3. Choose the type of audio file you want to open by using the Files Of Type drop-down list.

4. Select the file you want to open from the displayed list of files.

> **TIP**
> You can also open multiple separate files at the same time by holding down the Ctrl key on your computer keyboard while you select the files with your mouse. Sound Forge opens each file in a separate Data Window.

5. If the Auto Play option is activated, Sound Forge plays the selected file before opening it. If you deactivate the Auto Play function, you can also play the file manually by clicking the Play button. To stop playback, click the Stop button.

6. To find out some specifics about the selected file, look at the bottom section of the Open dialog box. Here, you'll find displayed the file type, the file length (in minutes, seconds, frames, and samples), the format of the data (PCM, ADPCM, etc.), the attributes of the data (sampling rate, bit depth, monophonic or stereo), whether the data has sample loop properties (such as a unity note and loop type), the SMPTE offset assigned to the data, whether the file contains any Region or Playlist attributes, and any comments attached to the file in the form of text. (Don't worry if I've mentioned some things here that you don't understand just yet. I talk about them later in the book.)

7. For even more details about the file, click the More button to open the Properties dialog (see Figure 4.3). Click Cancel to close the dialog box after you've finished examining its properties.

Figure 4.3
The Properties dialog
box displays detailed
information about your
selected audio file

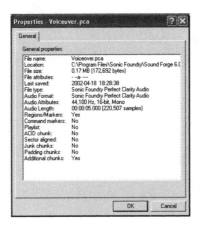

8. If you simply need to copy some data from the file without doing any other edits, and you want to take extra care not to alter the file, you can open it in read-only mode. Just put a check mark next to the Open As Read-Only option to activate it. This allows you to open the file for playback or data copying, but you won't be able to alter the file in any way.

9. Click the Open button to open your file(s).

After you've opened your file(s), Sound Forge displays the Data Window(s). It also shows attributes and file length in the currently selected Data Window in the status bar at the bottom of the Workspace. In addition, you can see how much hard disk space you have left after opening your file(s) by checking the number of megabytes display, which is also located in the status bar.

TIP
One other way to open files with Sound Forge is to simply drag and drop them from the Windows Explorer or Desktop on to the Sound Forge Workspace.

Opening RAW Files

Because a RAW file is nothing more than pure audio data, Sound Forge can't tell the file's attributes when opening the file. Instead, you have to tell Sound Forge what attributes to use when opening a RAW file. So, after you click the Open button in the Open dialog box (discussed earlier), you need to make some additional option choices. Here are the steps you should take:

1. After you select the RAW file and click the Open button in the Open dialog box, the Raw File Type dialog box is displayed (see Figure 4.4).

Figure 4.4
The Raw File Type
dialog box lets you
select the attributes of
the RAW file that you
want to work with in
Sound Forge

2. Select a sampling rate for the audio file using the Sample Rate drop-down list.

3. Select sample type or bit depth for the audio file by selecting one of the options in the Sample Type section.

4. Select a format for the audio file in the Format section. This option is a bit technical. You use it to tell Sound Forge whether the bits of audio data are stored as Unsigned or Signed. Most files utilize the Signed option.

5. Select whether the audio file is monophonic or stereo by selecting an option in the Channels section.

6. Select how the audio data bytes are ordered in the file by selecting an option in the Byte Order section. If it is a PC-based audio file, select the Little Endian option. If it is a Mac-based audio file, select the Big Endian option.

7. If you know that there is other data stored in the file before the audio data, specify how many bytes of nonaudio data is included by entering a number in the Header field.

8. If you know that there is other data stored in the file after the audio data, specify how many bytes of nonaudio data is included by entering a number in the Trailer field.

9. Click OK.

Sound Forge then opens the RAW file using the attributes that you selected. If the attributes you specified are wrong, Sound Forge opens the file, but you get nothing but junk data. If you try playing the file, it just sounds like noise. So, if anyone ever sends you a RAW audio data file, be sure they tell you the attributes of the file to save yourself a lot of trial and error, not to mention frustration.

File Crash Recovery

Sound Forge automatically creates temporary edit files for the files you open. If at any time during your audio editing session, your computer crashes, Sound Forge has the ability to recover the temporary files containing your edited audio data. I really like this feature, because I never know when Windows is going to decide to crash.

Here's how the file recovery feature works:

1. After your computer crashes, reboot and then run Sound Forge.
2. When you start the program, it automatically detects any temporary audio files that might still be on your hard drive. If any are found, Sound Forge displays the Crash Recovery dialog box (see Figure 4.5).

Figure 4.5
The Crash Recovery dialog box allows you to recover temporary audio files that may have been left on your hard drive during a computer system crash

3. In the list of files displayed, select the files that you want to recover, and click the Recover button.
4. If you know you don't need the files, you can just delete them by clicking the Cancel button.

After you recover your files, Sound Forge opens them in Data Windows and brings you back to the point you were at in your editing session right before your computer crashed.

Creating New Audio Files

Creating a new audio file with Sound Forge is one of the easiest tasks you'll ever perform with the software. It's really just a simple matter of using the File > New function and defining the attributes of your new file. Here are the steps you need to take:

1. Choose File > New (or press Ctrl + N on your computer keyboard) to open the New Window dialog box (see Figure 4.6).

Figure 4.6
The New Window dialog box allows you to define the attributes of the new audio file you want to create with Sound Forge

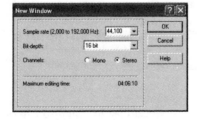

2. Select a sampling rate for the new file by using the Sample Rate drop-down list.
3. Select a bit depth for the new file by using the Bit-Depth drop-down list.
4. Select whether the file will be monophonic or stereo by choosing an option in the Channels section.

NOTE

As you change each of the parameters, Sound Forge displays an estimate (via the Maximum Editing Time feature) of how long (in hours, minutes, and seconds) of a file you can create, taking into account the remaining space on your hard drive.

5. Click OK.

Sound Forge then opens a new, blank Data Window ready and waiting for you to fill it with audio data.

NOTE

You can also create new audio files by using Sound Forge's audio recording feature, which automatically creates a new audio file with the data that you record. I talk more about that in Chapter 6.

Saving Audio/Video Files

Sound Forge provides three different commands for saving files: Save, Save All, and Save As. The Save command provides a quick way to save the file with which you're currently working. Simply choose File > Save (or press Ctrl + S on your computer keyboard) and the file is saved. The Save All command provides a quick way to save all of the currently open files (if you have more than one open). Simply choose File > Save All. Sound Forge asks you if you're sure you want to save each individual file.

TIP

If you hold down the Shift key on your computer keyboard when you choose the File > Save All command, Sound Forge does not confirm the saving of each open file. All of the files are simply saved. This method is much quicker.

The Save As command allows you to specify the format to which you want to save the currently open file. To use this command, follow these steps:

1. Choose File > Save As to display the Save As dialog box (see Figure 4.7). Notice that this dialog box provides a bit more functionality than the standard Windows Save As dialog box.

Figure 4.7
You can specify the
format to which you
want to save the
currently open file using
the Save As dialog box

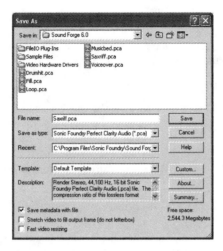

2.   Locate the folder into which you want to save the file using the Save In drop-
     down list. Or, for a list of recently accessed folders, use the Recent drop-down
     list.

3.   Enter a name for the file (if it doesn't already have one) into the File Name field.

4.   Choose the file type that you want to save the file as by using the Save As Type
     drop-down list.

5.   Choose the format (PCM, ADPCM, etc.) that you want to save the file as by using
     the Template drop-down list.

NOTE
Templates provide a quick and easy way to choose the attributes for your file
(including sample rate, bit depth, etc). Each file type provides different
attributes that can be set. There are predefined templates for each file type,
but you can also create your own. I talk about this later in this chapter.

6.   If you have created Regions or a Playlist for your file (I talk more about these
     features in Chapters 5 and 6) or defined summary information for the file, you
     can save this information within the file by activating the Save Metadata With
     File option.

7.   To edit or view the summary information for a file, click the Summary button to
     open the Properties dialog box (see Figure 4.8).

Figure 4.8
The Properties dialog
box allows you to edit
and view the summary
information for a file

8. Edit the Title, Subject, Engineer, Copyright, and Comments information for the file.

9. You can also attach a picture to the file by clicking the Picture button. In the Open Picture dialog box, simply select a Windows Bitmap (.BMP), Windows Cursor (.CUR), or Windows Icon (.ICO) file to attach, and then click the Open button.

TIP

Most Windows graphics applications allow you to create your own Windows Bitmap (.BMP) files. For identification purposes, you could take a picture of yourself, scan it into your computer, save it as a Windows Bitmap, and then attach it to all your audio files.

10. If you want to include even more information in your file, click the Extended button to open the Extended Summary dialog box (see Figure 4.9).

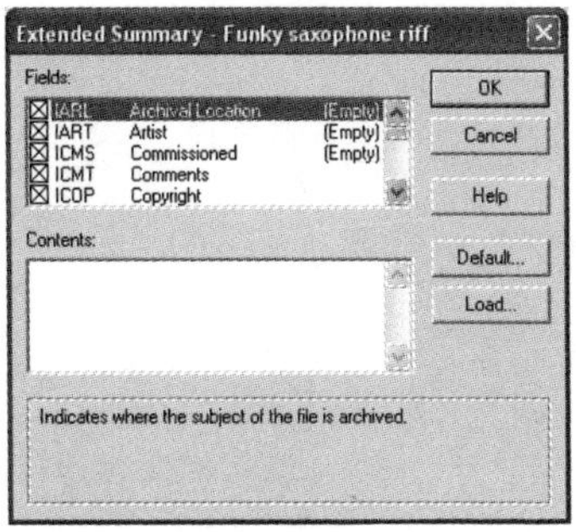

Figure 4.9
The Extended Summary
dialog box allows you to
enter even more textual
data to be embedded in
your file

11. In the Fields section is a list of all the additional information you can include in your file. To include a specific piece of information, put an X next to it in the list. Then enter the text for the information in the Contents section. To see a description of each item listed in the Field section, just highlight the item and read the description at the bottom of the dialog box.

TIP

Whenever you save a file in Sound Forge, a default set of summary information is included in the file. If you want to set the current file's summary information to be the default information for newly saved files, just click the Default button, and then click Yes.

12. Click OK in the Extended Summary dialog box.

13. Click OK in the Properties dialog box.

14. Click the Save button to save your file.

Sound Forge then saves your file with all of the settings that you specified.

File Save Templates

In past versions of Sound Forge, you had to specify individual parameter settings for each file type whenever you saved a file. With Sound Forge 6, this process is made much easier through the use of templates. Now, instead of having to set the compression format, sample rate, bit depth, and channels when saving a WAV file, you simply choose a template, which defines those settings for you.

Sound Forge ships with a number of predefined templates for each file type. Of course, some of these templates may not serve your needs. In this case, you may have to create a new template. To create a new template, you simply click the Custom button in the Save As dialog box. This opens the Custom Settings dialog box. But this box does not always look the same. Each file type has different parameter settings available, so creating a template can sometimes be different for each one. In the following sections, I show you how to create a template for the file types available within Sound Forge.

Audio Interchange File Format (AIFF) Templates

To create a template for this file type, do the following:

1. With the Save As dialog box open, click the Custom button to open the Custom Settings dialog box (see Figure 4.10).

Figure 4.10
Use the Custom Settings dialog box to create a template for the AIFF file format

2. Enter a name for the template in the Template parameter.
3. Enter a description for the template in the Description parameter.
4. Enter a sampling rate using the Sample Rate drop-down list.
5. Enter a bit depth using the Bit-Depth drop-down list.
6. Enter whether the file should be mono or stereo using the Channels drop-down list.
7. To save the template, click the Save Template button (shown as a small disk icon to the right of the Template field).
8. If you want to delete the template, click the Delete Template button (shown as a small X icon to the right of the Template field).
9. Click OK.

Intervoice File Templates

To create a template for this file type, do the following:

1. With the Save As dialog box open, click the Custom button to open the Custom Settings dialog box (see Figure 4.11).

Figure 4.11
Use the Custom Settings dialog box to create a template for the Intervoice file format

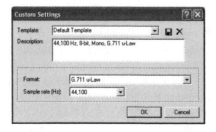

2.   Enter a name for the template in the Template parameter.

3.   Enter a description for the template in the Description parameter.

4.   Choose the type of audio compression to be associated with this template using the Format drop-down list.

5.   Enter a sampling rate using the Sample Rate drop-down list.

6.   To save the template, click the Save Template button (shown as a small disk icon to the right of the Template field).

7.   If you want to delete the template, click the Delete Template button (shown as a small X icon to the right of the Template field).

8.   Click OK.

MP3 Audio File Templates

To create a template for this file type, do the following:

1.   With the Save As dialog box open, click the Custom button to open the Custom Settings dialog box (see Figure 4.12).

Figure 4.12
Use the Custom Settings dialog box to create a template for the MP3 file format

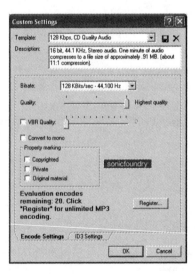

2.   Enter a name for the template in the Template parameter.

3.   Enter a description for the template in the Description parameter.

4.   Under the Encode Settings tab, enter a bit rate using the Bitrate drop-down list. The bit rate lets you set how much data needs to be read from the file to achieve reliable playback. The higher the bit rate, the better the quality of the sound, but the bigger the file. The lower the bit rate, the worse the quality of the sound, but the smaller the file. Most MP3 files that you find on the Internet use a 128 kbits/sec bit rate. This setting provides a good balance between sound quality and file size.

5. Set the Quality slider. This parameter determines the quality and speed of the encoding process. The higher the Quality slider setting, the better the encoding process and the better your file sounds. This setting makes the encode process take more time, but not so much of a difference from a lower Quality slider setting. I always leave this set to Highest Quality.

6. Set the VBR Quality option. Activating this option tells Sound Forge to vary the bit rate during the encoding process. Sometimes this can yield a higher quality sound and a smaller file size, but it depends on the material you are encoding. You'll have to experiment with this setting to see if it is worth using. Personally, I usually leave this option deactivated.

7. If your original audio file is in stereo and you want to convert it to mono during the MP3 encoding process, activate the Convert To Mono option. This can reduce the file size and sometimes improve the sound quality with voice-only material. But other than that, you'll probably want to leave this option deactivated.

8. If you want to apply property markings to be included in the file that indicate the audio material is copyrighted, private, or original, activate the Copyrighted, Private, or Original Material options. These options don't affect the sound at all, they just tell the player software used to play the MP3 file that the file has certain characteristics.

9. Click the ID3 Settings tab.

10. If you want to save some descriptive textual information in the template, activate the Save ID3 Tag To File option.

11. Choose ID3 Version 1 to add information regarding Title, Artist, Album, Comments, Year, and Genre. Choose ID3 Version 2 to add all of the previous information, plus a Copyright notice. You can also choose to include both versions of the ID3 tag. This information can be displayed by the MP3 player software during playback of the file.

12. To save the template, click the Save Template button (shown as a small disk icon to the right of the Template field).

13. If you want to delete the template, click the Delete Template button (shown as a small X icon to the right of the Template field).

14. Click OK.

CHAPTER 4

Ogg Vorbis File Templates

To create a template for this file type, do the following:

1. With the Save As dialog box open, click the Custom button to open the Custom Settings dialog box (see Figure 4.13).

Figure 4.13
Use the Custom Settings dialog box to create a template for the Ogg Vorbis file format

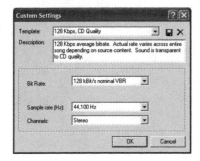

2. Enter a name for the template in the Template parameter.

3. Enter a description for the template in the Description parameter.

4. Enter a bit rate using the Bit Rate drop-down list. The bit rate lets you set how much data needs to be read from the file to achieve reliable playback. The higher the bit rate, the better the quality of the sound, but the bigger the file. The lower the bit rate, the worse the quality of the sound, but the smaller the file. If you want your Ogg Vorbis file to have CD quality sound, use a 128 kbits/sec bit rate. This setting provides a good balance between sound quality and file size.

5. Enter a sampling rate using the Sample Rate drop-down list. For CD quality sound, use a setting of 44,100 Hz.

6. Enter whether the file should be mono or stereo using the Channels drop-down list.

7. To save the template, click the Save Template button (shown as a small disk icon to the right of the Template field).

8. If you want to delete the template, click the Delete Template button (shown as a small X icon to the right of the Template field).

9. Click OK.

RAW File Templates

To create a template for this file type, do the following:

1. With the Save As dialog box open, click the Custom button to open the Custom Settings dialog box (see Figure 4.14).

Figure 4.14
Use the Custom Settings
dialog box to create a
template for the RAW
file format

CHAPTER 4

2. Enter a name for the template in the Template parameter.

3. Enter a description for the template in the Description parameter.

4. Select sample type or bit depth for the audio file by selecting one of the options in the Sample Type section.

5. Select a format for the audio file in the Format section. This option is a bit technical. You use it to tell Sound Forge whether the bits of audio data are stored as Unsigned or Signed. Most files utilize the Signed option.

6. Select whether the audio file is monophonic or stereo by selecting an option in the Channels section.

7. Select how the audio data bytes are ordered in the file by selecting an option in the Byte Order section. If it is a PC-based audio file, select the Little Endian option. If it is a Mac-based audio file, select the Big Endian option.

8. To save the template, click the Save Template button (shown as a small disk icon to the right of the Template field).

9. If you want to delete the template, click the Delete Template button (shown as a small X icon to the right of the Template field).

10. Click OK.

RealMedia File Templates

To create a template for this file type, do the following:

1. With the Save As dialog box open, click the Custom button to open the Custom Settings dialog box (see Figure 4.15).

Figure 4.15
Use the Custom Settings dialog box to create a template for the RealMedia file format

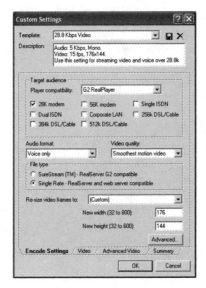

2. Enter a name for the template in the Template parameter.

3. Enter a description for the template in the Description parameter.

4. Under the Encode Settings tab, tell Sound Forge what player software your Web site visitors will be using by utilizing the Player Compatibility drop-down list. This allows you to create files that are compatible with older player software if need be. More than likely, you'll want to leave this set to G2 RealPlayer most of the time.

5. Choose the connection speed your Web site visitors will be using to access the Internet. You can select from 28 K modem up to 512 k DSL/Cable. It's usually best to go with a lower setting unless you know all your visitors have high-speed Internet access.

6. Choose the type of audio data you are encoding by making a selection in the Audio Format drop-down list.

7. Choose the type of video data you are encoding by making a selection in the Video Quality drop-down list.

8. In the File Type section, choose SureStream if you will be using a RealServer to transmit your file over the Internet. Or, choose Single Rate if you will be using a regular Web server to transmit your file over the Internet.

9. If you want to change the size of the video frames to something other than the original size, you can do so by selecting a new frame size from the Re-size Video Frames To drop-down list. You can also set a custom video frame size by selecting Custom from the drop-down list and then entering values for the New Width and New Height parameters.

10. If you want to make even more specific settings to control the encoding of your data, click the Advanced button. More often than not, however, you won't have to deal with these settings.

11. Under the Video tab, set the Enable 2-Pass Encoding option. Activating this option tells Sound Forge to spend more time examining the data, thus yielding better quality. So, if you don't mind spending a little extra time encoding your file, turn this option on.

12. Set the Enable Variable Bit Rate Encoding option. This setting also increases the quality of your data, but it may introduce a slight pause during the startup of playback.

13. Set the Enable Loss Protection option. This feature embeds special codes in your data that can prevent data loss during playback over a bad Internet connection. You'll probably want to turn this option on as well.

14. Under the Advanced Video tab, leave these settings alone. The default values are usually the best ones to use.

15. Under the Summary tab, set the Enable Perfect Play option. If activated, this forces the G2 player to first download the entire file before playback begins. This way, the file plays off of the visitor's hard drive for better playback rather than streaming over the Internet, which can introduce glitches because of Internet congestion.

16. Set the Allow Download option. If activated, this allows listeners to download your file and play it on a mobile audio player. This option only applies to G2 audio files.

17. Set the Allow Recording option. If activated, this allows the people who are listening to your streaming audio on the Internet to record the audio for saving onto their hard drives.

18. Enter any text information you want to incorporate into the template, including Title, Author, Copyright, and Comments.

19. To save the template, click the Save Template button (shown as a small disk icon to the right of the Template field).

20. If you want to delete the template, click the Delete Template button (shown as a small X icon to the right of the Template field).

21. Click OK.

CHAPTER 4

Perfect Clarity Audio File Templates

To create a template for this file type, do the following:

1. With the Save As dialog box open, click the Custom button to open the Custom Settings dialog box (see Figure 4.16).

Figure 4.16
Use the Custom Settings dialog box to create a template for the Perfect Clarity Audio file format

2. Enter a name for the template in the Template parameter.
3. Enter a description for the template in the Description parameter.
4. Enter a sampling rate using the Sample Rate drop-down list.
5. Enter a bit depth using the Bit-Depth drop-down list.
6. Enter whether the file should be mono or stereo using the Channels drop-down list.
7. To save the template, click the Save Template button (shown as a small disk icon to the right of the Template field).
8. If you want to delete the template, click the Delete Template button (shown as a small X icon to the right of the Template field).
9. Click OK.

Video For Windows (AVI) File Templates

To create a template for this file type, do the following:

1. With the Save As dialog box open, click the Custom button to open the Custom Settings dialog box (see Figure 4.17).

Figure 4.17
Use the Custom Settings
dialog box to create a
template for the Video
For Windows file format

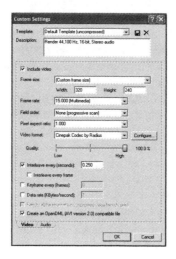

2. Enter a name for the template in the Template parameter.
3. Enter a description for the template in the Description parameter.
4. If you want to use this template to save video data, activate the Include Video option under the Video tab.
5. If you want to change the size of the video frames to something other than the original size, you can do so by selecting a new frame size from the Frame Size drop-down list. You can also set a custom video frame size by selecting Custom Frame Size from the drop-down list and then entering values for the Width and Height parameters.
6. Set the frame rate for the video using the Frame Rate drop-down list. The higher the frame rate, the smoother the video motion. There are certain frame rates that should be used with certain video material. For instance, a frame rate of 15 is used for multimedia content; a frame rate of 24 is used for film; a frame rate of 25 is used for European television; and a frame rate of 29.970 is used for American television.
7. Set the field order using the Field Order drop-down list. You need to consult the user's manual of your video capture card for information on what setting to use here. For most purposes, just leave it set to None.
8. Set the pixel aspect ratio using the Pixel Aspect Ratio drop-down list. You need to consult the user's manual of your video capture card for information on what setting to use here. For most purposes, just leave it set to 1.000.

9. Select a compression scheme for your video using the Video Format drop-down list. This parameter allows you to apply compression to your video data to make the video file smaller in size. Be aware that this does affect the quality of the video and different compression schemes yield different results.

10. Depending on the compression scheme you select, the Quality, Keyframe Every, and Data Rate parameters may or may not be available. If they are available, set them to the appropriate values. The Quality parameter allows you to set the amount of compression that you want to apply to the video data. The Keyframe Every parameter allows you to set the number of key frames that will be included in the video data. Key frames are individual video frames that have less compression or no compression at all applied to them. The more key frames included in the video data, the higher the quality of the video but the lower the amount of compression (less compression means a bigger file size). The Data Rate parameter allows you to set the amount of data per second that will be required to play back the AVI file in real time. The standard data rate for a CD-ROM drive is 150 K per second, but with most modern drives able to transfer data at quadruple or higher speeds, you shouldn't have any trouble with higher rates. Plus, hard drives transfer data even faster, so setting the data rate depends on where you plan to play back your AVI file.

11. Some of the compression schemes also come with additional parameters that you can configure. You can access these parameters by clicking the Configure button. Unfortunately, there are so many different compression schemes available, it is impossible for me to cover them all, so you are on your own here.

12. Set the Interleave Every parameters. Activating the Interleave Every parameters structures the data in the AVI file so that segments of the audio and video data are interspersed and read sequentially during playback. This is a good way to improve the playback performance of your AVI files, especially if they are destined for CD-ROM. The seconds value of the Interleave Every (Seconds) parameter allows you to specify the interval between audio and video segments. I find, however, that activating the Interleave Every Frame parameters works best. This setting interleaves the data at every video frame.

13. Click the Audio tab.

14. If you want to use this template to save audio data, activate the Include Audio option.

15. Select a compression scheme for the audio data using the Audio Format drop-down list.

16. Depending on your choice in the Audio Format drop-down list, you can set the sampling rate, bit depth, and channels of the audio data using either the Attributes drop-down list or the Sample Rate, Bit-Depth, and Channels drop-down lists.

17. To save the template, click the Save Template button (shown as a small disk icon to the right of the Template field).

18. If you want to delete the template, click the Delete Template button (shown as a small X icon to the right of the Template field).

19. Click OK.

Wave (WAV) File Templates

To create a template for this file type, do the following:

1. With the Save As dialog box open, click the Custom button to open the Custom Settings dialog box (see Figure 4.18).

Figure 4.18
Use the Custom Settings dialog box to create a template for the WAV file format

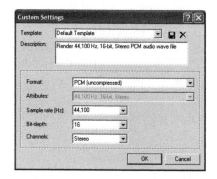

2. Enter a name for the template in the Template parameter.
3. Enter a description for the template in the Description parameter.
4. Select a compression scheme for the audio data using the Format drop-down list.
5. Depending on your choice in the Format drop-down list, you can set the sampling rate, bit depth, and channels of the audio data using either the Attributes drop-down list or the Sample Rate, Bit-Depth, and Channels drop-down lists.
6. To save the template, click the Save Template button (shown as a small disk icon to the right of the Template field).
7. If you want to delete the template, click the Delete Template button (shown as a small X icon to the right of the Template field).
8. Click OK.

Windows Media Audio File Templates

To create a template for this file type, do the following:

1. With the Save As dialog box open, click the Custom button to open the Custom Settings dialog box (see Figure 4.19).

Figure 4.19
Use the Custom Settings dialog box to create a template for the Windows Media Audio file format

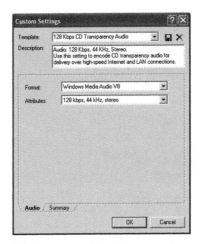

2. Enter a name for the template in the Template parameter.

3. Enter a description for the template in the Description parameter.

4. Under the Audio tab, select a compression scheme for the audio data using the Format drop-down list.

5. Set the bit rate, sampling rate, and channels of the audio data using the Attributes drop-down list.

6. Click the Summary tab.

7. Enter any textual data you want to incorporate into the template, including Title, Author, Copyright, Description, and Rating.

8. To save the template, click the Save Template button (shown as a small disk icon to the right of the Template field).

9. If you want to delete the template, click the Delete Template button (shown as a small X icon to the right of the Template field).

10. Click OK.

Windows Media Video File Templates

To create a template for this file type, do the following:

1. With the Save As dialog box open, click the Custom button to open the Custom Settings dialog box (see Figure 4.20).

Figure 4.20
Use the Custom Settings dialog box to create a template for the Windows Media Video file format

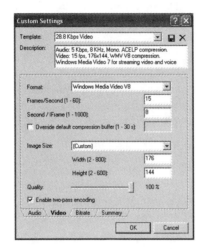

2. Enter a name for the template in the Template parameter.

3. Enter a description for the template in the Description parameter.

4. Under the Audio tab, select a compression scheme for the audio data using the Format drop-down list.

5. Set the bit rate, sampling rate, and channels of the audio data using the Attributes drop-down list.

6. Click the Video tab.

7. Select a compression scheme for your video using the Format drop-down list. This parameter allows you to apply compression to your video data to make the video file smaller in size. Be aware that this does affect the quality of the video and different compression schemes yield different results.

8. Set the frame rate for the video using the Frames/Second parameter. The higher the frame rate, the smoother the video motion. There are certain frame rates that should be used with certain video material. For instance, a frame rate of 15 is used for multimedia and Internet content.

9. By activating the Override Default Compression Buffer option, you can specify the number of seconds of video data that the player software will download before it begins to play the video. This can result in better playback sometimes, but most often, the user sets their own buffer settings in the player software, so it's usually best to leave this option deactivated.

10. If you want to change the size of the video frames to something other than the original size, you can do so by selecting a new frame size from the Image Size drop-down list. You can also set a custom video frame size by selecting Custom from the drop-down list and then entering values for the Width and Height parameters.

11. Set the Quality parameter. This parameter allows you to set the amount of compression that you want to apply to the video data. The more compression, the lower the quality of the video but the smaller the file size. The less compression, the higher the quality of the video but the larger the file size.

12. Set the Enable Two-Pass Encoding option. Activating this option tells Sound Forge to spend more time examining the data, thus yielding better quality. So, if you don't mind spending a little extra time encoding your file, turn this option on.

13. Click the Bitrate tab.

14. Choose the target bit rates that you want to use for the video data depending on what connection speeds your visitors will be using to view your Web site.

15. Click the Summary tab.

16. Enter any textual data you want to incorporate into the template, including Title, Author, Copyright, Description, and Rating.

17. To save the template, click the Save Template button (shown as a small disk icon to the right of the Template field).

18. If you want to delete the template, click the Delete Template button (shown as a small X icon to the right of the Template field).

19. Click OK.

5

Getting Around in Sound Forge

To record, play, and edit your audio in Sound Forge, you have to know how to navigate your way through the data in your file. As you learned in Chapter 2, Sound Forge provides a Data Window that allows you to examine and manipulate your audio data. Sound Forge also provides a number of other features that allow you to navigate through your audio within the Data Window. In this chapter, you'll learn how to:

▶ Use the Current Position

▶ Use the Go To function

▶ Set place marks in your audio file

▶ Search for specific audio data in your file

The Current Position

You learned a little about timing in Chapter 1. Essentially, you learned that in addition to the audio data itself, the timing of the sounds is tracked during recording. What this means is that Sound Forge keeps track of exactly when a sound occurs while you are recording, so that later during playback, your audio is played accurately and sounds exactly as it did during recording.

To give you access to your data in a file, Sound Forge provides a feature known as the Current Position. The Current Position is essentially a pointer that indicates your current time location within an audio file. For example, the beginning of a file has a Current Position of 00:00:00 (when measured in hours, minutes, and seconds). If you want to view the data at two minutes and five seconds, for example, set the Current Position to 00:02:05. In addition, you can get even more precise by specifying milliseconds, such as in a Current Position of 00:05:02:010, which is five minutes, two seconds, and ten milliseconds.

The Current Position is also updated in real time, which means that it changes constantly during recording or playback of an audio file. So, for example, as you play your file, the Current Position counts along and shows you the current timing while you listen to your audio.

Show Me the Current Position

You can view the Current Position in several different ways. Numerically, the Current Position is displayed in the Playbar of the Data Window (see Figure 5.1).

Figure 5.1
You can view the Current Position in the Playbar of the Data Window

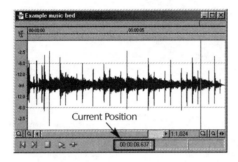

You can also use the Time Display to view the Current Position (see Figure 5.2). To open the Time Display, simply choose View > Time Display (or press Alt + 5 on your computer keyboard).

Figure 5.2
The Current Position is also shown in the Time Display

$$00{:}00{:}08.614$$

TIP

If you're like me, and you have some of your equipment set up in your home studio a fair distance away from your computer, you might have trouble reading the small Current Position in either the Data Window Playbar or the Time Display. To remedy this situation, Sound Forge allows you to change the size of the Time Display. Just drag any of its sides or corners, like you do with any window in Windows. Sound Forge scales the size of the Current Position accordingly, as shown in Figure 5.3.

Figure 5.3
By manipulating the
Time Display, you can
view the Current
Position in a variety of
sizes on your computer
screen

The Current Position Cursor

In addition to being displayed numerically, the Current Position is displayed graphically within Sound Forge's Data Windows. In the Data Window, the Current Position is displayed as a vertical line cursor that extends from the top to the bottom of the window. As the Current Position changes—either from being set manually or in real time during playback—the cursor follows along and indicates graphically the place in the audio file that the Current Position is currently pointing. To demonstrate what I mean, try the following:

1. Choose File > Open (or press Ctrl + O on your computer keyboard), and load one of the sample files that comes with Sound Forge. For this example, choose MUSICBED.PCA (see Figure 5.4).

Figure 5.4
This screen shows the
Data Window for the
MUSICBED.PCA audio
file

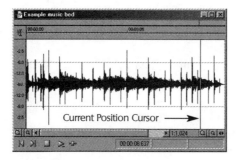

Current Position Cursor ⟶

2. Choose Special > Transport > Play (or press the space bar on your computer keyboard) to start playing the file.

3. Look at the Data Window. See the Current Position cursor moving across the screen as the audio plays?

4. Notice the row of numbers above the place where the Current Position cursor is moving; this is the Time Ruler. The Time Ruler displays the time in the current audio file. By lining up the top of the Current Position cursor with the Time Ruler, you can get a quick estimate of the Current Position.

Set the Current Position

As you've just seen, the Current Position changes automatically as an audio file is played, but you can also set the Current Position manually while a file isn't playing. Sound Forge gives you this capability so that you can access different parts of your file for editing, which I talk about in Chapter 7.

Numerically

Changing the Current Position is easy. If you want to set the Current Position to a precise numerical value, you can use the Go To function. Here's how:

1. Choose Edit > Go To (or press Ctrl + G on your computer keyboard) to open the Go To dialog box, as shown in Figure 5.5.

Figure 5.5
You can change the Current Position using the Go To function via the Go To dialog box

2. Sound Forge gives you quick access to a number of predefined points in a file via the Go To drop-down list. To use one of these, just make a selection from the list, and skip to Step 5.

3. For precise positioning, enter a time value in the Position field.

TIP

If you want to quickly set the Current Position to a particular time, you don't have to enter all the numerical values. For example, to set the Current Position to five seconds and ten milliseconds, type 5.010. That's it. There's no need to enter values for the hours or minutes because they're just zero anyway.

4. If you want to set the Current Position using a different type of time measurement, you can change the measurement using the Input Format drop-down list. In addition to time, you can choose to enter a value in a number of different formats, including samples (refer to Chapter 1), measures and beats, or SMPTE/frames.

NOTE

SMPTE (which stands for the Society of Motion Picture and Television Engineers) is a special timing code used for synchronizing audio and video data, although it can be used for other purposes, too. The technology was originally developed by NASA because it needed a precise method of keeping track of space mission data. In Sound Forge, you can use SMPTE to keep track of the timing of your audio file. Sound Forge automatically converts the regular time values in a file to the hours, minutes, seconds, and frames format used by SMPTE. The frames parameter comes from the fact that SMPTE is used extensively with video, film, and television. Video is created by recording a series of still picture frames very quickly. When these frames are played back, you see them as a moving picture. SMPTE can be used to time video data accurately right down to a single frame. Every second of video data usually has thirty frames, but the number depends on the format of the data. You learn more about using SMPTE in Chapter 6. For now, just know that you can view and set the Current Position of your file in a number of different ways, including in hours, minutes, seconds, and frames.

5. When you've entered the value you want to use, click OK.

Sound Forge changes the Current Position to the value you entered, and it also moves the Current Position cursor to the appropriate place within your file.

Graphically

Remember earlier when I described the Time Ruler in the Data Window in "The Current Position Cursor" section? Well, you can quickly change the Current Position by simply clicking within the Waveform Display area of the Data Window (the large area below the Time Ruler). For example, you can do the following:

1. Like you did earlier, choose File > Open (or press Ctrl + O on your computer keyboard), and load one of the sample audio files included with Sound Forge. For this example, choose MUSICBED.PCA.

2. Click in the Waveform Display area of the Data Window, as shown in Figure 5.6.

Figure 5.6
By clicking within the Waveform Display area of the Data Window, you can change the Current Position

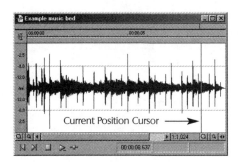

CHAPTER 5

TIP

You can also use the left and right arrow keys on your computer keyboard to move the Current Position cursor one time unit to the left or right.

3. Click once more in a different place. See how the Current Position changes? Depending on where you click within the Waveform Display, the Current Position changes to the appropriate value as measured on the Time Ruler.

TIP

As I mentioned earlier, you can enter a time value in the Go To dialog box using a number of different formats. Well, you can also change the Time Ruler to display its values in any of those formats. Just right-click the Time Ruler (or choose Options > Status Format) and select the type of format you want to use.

The Overview Area

Another quick way to set the Current Position graphically is to use the Overview Bar. The Overview Bar is part of the Data Window, located just above the Time Ruler (see Figure 5.7). To use the Overview Bar, just click within it like you did earlier with the Waveform Display. That's it.

Figure 5.7
You can also set the Current Position graphically by clicking in the Overview Bar

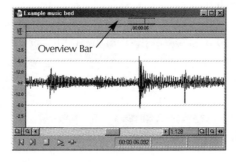

NOTE
The Overview Bar does offer a few other options, some of which I talk about later in the book. But for navigational purposes, the Overview Bar gives you access to your entire audio file even if part of it is located off of the screen. For example, if you open a very long audio file, all of the data can't be displayed inside the Data Window. To change the Current Position to a part of the file that isn't being displayed, you first have to scroll the Data Window (I also talk about this later in the book) to the appropriate place and then click in the Waveform Display. With the Overview Bar, you can just click once to change the Current Position even if it's off of the screen. And you can simply double-click within the Overview Bar to both change the Current Position and scroll the Data Window so that you can view the new area of your audio file.

The Transport Menu

In addition to allowing you to set the Current Position both numerically and graphically, Sound Forge provides a few special functions that let you quickly change the Current Position within an audio file. All these functions are part of the Transport menu. To activate them, simply choose Special > Transport, and choose the appropriate function. Following is a list of the functions, along with explanations for each of them:

Go To Start

This function is pretty self-explanatory. Simply put, it allows you to set the Current Position to the time that corresponds to the beginning of your audio file.

Rewind

The Rewind function sets the Current Position by subtracting a time value from its current value, thus moving the Current Position cursor closer to the beginning of your audio file. The time value subtracted depends on the zoom level you are currently using. I talk more about Sound Forge's Zoom features in Chapter 7.

Forward

The Forward function sets the Current Position by adding a time value from its current value, thus moving the Current Position cursor closer to the end of your audio file. The time value added depends on the zoom level you are currently using.

Go To End

This function is also self-explanatory. It allows you to set the Current Position to the time that corresponds to the end of your audio file.

TIP

Instead of using the Transport menu, you can use your computer keyboard for even quicker access to the previously mentioned functions. For Go To Start, just press Ctrl + Home. For Go To End, just press Ctrl + End. For Rewind, just press Page Up. For Forward, just press Page Down. And, if you want to Rewind or Forward the Current Position precisely by the smallest value possible, just press either the left arrow (Rewind) or right arrow (Forward) keys on your computer keyboard.

Markers, Oh My!

All the methods for setting the Current Position that I've described so far have either been based on numbers or predefined designations, such as the beginning or end of an audio file. These methods are fine when you already have the material for your file mapped out so you know exactly where everything occurs ahead of time, but what if you're creating material from scratch simply by recording on the fly? In this case, being able to put names to certain locations within a file is very helpful, and that's exactly what Markers allow you to do.

With Markers, you can assign a name to any exact point in time within an audio file. They're great for designating the places at which certain passages of a vocal recording occur. In addition, they make it very easy for you to jump to any point within a file that you specify simply by name.

Make Your Mark(ers)

Creating Markers is a simple process. Essentially, you just need to set the Current Position to the time at which you want to place the Marker in the file, activate the Insert Marker/Region dialog box, and type in a name. To create a Marker, just follow these steps:

1. Set the Current Position to the time at which you want to place the Marker in the audio file. As you learned earlier, you can set it either numerically or graphically.

2. Right-click in the Ruler Tag area (located just below the Time Ruler in the Data Window), as shown in Figure 5.8.

Figure 5.8
The Ruler Tag area is located just below the Time Ruler in the Data Window

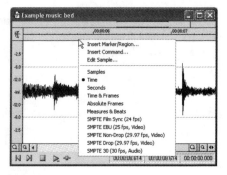

3. Choose Insert Marker/Region from the shortcut menu to open the Insert Marker/Region dialog box, as shown in Figure 5.9.

Figure 5.9
Using the Insert Marker/Region dialog box, you can create a Marker

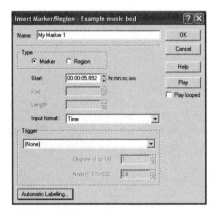

TIP

Instead of right-clicking in the Ruler Tag area, you can simply choose Special > Regions List > Insert to open the Insert Marker/Region dialog box.

4. Type a name for the Marker.

5. Make sure the Marker option in the Type section is activated. I talk about the Region option later in this chapter.

6. Because you've already set the Current Position, you don't need to change the position of the Marker, but if you want to make adjustments, enter a new time in the Start field. As with the Go To dialog box (mentioned earlier), you can select the format you want to use for entering the position value via the Input Format drop-down list.

7. Remember when I talked about MIDI Triggers back in Chapter 3? Well, in addition to many of its other functions, Sound Forge allows you to assign MIDI Triggers to Markers, too. This feature allows you to start playback from any point in your audio file via an external MIDI device such as a synthesizer keyboard. To assign a MIDI Trigger to your Marker, choose an option from the Trigger drop-down list. MIDI: Note On – Play triggers playback via a specified Note On message. MIDI: Note On – Play / Note Off – Stop triggers playback via a specified Note On message and stops playback upon receiving a follow-up Note Off message. MIDI: Note On – Queue / Note Off – Play triggers the Current Position to be set to the Marker position and starts playback upon receiving a follow-up Note Off message.

8. Enter the number of the MIDI channel you want to use for your MIDI Trigger via the Channel parameter.

9. Enter the pitch of the MIDI note you want to use for your MIDI Trigger via the Note parameter.

10. Click OK.

When you're finished, your Marker (and its name) is added to the Ruler Tag area (just below the Time Ruler) in the Data Window.

TIP

Usually, you add Markers to an audio file while no real-time activity is going on, but you can also add Markers while a file is playing. Simply press the M key on your computer keyboard, and Sound Forge creates a Marker at the present Current Position. The new Marker is automatically assigned a temporary name, which you can later change.

If you want, you can also adjust how the temporary Marker names are created. Just click the Automatic Labeling button in the Insert Marker/Region dialog box to display the Automatic Labeling dialog box. In the Markers section, you can have your Markers automatically labeled using the Current Position value or via a custom labeling scheme by activating the appropriate option. If you choose the Custom Label option, you can have a prefix added to each Marker name by using the New Marker Prefix option. You can also have each Marker name use a consecutive number by using the Use Counter And Start At and Insert Leading Zeros In Field Width Of options.

Edit the Markers

Editing existing Markers is just as easy as creating new ones. You can change their names, times, and MIDI Triggers, make copies of them, and delete them.

Name and Trigger Change

To change the name or MIDI Trigger of a Marker, follow these steps:

1. Right-click the Marker in the Ruler Tag area of the Data Window and choose Edit from the shortcut menu to open the Edit Marker/Region dialog box (which is exactly the same as the Insert Marker/Region dialog box). Alternatively, choose View > Regions List (or press Alt + 1 on your computer keyboard) to open the Regions window (see Figure 5.10), and double-click on the Marker in the list to open the Edit Marker/Region dialog box.

Figure 5.10
The Regions window displays a list of all the Markers in an audio file

2. Type a new name for the Marker.

3. Select new MIDI Trigger settings for the Marker.

4. Click OK.

Time Change

Follow these steps to change the time value of a Marker numerically:

1. Right-click the Marker in the Ruler Tag area of the Data Window and choose Edit from the shortcut menu to open the Edit Marker/Region dialog box (which is exactly the same as the Insert Marker/Region dialog box). Alternatively, choose View > Regions List (or press Alt + 1 on your computer keyboard) to open the Regions window, and double-click the Marker in the list to open the Edit Marker/Region dialog box.

2. Select the format you want to use via the Input Format drop-down list.

3. Enter a new time value via the Start parameter for the Marker.

4. Click OK.

You can also change the time value of a Marker graphically by simply dragging the Marker within the Ruler Tag area of the Data Window with your mouse. Drag the Marker to the left to decrease its time value, or drag it to the right to increase its time value. Simple, no? In addition, you can quickly change the Marker's position to the Current Position by right-clicking the Marker and choosing Update from the shortcut menu. The Go To selection in the shortcut menu does the exact opposite: It quickly sets the Current Position to the same value as the Marker.

Make a Copy

To make a copy of a Marker, follow these steps:

1. Click the Marker to select it in the Ruler Tag area of the Data Window. Alternatively, choose View > Regions List (or press Alt + 1 on your computer keyboard) to open the Regions window, and click the Marker to select it in the list.

2. Choose Special > Regions List > Replicate to make an exact copy of the Marker. Alternatively, right-click the Marker in the Regions window and select Replicate from the shortcut menu.

3. Initially, the new Marker has the exact same characteristics (including name and time value) as the original. So, edit the new Marker to change its settings.

Delete a Marker

You can delete a Marker in one of two ways—either directly in the Data Window or via the Regions window. Here's the exact procedure:

1. If you want to use the Data Window, click the Marker that you want to delete to select it.

2. If you want to use the Regions window, select View > Regions List (or press Alt

+ 1 on your computer keyboard) to open the Regions window. Then, select the Marker that you want to delete from the list.

3.   Right-click the Marker and select Delete from the shortcut menu. Alternatively, you can choose Special > Regions List > Delete.

Navigate with Markers

Of course, what good is creating Markers if you can't use them to navigate through the data in your file? What's more, all you need to do is select the name of a Marker, and the Current Position is automatically set to the exact time of that Marker. You can move to a specific Marker in a file in two different ways: either by using the Regions window or the Go To function.

Use the Regions Window

To jump to a specific Marker using the Regions window, do the following:

1.   Choose View > Regions List (or press Alt + 1 on your computer keyboard) to open the Regions window.

2.   Select the Marker that you want to jump to from the list.

3.   Sound Forge then sets the Current Position to the time corresponding to that Marker, and the Current Position cursor in the Data Window jumps to the appropriate location.

Use the Go To Function

To jump to a specific Marker using the Go To function, do the following:

1.   Choose Edit > Go To (or press Ctrl + G on your computer keyboard) to open the Go To dialog box.

2.   Select a Marker from the Go To drop-down list.

3.   Click OK.

Sound Forge then sets the Current Position to the time corresponding to that Marker, and the Current Position cursor in the Data Window jumps to the appropriate location.

TIP

To quickly jump to the next or previous Marker in the Data Window, simply press the CTRL + Left Arrow or CTRL + Right Arrow keys on your computer keyboard.

What About Regions?

In addition to Markers, Sound Forge allows you to label different sections of your audio file using its Regions feature. The only difference between Markers and Regions is that Markers specify a single point within a file, whereas Regions specify an entire area. In addition to a starting point, Regions also have an ending point and length associated with them. Regions are great for specifying certain areas of your file for easy playback or editing. And just like with Markers, you can assign a name to any section of your file. So, for example, if you are working with a vocal recording, you can easily mark the different lyric passages within the file. Then, you can easily jump to or edit any passage in the file.

Make Your Regions

You can create Regions in one of two ways: by manually using the Insert Marker/Region dialog box or by automatically using Sound Forge's Auto Region function.

Use the Insert Marker/Region Dialog Box

To create a Region using the Insert Marker/Region dialog box, do the following:

1. Click and drag your mouse within the Waveform Display of the Data Window to select the portion of your audio file around which you want to create a Region, as shown in Figure 5.11. I talk more about selecting data in Chapter 7.

Figure 5.11
To create a Region, first select a portion of your audio file

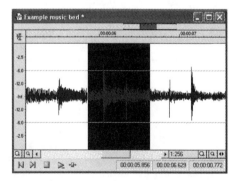

CHAPTER 5

TIP
You can also select data using your computer keyboard by simply holding down the Shift key while using the navigation keyboard shortcuts that I mentioned earlier. For example, hold down the Shift key and press the Left Arrow key to make a selection from the Current Position towards the beginning of the audio file.

2. Choose Special > Regions List > Insert (or press the R key on your computer keyboard) to open the Insert Marker/Region dialog box, as shown in Figure 5.12.

Figure 5.12
In addition to
Markers, the Insert
Marker/Region dialog
box can be used to
create Regions

3. Type a name for the Region.

4. Make sure the Region option in the Type section is activated.

5. Because you've already selected a portion of your audio file, the Start, End, and Length parameters should already be set. However, if you want to make adjustments, enter new values into any of the fields. As with the Go To dialog box (mentioned earlier), you can select the format you want to use for entering position values via the Input Format drop-down list.

6. As with Markers, you can set up a MIDI Trigger for your new Region. Triggering Regions is even more useful than triggering Markers, because when you play, a Region, Sound Forge only plays the audio data contained within the Regions boundaries. So, for example, you could have an audio file containing a number of different vocal passages that could be triggered during a live performance or recording session in any order that you choose.

7. Click OK.

When you're finished, your new Region and its name is added to the Ruler Tag area (just below the Time Ruler) in the Data Window.

TIP

For a really quick way to create a Region, just make a data selection and press Shift + R on your computer keyboard. A new Region is created and is automatically assigned a temporary name, which you can later change.

If you want, you can also adjust how the temporary Region names are created. Just click the Automatic Labeling button in the Insert Marker/Region dialog box to display the Automatic Labeling dialog box. In the Regions section, you can have your Regions automatically labeled using the Current Position value or via a custom labeling scheme by activating the appropriate option. If you choose the Custom Label option, you can have a prefix added to each Region name by using the New Region Prefix option. You can also have each Region name use a consecutive number by using the Use Counter And Start At and Insert Leading Zeros In Field Width Of options.

Use the Auto Region Function

The Auto Region function automatically creates Regions for you by scanning the data in your audio file for certain characteristics that you specify. To detect these characteristics, the Auto Region function uses a digital noise gate. Depending on your parameter settings, this noise gate opens up when the Auto Region function comes upon a section in your audio that has an amplitude (volume) level greater than the one you set. It identifies this part of the audio as acceptable sound (or the beginning of a Region) and lets it pass through. When the level of audio dips below a certain amplitude level that you set, the noise gate identifies that part of the audio as the end of a Region, and it closes to stop it from passing through. At that point, the Auto Region function creates a new Region from the acceptable data. This process happens over and over until the entire audio file has been scanned.

To create new Regions using the Auto Region function, do the following:

1. Choose Tools > Auto Region to open the Auto Region dialog box, as shown in Figure 5.13.

Figure 5.13
Before Auto Region can do its magic, you need to specify the characteristics you want to use via the Auto Region dialog box

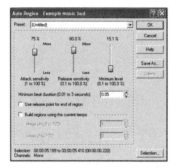

2. Set the Minimum Level parameter by dragging its slider up or down. This parameter determines how loud the audio data has to be to make the noise gate open, thus identifying the data as acceptable sound and the start of a new Region.

3. Set the Attack Sensitivity parameter by dragging its slider up or down. This parameter determines how quickly the noise gate opens and thus creates the start of a Region. If you set this parameter too high, the noise gate reacts to any small amplitude increases and ends up creating Regions where you don't want them. If you set this parameter too low, the noise gate may not detect all the Regions that you want it to. You should experiment to find the right setting depending on the material you are scanning.

4. Set the Release Sensitivity parameter by dragging its slider up or down. This parameter is similar to the Attack Sensitivity parameter but in reverse. It determines how quickly the noise gate closes and thus creates the end of a Region. If you set this parameter too high, the noise gate reacts to any small amplitude decreases and ends some Regions where you don't want them to end. If you set this parameter too low, the noise gate may not detect the end of some

Regions. Again, you should experiment to find the right setting depending on the material you are scanning.

5. Set the Minimum Beat Duration parameter. This parameter determines how long (in seconds) the noise gate remains open even when a dip in the amplitude level is detected. Basically, it means that this amount of time must elapse before a new Region can be detected/created. Setting this parameter low allows the noise gate to detect quick amplitude changes, such as drum beats. Setting this parameter high prevents the noise gate from detecting this type of data.

6. Activate the Use Release Point For End Of Region option if you don't want low amplitude sections of your audio (such as silence) included in your Regions. Deactivate this option if you only want the end of a Region created when the start of a new Region is detected.

7. Click OK.

Sound Forge scans your audio file and then creates new Regions according to the settings that you specified.

TIP

For some examples on how the Auto Region parameters should be set, be sure to check out the default presets provided by Sound Forge. To access them, click in the Preset drop-down list at the top of the dialog box.

You can also have the Auto Region function create Regions for you based on musical designations, such as tempo, measures, and beats. To do this, you have to determine the tempo of your audio data, and then tell the Auto Region function at what measures and beats you want new Regions to be created. Here's how:

1. Click and drag your mouse within the Waveform Display of the Data Window to select a portion of your audio file that is equal to one measure of musical data. You may have to listen to the audio a few times to find the right area to highlight.

2. Choose Special > Edit Tempo to open the Edit Tempo dialog box, as shown in Figure 5.14.

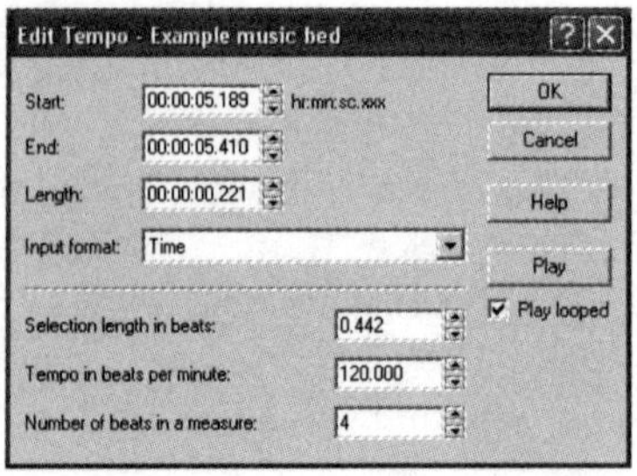

Figure 5.14
You can tell Sound Forge the tempo of your music using the Edit Tempo dialog box

3. Because you've already made a data selection, the Start, End, and Length parameters should be set, but you can make adjustments to them if you want.

4. Set the Number Of Beats In A Measure parameter. For example, if your music is in 4/4 time, then the number of beats in a measure is 4.

5. Set the Selection Length In Beats parameter. This tells Sound Forge how many beats are in the portion of data you selected. For example, if your music has four beats in a measure, and you selected one measure's worth of data, then you would set this parameter to 4.

6. Sound Forge should then automatically adjust the Tempo In Beats Per Minute parameter. If this isn't correct, adjust it. When you adjust this parameter, the Selected Length In Beats Parameter is adjusted automatically, and vice versa.

7. When you're satisfied with the parameter settings, click OK.

8. In the Data Window, change the Time Ruler to display its measurements in measures and beats by right-clicking the Time Ruler and choosing Measures & Beats from the shortcut menu (or choosing Options > Status Format > Measures & Beats).

9. Choose Tools > Auto Region to open the Auto Region dialog box.

10. Activate the Build Regions Using The Current Tempo option.

11. Set the Measures parameter and the Beats parameter. These parameters work together, and they specify at what intervals you want Regions to be created in your file. For example, if you want Regions to be created at every beat, then set Measures to 0 and Beats to 1. If you want Regions to be created at every measure, set Measures to 1 and Beats to 0. If you want Regions to be created at every 7 beats, set Measures to 1 and Beats to 3. All of these examples are based on your music having 4 beats per measure. You get the idea.

12. Click OK.

Sound Forge creates new Regions according to the tempo, measure, and beat settings that you specified, and the Start and End points of the Regions should line up with the measurements in the Time Ruler.

TIP
There is one additional way to create Regions in Sound Forge. If your file contains existing Markers, you can convert those Markers to Regions by choosing Special > Regions List > Markers To Regions.

Edit the Regions

Just as with Markers, you can edit the Regions you create. You can change their names, start, and end times, make copies of them, split them into smaller Regions, and delete them.

Name and Trigger Change

To change the name or MIDI Trigger of a Region, follow these steps:

1. Right-click on either of the tags of the Region in the Ruler Tag area of the Data Window and choose Edit from the shortcut menu to open the Edit Marker/Region dialog box. Alternatively, choose View > Regions List (or press Alt + 1 on your computer keyboard) to open the Regions window, and double-click on the Region in the list.

2. Type a new name for the Region.

3. Select new MIDI Trigger settings for the Region.

4. Click OK.

Time Change

Follow these steps to change the time values of a Region numerically:

1. Right-click on either of the tags of the Region in the Ruler Tag area of the Data Window and choose Edit from the shortcut menu to open the Edit Marker/Region dialog box. Alternatively, choose View > Regions List (or press Alt + 1 on your computer keyboard) to open the Regions window, and double-click on the Region in the list.

2. Select the format you want to use via the Input Format drop-down list.

3. Enter new values for the Start and End parameters. Changing these parameters automatically changes the Length parameter. If you change the Length parameter, the End parameter is automatically adjusted.

4. Click OK.

You can also change the time values of a Region graphically by simply dragging the Start and End tags within the Ruler Tag area of the Data Window with your mouse. Drag the tags to the left to decrease their values, or drag them to the right to increase their values. Just as with Markers, it's a simple procedure. In addition, you can quickly select the data within a Region by right-clicking on either of the Region's tags and choosing Select from the shortcut menu.

Make a Copy

To make a copy of a Region, follow these steps:

1. Right-click on either of the tags of the Region in the Ruler Tag area of the Data Window and choose Select from the shortcut menu. Alternatively, choose View > Regions List (or press Alt + 1 on your computer keyboard) to open the Regions window, and click on the Region to select it in the list.

2. Choose Special > Regions List > Replicate to make an exact copy of the Region. Alternatively, right-click on the Region in the Regions window and select Replicate from the shortcut menu. By the way, this does not make a copy of the data outlined in the Region, just a copy of the Region tags. Remember, Regions just mark areas of your data, they don't contain audio data themselves.

3. Initially, the new Region will have the exact same characteristics (including name and time values) as the original. So, edit the new Region to change its settings.

Split a Region

In addition to copying a Region, you can also split it into two new Regions. For example, if you have a Region that outlines two measures of data and you'd rather break that Region down so that you have one measure per Region, this function makes the process easy. To split a Region, follow these steps:

1. Change the Current Position to the point within the Region at which you want it to be split. This point becomes the end of one of the new Regions and the start of the other.

2. Right-click on either of the tags of the Region in the Ruler Tag area of the Data Window and choose Split from the shortcut menu.

Sound Forge creates two new Regions from the old Region.

Delete a Region

You can delete a Region in one of two ways, either directly in the Data Window or via the Regions window. Here's the procedure:

1. If you want to use the Data Window, right-click on either of the Region's tags and choose Select from the shortcut menu to select the Region.

2. If you want to use the Regions window, choose View > Regions List (or press Alt + 1 on your computer keyboard) to open the Regions window. Then, select the Region that you want to delete from the list.

3. Right-click on one of the tags in the Data Window or the Region in the Regions window and choose Delete from the shortcut menu. Alternatively, you can choose Special > Regions List > Delete.

TIP
You can also delete all the Regions in a file by simply choosing Special > Regions List > Clear.

Navigate with Regions

Just as with Markers, you can use Regions to navigate through the data in your audio file. You can move to a specific Region in a file in two different ways: either by using the Regions window or the Go To function.

Use the Regions Window

To jump to a specific Region using the Regions window, do the following:

1. Choose View > Regions List (or press Alt + 1 on your computer keyboard) to open the Regions window.

2. Select the Region that you want to jump to from the list.

3. Sound Forge then sets the Current Position to the time corresponding to the Start tag of that Region, and the Current Position cursor in the Data Window jumps to the appropriate place.

Use the Go To Function

To jump to a specific Region using the Go To function, do the following:

1. Choose Edit > Go To (or press Ctrl + G on your computer keyboard) to open the Go To dialog box.

2. Select a Region from the Go To drop-down list.

3. Click OK.

Sound Forge then sets the Current Position to the time corresponding to the Start tag of that Region, and the Current Position cursor in the Data Window jumps to the appropriate place.

TIP

To quickly jump to the next or previous Region tag in the Data Window, simply press the CTRL + Left Arrow or CTRL + Right Arrow keys on your computer keyboard.

Saving and Loading Regions

When you save your audio file in certain formats, your Region markings get saved along with it. But, unfortunately, not all file formats (discussed in Chapter 4) allow you to store Region data along with your audio data. What if you want to save your audio in an incompatible format and still keep the Region markings? To remedy this problem, Sound Forge allows you to save and load Region data as separate files.

Save your Region Data

To save your Region data as a separate file, do the following:

1. Choose Special > Regions List > Save As to open the Save As Regions/Playlist dialog box. This box is just like any other Windows file save dialog box.

2. Choose a folder location for your new file.

3. Type a name for your new file.

4. Click Save.

Load your Region Data

To load your Region data back into Sound Forge for use with your existing audio file, do the following:

1. Choose Special > Regions List > Open to display the Open Regions/Playlist

dialog box. This box is just like any other Windows file open dialog box.

2. Choose the folder location in which you will find your file.

3. Select a file type from the Files Of Type drop-down list to display only those types of files.

4. Choose the file you want to open.

5. Click Open.

TIP

The functions for loading and saving Region data can also be used for creating more than one set of Regions for the same audio file. For example, if you are editing a vocal recording, you can use one set of Regions to outline all the phrases and another set of Regions to outline all the syllables in each phrase. This is especially useful in playback and editing, which I talk about in a number of other chapters in the book.

The Extract Regions Function

Another useful function that is related to Regions is the Extract Regions function. This function is especially useful for editing purposes because it allows you to break up your audio file into smaller files that are based on the Regions in your original file. For example, suppose you are editing a vocal performance and you have Regions set up that outline all of the phrases in the performance. You might want to split each phrase into its own audio file for use as individual sounds in your MIDI sampler device. The Extract Regions function makes this very easy. Here's how it works:

1. After you have defined all the Regions in your file, choose Tools > Extract Regions to open the Extract Regions dialog box, as shown in Figure 5.15.

Figure 5.15
The Extract Regions function allows you to create new audio files from the data outlined by the Regions in your original audio file

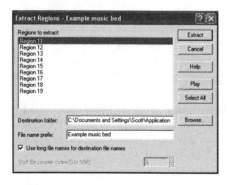

2. Choose the Regions you want to extract by selecting them in the list. If you want to extract them all, click the Select All button.

CHAPTER 5

3. Choose a folder in which the new audio files will be saved by either typing a file path in the Destination Folder parameter or using the Browse button.

4. Type a word or phrase that you want the names of each new file to begin with into the File Name Prefix parameter.

5. If you want to use long file names, activate the Use Long File Names For Destination File Names option. Otherwise, enter a number for the Start File Counter Index parameter. This parameter tells Sound Forge to append a number to each file name starting with the number that you entered.

6. Click Extract.

Sound Forge then saves the audio data outlined in each of the Regions that you selected as new audio files in the WAV format. Your original audio file remains unchanged.

Where's That Sound?

Until now, I have been describing how to navigate through the data in a file by somehow specifying the Current Position, with the result being that you go to a specific point within a file. Well, what happens when you don't know the exact position in a file to which you want to move? For instance, suppose you hear an annoying click or pop in your audio file but you can't quite pinpoint its location? Instead of playing the file and trying to listen for the click via trial and error, you can use Sound Forge's Find function.

The Find function allows you to automatically examine the data in your audio file and find a number of different kinds of amplitude-related (volume) sounds. These sounds include glitches that come in the form of unwanted clicks and pops, amplitude levels that are equal to or above a level that you specify, silent sections or passages in the audio, and the highest amplitude levels in a file. This function is very useful for finding certain points within a file (such as the silent sections of a vocal performance) and placing Markers or Regions there. The function is also useful for precision-editing tasks, which you learn more about in Chapter 7. In the meantime, you can use the Find function for navigational purposes like this:

1. Choose Special > Transport > Go To Start (or press Ctrl + Home on your computer keyboard) to set the Current Position to the beginning of the file. If you don't take this step, the Find function begins looking at your data starting at the immediate Current Position, not at the beginning of the file. This means that if the Current Position is set to 00:00:10, the Find function does not look at any of the data contained in the first ten seconds.

2. Choose Tools > Find to open the Find dialog box, as shown in Figure 5.16.

Figure 5.16
In the Find dialog box, you specify the criteria for your search

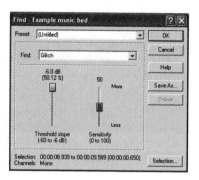

3. Select the kind of amplitude data for which you want to search via the Find drop-down list. Choose Glitch to find any clicks or pops in your audio that may have occurred from bad editing procedures, or perhaps from material that originated as a vinyl recording. Choose Level Equal To Or Above to find any amplitude level in your audio that is equal to or above the level that you specify. The Level Equal To Or Above option can be useful in finding clipped or distorted material in your audio file. Choose End Of Silent Region to find the end of the next silent section in your audio file. The End Of Silent Region option can be useful in finding (and marking) different passages in a vocal performance or even different beats in a percussion performance. Choose Largest Peak to find the highest amplitude level in your audio file. The Largest Peak option can be useful when you're trying to match the overall amplitude levels between multiple audio files, such as all the songs you want to include on the same CD.

NOTE

Clipping (or distortion) occurs when the amplitude level of audio data is raised higher than 100 percent (or 0 dB, which I talk about shortly). The top and bottom of the audio waveform becomes clipped, and when you play the audio, it sounds distorted.

4. Set the Threshold Slope parameter. Depending on which option you choose via the Find drop-down list, the Threshold Slope parameter works differently. If you choose Glitch, the Threshold Slope parameter determines the slope (steepness) of the glitch. (Glitches—or pops and clicks—in audio data look like big spikes in the audio waveform, and these spikes have a slope—or steepness—to them.) If you choose Level Equal To Or Above, the Threshold Slope parameter determines the amplitude (volume) for which you want to search. If you choose End Of Silent Region, the Threshold Slope parameter determines the amplitude level at which the audio data falls below and then rises above. This signifies a silent or quiet section in the audio. If you choose Largest Peak, the Threshold Slope parameter does not have to be set.

CHAPTER 5

NOTE

The Threshold Slope parameter is set in decibels (dB). Decibel is a very complicated term to describe, especially in a beginning to intermediate text such as this one. The most basic explanation is that a decibel is a unit of measurement used to determine the loudness of sound. In regard to digital audio, the highest possible level you can use is 0 dB. Anything higher, and you introduce clipping into your data. For a more detailed explanation, in Sound Forge, choose Help > Contents And Index. Then click Glossary and scroll down to the section labeled Decibel (dB).

5. Set the Sensitivity parameter. This parameter is only relevant if you choose Glitch in the Find drop-down menu. The Sensitivity parameter determines how closely Sound Forge examines the audio data when searching for glitches. A high setting tells Sound Forge that any audio with a slope above the Threshold Slope setting should be considered a glitch. A low setting tells Sound Forge that not all audio with a slope above the Threshold Slope setting should be considered a glitch, and that it should look more closely during the search process.

TIP

If you can hear glitches in the audio but Sound Forge doesn't detect them, try lowering the Threshold Slope and raising the Sensitivity. If you find that Sound Forge is detecting glitches where there are none, try raising the Threshold Slope and lowering the Sensitivity.

6. Click OK.

Sound Forge searches through the audio in your file and finds the appropriate data that you specified via your parameter settings. It also changes the Current Position and the Current Position cursor to the appropriate location within the file.

TIP

To quickly perform the Find function again using the same parameter settings without having to access the Find dialog box, just press Ctrl + Y on your computer keyboard.

6

Recording and Playback

As I mentioned in Chapter 3, Sound Forge doesn't provide multitrack recording or playback. What this means is that you are only allowed to record or play a single stereo audio file at a time. This is how most audio editing applications work. Their main purpose is editing, but they also provide recording for tasks such as making a stereo recording of a live performance or creating new sounds for a MIDI sampling device. Sound Forge provides a vast number of recording and playback features. In this chapter, you'll learn to:

▶ Identify which parameters need to be set prior to recording

▶ Record audio using various available methods

▶ Play audio using various available methods

▶ Correct mistakes using Punch-In

▶ Define and use synchronization

Preliminary Parameters

Before you do any actual recording with Sound Forge, you need to be aware of a number of parameter settings. These parameters allow you to configure Sound Forge for a variety of recording situations. The parameters include recording attributes, DC offset adjustment, and gap detection. All of the parameters are accessed via the Record dialog box (see Figure 6.1).

Figure 6.1
Recording audio in
Sound Forge should be
preceded with a few
parameter settings

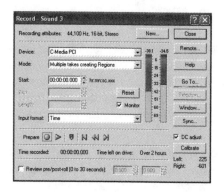

As a matter of fact, all audio recording within Sound Forge is done via the Record dialog box. To access the Record dialog box, choose Special > Transport > Record (or press Ctrl + R on your

computer keyboard). I talk more about the actual recording procedures later in this chapter. For now, I explain the what, why, and how of each parameter that needs to be set prior to recording.

Recording Attributes

First and foremost, you need to tell Sound Forge the specifications of the audio data that you want to record. In other words, you need to set the bit depth, sampling rate, and number of channels for your new recording. When you first open the Record dialog box, these parameters are automatically set to the current defaults (usually 16-bit, 44,100 Hz, stereo). To use different settings, click the New button in the Recording Attributes section of the Record dialog box to access the New Window dialog box (see Figure 6.2).

Figure 6.2
Change the bit depth, sampling rate, and channel parameters of your recording via the New Window dialog box

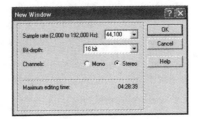

Sampling Rate and Bit Depth

You learned about the meanings of the terms sampling rate and bit depth in Chapter 1. Sound Forge enables you to set the sampling rate and bit depth used for the audio data that you record. Depending on the sophistication of your sound card, you can set the sampling rate up to 192,000 Hz and the bit depth up to 64 bits.

So, what settings should you use? Well, the higher the sampling rate and bit depth, the better the quality of your recorded audio. Higher settings also put more strain on your computer system, however, and the data takes up more memory and hard disk space. Plus, if your input signal is already bad (if you use a low-end microphone to record your vocals, for instance), higher settings won't make it sound any better.

In my opinion, if your computer has enough power, memory, and hard disk space, then you should use at least a 96,000 Hz sampling rate and a 24-bit bit depth. Using these settings ensures a very high-quality recording. Of course, you can use even higher settings, and higher always results in a better quality audio signal. However, it's very doubtful that most people will hear the difference, especially because if you want to put your audio on CD, you have to lower the quality anyway. For CD, the audio needs to have a sampling rate of 44,100 Hz and a bit depth of 16 bits.

Why record at higher settings if you're ultimately going to put your audio on CD? Well, the main reason is because of mathematical errors. You see, when audio is recorded as digital data, a finite range of numbers is used to represent the audio signal. When you edit or process your audio, Sound Forge (and other digital audio editors) applies mathematical calculations to the data to achieve different results. Each mathematical process results in tiny errors, because the data has to be rounded or truncated. These errors result in small amounts of noise or other artifacts added to your audio signal. Most of the time, this noise isn't really noticeable, but if you do enough processing and editing, the noise eventually becomes audible.

To set the sampling rate and bit depth for your new recording, simply select the appropriate values for the Sample Rate and Bit-Depth parameters in the New Window dialog box.

NOTE

As I mentioned earlier, to store music on a CD, the audio data is required to have a sampling rate of 44,100 Hz and a bit depth of 16 bits. These values cannot be higher or lower. They must be exact. Of course, you can start off by recording your audio with different settings. For example, if your computer has a limited amount of memory or hard disk space, you might want to use smaller values. I don't recommend this, though, unless it's absolutely necessary, because lower values mean lower-quality audio. You can also record by using higher values, which raises the quality of your audio data. When it comes times to put the audio on CD, however, you must convert the sampling rate and bit depth to the values just mentioned. By using Sound Forge's Resample and Bit-Depth Converter features, you can convert the sampling rate and bit depth of your audio file. I talk more about these features in Chapter 8.

Number Of Channels

Because Sound Forge does not provide any kind of multitrack recording capabilities (meaning you can't record different instruments separately and then play them back via separate but synchronized audio tracks), you are only given two choices for the type of audio file you want to create: mono (one channel) or stereo (two channels). To set the number of channels for your new recording, select the appropriate option in the Channels section of the New Window dialog box.

TIP

Although Sound Forge only allows you to record monophonic or stereo audio, you can do a sort of pseudo-multitrack recording by recording in stereo. Because stereo is comprised of two distinct audio channels (one for the left speaker and one for the right), you can simply record one audio source into the left channel and another audio source into the right channel simultaneously. This might come in handy, for example, if you need to record two different voices at the same time. Sound Forge allows you to edit and process each channel of a stereo recording separately, so you can easily manipulate the data for each voice recording independently.

DC Offset

Depending on the quality of your sound card, your audio may not get recorded as accurately as it should. Many times (especially with less expensive sound cards, such as the Sound Blaster), an electrical mismatch may occur between a sound card and the input device. When this happens, an excess of current is added to the incoming signal and the resulting audio waveform is offset from the zero axis. This is known as DC offset.

NOTE

An audio waveform is a graphical representation of sound. Let me try to explain by using the cup and string analogy. Remember when you were a kid, and you set up your own intercom system between your bedroom and your tree house by using nothing but a couple of paper cups and a long piece of string? You poked a hole in the bottom of each cup and then tied one end of the string to one cup and the other end of the string to the other cup. Your friend would be in the tree house with one of the cups, and you would be in your bedroom with the other. As you talked into your cup, your friend could hear you by putting his cup to his ear, and vice versa. Why did it work?

Well, when you talked into the cup, the sound of your voice vibrated the bottom of the cup, making it act like a microphone. This movement, in turn, vibrated the string up and down, and the string carried the vibrations to the other cup. This movement made the bottom of that cup vibrate so that it acted like a speaker, thus enabling your friend to hear what you said. If it were possible for you to freeze the string while it was in motion and then zoom in on it so that you could see the vibrations, it would look similar to the audio waveform shown in the Data Window (see Figure 6.3).

As you can see, a waveform shows up and down movements just like a vibrating string. A line, called the zero axis, runs horizontally through the center of the waveform. The zero axis represents the point in a waveform at which there are no vibrations or there is no sound, so the value of the audio data at the zero axis is the number zero (also known as zero amplitude). When a waveform moves above or below the zero axis, vibrations occur, and thus there is sound. The amplitude value of a waveform in these places depends on how high above or how far below the zero axis the waveform is at a certain point in time (shown on the Time Ruler in the Data Window). You can read the value of a waveform by using the Level Ruler in the Data Window. I talk more about the different features of the Data Window in Chapter 7.

Figure 6.3

An audio waveform is similar to that of a vibrating string, if you could freeze it and zoom in on it to observe the vibrations

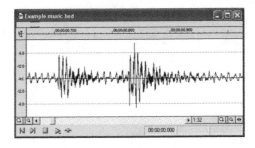

If your audio waveform is offset from the zero axis because of DC offset, you can introduce noise and other anomalies into your data during editing and processing.

To remove DC offset during recording, you simply need to calibrate Sound Forge so that it adds a constant value to your audio samples during recording. Doing so ensures your waveform is centered on the zero axis. In the Record dialog box, activate the DC Adjust option and click the Calibrate button. That's all there is to it.

NOTE

Whenever you change sound cards, or sound card inputs, or even alter the recording attributes (described earlier), you may want to recalibrate for DC offset. Any changes of this type can sometimes cause DC offset to occur.

Gap Detection

If you have a slow computer system, your sound card can sometimes produce audio faster than Sound Forge is able to record it. This can cause gaps (as in glitches or very short spans of silence) to occur during the recording process. Gaps can also occur because of sound card driver conflicts. During recording, you can have Sound Forge handle gaps in one of three ways: ignore them, mark them, or stop recording when gaps occur. Right-click on any blank area within the Record dialog box and a shortcut menu appears with a number of choices (see Figure 6.4).

Figure 6.4
Set the Gap Detection parameter by right-clicking within the Record dialog box

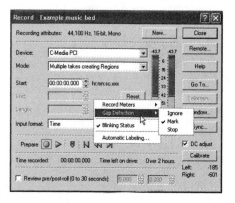

If you want Sound Forge to simply ignore any gaps that occur, choose Gap Detection > Ignore. If you want Sound Forge to place a Marker at every point in the audio file where a gap occurs, choose Gap Detection > Mark. If you want Sound Forge to stop recording whenever a gap occurs, choose Gap Detection > Stop.

CHAPTER 6

TIP

If you have trouble with gaps during recording, you may need to upgrade your computer system. The most helpful upgrades are memory and hard drive speed. These two are the most important aspects for digital audio recording. Of course, a faster CPU can also make a big difference. But before you start spending your hard-earned money, you may want to try a few techniques to optimize the performance of your audio PC. Check out my feature article (titled "Optimizing Your Audio PC") in Issue 14 of DigiFreq. You can download the issue for free at:

http://www.digifreq.com/digifreq/issues.asp.

Basic/Auto Retake Recording

You're now ready to start recording with Sound Forge. Nothing is really complicated about the process, but you should follow a number of steps to make sure that everything goes smoothly. Here, and in the following sections, I show you step-by-step how to record audio with Sound Forge in a variety of ways. First, let's tackle a basic recording. To get started, do the following:

1. Create a new audio file by choosing File > New (or pressing Ctrl + N on your computer keyboard) to open the New Window dialog box.

2. Set the sampling rate, bit depth, and number of channels you want to use for your new file. Then click OK.

3. Choose Special > Transport > Record (or press Ctrl + R on your computer keyboard) to open the Record dialog box.

4. Activate the DC Adjust option, and click the Calibrate button to compensate for any DC offset that may be present because of your audio hardware.

5. Select the recording device you want to use via the Device drop-down list. If you have more than one sound card or you have a sound card with multiple audio inputs, you can choose which input you want to use for recording.

NOTE

Making a selection via the Device drop-down list in the Record dialog box is the same as choosing a Record device in the Options > Preferences > Wave dialog box, which I talk about in Chapter 3.

6. Select the Automatic Retake recording mode via the Mode drop-down list (see Figure 6.5). I explain Automatic Retake later.

Figure 6.5
Choose the recording
mode you want to use
by selecting an option
from the Mode drop-
down list

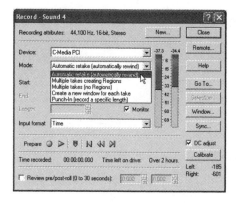

7. Activate the Monitor option. You should see the recording meters display your current audio input signal level in decibels (see Figure 6.6).

TIP
Right-click on the meters to set a different range, and determine whether signal level peaks and valleys are displayed longer. You can also reset the meters by selecting Reset Clip or by clicking the Reset button. In addition, the Aggressive Update option determines whether the meters will be given priority processing to show a more accurate level. If activated, Aggressive Update takes more computer processing power, but not really enough for you to notice it, except possibly on a really slow machine.

Figure 6.6
The recording meters
display your current
audio input signal level
in decibels

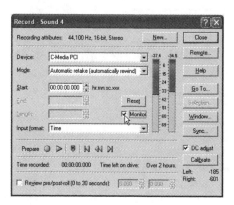

CHAPTER 6

NOTE

Decibel is a very complicated term to describe, especially in a beginning to intermediate text such as this. The most basic explanation is that a decibel is a unit of measurement used to determine the loudness of sound. For a more detailed (and complicated) explanation, search for the subject "Digital Levels" in the Sound Forge Help file.

8. Set the audio input level for your sound card so that it's not too loud, but also not too soft. To do so, you have to use the software mixer that came with your sound card. In the Windows Taskbar, you should see a small, speaker icon. Double-click the speaker icon to open your sound card mixer. Then, choose Options > Properties to open the sound card mixer Properties dialog box. In the Adjust Volume For section, select Recording, make sure all boxes below are checked, and click OK to display the recording controls for your sound card mixer (see Figure 6.7).

Figure 6.7
Use your sound card mixer to adjust the input levels for your sound card

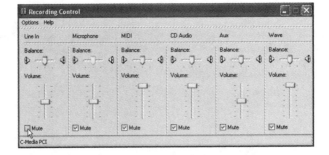

9. For the set of controls labeled Line In, deactivate the Mute option. For all other controls, keep the Mute option activated. This option tells your sound card that you want to record audio by using its line input connection. If you want to use a different connection (such as a microphone or internal CD player), use the set of controls associated with that connection.

NOTE

These steps show how to use a standard Windows XP sound card for recording. You might have a sound card that uses a different method for setting audio input levels. In that case, you need to read the documentation for your sound card to find out how to use it correctly.

10. When you have access to the input level controls for your sound card, begin playing the material you want to record. Be sure the material is played at the loudest level at which you plan to record. As the material plays, the recording meters in the Record dialog box light up, displaying the current audio input signal level. You should adjust the input level (by manipulating the Volume fader for the Line-In connection in your sound card mixer) so that when the loudest part of your material is playing, the recording meters do not turn red. If they turn red, you have overloaded the input, and if you record at that level, your audio signal will be distorted. If the recording meters light up at around –6dB during the loudest portion of your material, you have a good input level setting.

11. Click the Record button (or press R on your computer keyboard) to start recording.

NOTE

If you find that there's a bit of a delay from the time you click the Record button to the time that Sound Forge actually starts recording, click the Prepare button first. This tells Sound Forge to prepare its recording buffers and to prepare your sound card for recording. More than likely, you won't need to do this, but using the Prepare feature can yield more accurate results when using the Punch-In recording mode. I talk more about that later.

12. Play the material that you want to record. As you make your recording, the Time Recorded display shows how much time has elapsed during your recording; the Time Left On Drive display shows how much space you have left on your hard drive in the form of hours, minutes, seconds, and milliseconds. You can change the format of both the Time Recorded and Time Left On Drive displays by choosing a different option from the Input Format drop-down list.

TIP

By clicking the Marker button (the one with the letter M shown on it), you can drop Markers into your audio file while it's being recorded. This can be very useful if you need to keep track of different places within the audio or if you need to separate the file into different sections. An example might be if you are recording your own sound effects and you need to get a number of variations of the same sound, such as hitting a trash can to get a percussion effect. Each time you hit the trash can, you would pause and drop a Marker to indicate the different hits. After you finished recording all the hits, you could easily split the file into separate files (one for each hit variation) by using the Markers to Regions feature. Just choose Special > Regions List > Markers To Regions. I explain Markers and Regions in Chapter 5.

13. When you're finished, click the Stop button (or press R on your computer keyboard) to stop recording. The Stop button is actually located in the same place as the Record button. When Sound Forge is idle, the button acts as the Record button. As audio is being recorded, the button acts as the Stop button. After you've stopped recording, Sound Forge displays your new audio waveform in the Data Window you opened previously (see Figure 6.8). You may need to move the Record dialog box over a bit to see underneath.

Figure 6.8
After you finish recording, Sound Forge displays an audio waveform in the Data Window you open earlier

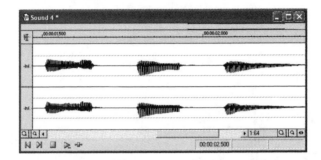

14. Listen to your new recording by clicking the Play button (or press P on your computer keyboard) in the Record dialog box. Earlier, I told you to set the recording mode to Automatic Retake. This tells Sound Forge to automatically "rewind" (or set the Current Position) back to the beginning of the file. So, if you don't like the recording, you can simply do it over again by going back to Step 8.

15. After you've got a recording that you like, just click Close to leave the Record dialog box.

CAUTION
Be sure to save your audio file after you've finished recording. This step isn't really mandatory, but it's a good precautionary measure because you never know when your computer might decide to crash on you. Rather than lose that really great recording, quickly choose File > Save (or press Ctrl + S on your computer keyboard) so you can rest easy in knowing that your data is safe.

TIP

If you have your home studio set up within a single room containing all of your equipment (including your computer), and you are recording audio by using a microphone, the microphone picks up the background noise made by your electronic devices (including the fan inside your computer). To remedy this situation, set up your microphone and one of your MIDI instruments in a different room, although keep them connected to your computer via longer cables. Then, you can set up some MIDI Triggers (you learned about them in Chapter 3) so that you can control Sound Forge remotely. This way, when you record the audio from your microphone, it won't pick up all that background noise.

Multiple Take Recording

When using the Automatic Retake mode, you can easily redo your recording, because Sound Forge automatically "rewinds" to the beginning of the file. But this also overwrites any existing data. What if you want to keep all of the different versions of your recording and then pick the best one after you've finished? You can do this by using any of the three available multiple take recording modes.

Multiple Takes Creating Regions

The Multiple Takes Creating Regions recording mode allows you to make multiple recordings one right after the other, and have them all stored within the same audio file, but separated into different Regions within that file. I talk about Regions in Chapter 5. To use this recording mode, do the following:

1. Create a new audio file by choosing File > New (or pressing Ctrl + N on your computer keyboard) to open the New Window dialog box.

2. Set the sampling rate, bit depth, and number of channels you want to use for your new file. Then click OK.

3. Select Special > Transport > Record (or press Ctrl + R on your computer keyboard) to open the Record dialog box.

4. Activate the DC Adjust option, and click the Calibrate button to compensate for any DC offset that may be present because of your audio hardware.

5. Select the recording device you want to use via the Device drop-down list. If you have more than one sound card or you have a sound card with multiple audio inputs, you can choose which input you want to use for recording.

6. Select the Multiple Takes Creating Regions recording mode via the Mode drop-down list.

7. Activate the Monitor option. You should see the recording meters display your current audio input signal level in decibels.

8. Set the audio input level for your sound card so that it's not too loud, but also not too soft. To do so, you have to use the software mixer that came with your sound card. In the Windows Taskbar, you should see a small, speaker icon. Double-click the speaker icon to open your sound card mixer. Then choose Options > Properties to open the sound card mixer Properties dialog box. In the Adjust Volume For section, select Recording, make sure all boxes below are checked, and click OK to display the recording controls for your sound card mixer.

9. For the set of controls labeled Line-In, deactivate the Mute option. For all other controls, keep the Mute option activated. This option tells your sound card that you want to record audio by using its line input connection. If you want to use a different connection (such as a microphone or internal CD player), use the set of controls associated with that connection.

NOTE

These steps show how to use a standard Windows XP sound card for recording. You might have a sound card that uses a different method for setting audio input levels. In that case, you need to read the documentation for your sound card to find out how to use it correctly.

10. When you have access to the input level controls for your sound card, begin playing the material you want to record. Be sure the material is played at the loudest level at which you plan to record. As the material plays, the recording meters in the Record dialog box light up, displaying the current audio input signal level. You should adjust the input level (by manipulating the Volume fader for the Line-In connection in your sound card mixer) so that when the loudest part of your material is playing, the recording meters do not turn red. If they turn red, you have overloaded the input, and if you record at that level, your audio signal will be distorted. If the recording meters light up at around −6dB during the loudest portion of your material, you have a good input level setting.

11. Click the Record button (or press R on your computer keyboard) to start recording.

12. Play the material that you want to record. As you make your recording, the Time Recorded display shows how much time has elapsed during your recording; the Time Left On Drive display shows how much space you have left on your hard drive in the form of hours, minutes, seconds, and milliseconds. You can change the format of both the Time Recorded and Time Left On Drive displays by choosing a different option from the Input Format drop-down list.

13. When you're finished, click the Stop button (or press R on your computer keyboard) to stop recording. The Stop button is actually located in the same place as the Record button. When Sound Forge is idle, the button acts as the Record button. As audio is being recorded, the button acts as the Stop button.

After you've stopped recording, Sound Forge displays your new audio waveform in the Data Window you opened previously. You may need to move the Record dialog box over a bit to see underneath.

14. Because we're using the Multiple Takes Creating Regions recording mode, Sound Forge keeps the Current Position located at the end of the current recording. So, to record another take/Region, just go back to Step 10.

15. After you've finished all of the takes that you need, just click Close to leave the Record dialog box.

Your audio file now contains all of the recordings that you made, separated into Regions within the same file. If you want to extract each Region into a separate file, just use the Extract Regions function (described in Chapter 5).

Multiple Takes (No Regions)

The Multiple Takes (No Regions) recording mode works in exactly the same way as the Multiple Takes Creating Regions recording mode, except that each take is not separated into a Region. Instead, you are left with having to either designate each take manually by inserting Markers or by recording some silence between each take to separate them. To use the Multiple Takes (No Regions) recording mode, just follow the same steps as when using the Multiple Takes Creating Regions recording mode. The only difference is that in Step 6, be sure to select the Multiple Takes (No Regions) recording mode from the Mode drop-down list.

Create a New Window

The Create A New Window For Each Take recording mode also works in the same way as the two previously mentioned recording modes, except that each take is put into a separate Data Window. To use the Create A New Window For Each Take recording mode, just follow the same steps as when using the Multiple Takes Creating Regions recording mode. The only difference is that in Step 6, be sure to select the Create A New Window For Each Take recording mode from the Mode drop-down list.

Punch-In Recording

If you make a mistake during a recording, you may think that the only way to correct it is to do the recording all over again. Not so. By using Sound Forge's Punch-In recording mode, you can rerecord only the part of your material that was messed up, leaving the good parts alone.

Using the Punch-In recording mode, you can set up Sound Forge to automatically start recording and stop recording at precise times within an audio file. You, therefore, can record over certain parts of your material without having to redo the entire thing. The Punch-In recording mode is very similar to the other recording modes, but with a few differences. Here's the step-by-step procedure:

1. Suppose you want to correct some mistakes on an audio file that you just recorded. To get started, select the Punch-In recording mode from the Mode drop-down list in the Record dialog box.

2. For the Start parameter, enter the hour, minute, second, and millisecond at which you want Sound Forge to begin recording. And for the End parameter, enter the hour, minute, second, and millisecond at which you want Sound Forge to stop recording. The section of the audio file that falls between the Start and End parameters should contain the part of your material in which the mistakes are located.

NOTE

For a much easier way to set the Start and End parameters, try creating a Region that contains the area of your audio file that you want to rerecord. You need to do this before you open the Record dialog box. I talk about creating Regions in Chapter 5. After you've created the Region, open the Record dialog box, and click the Selection button to open the Set Selection dialog box (see Figure 6.9). In the Set Selection dialog box, select your recently created Region from the Selection drop-down list. Then click OK. Your Start and End parameters are automatically set to the start and end of the Region. This technique is much easier than trying to guess and set the Start and End parameters manually.

Figure 6.9
Use the Set Selection dialog box for an easier way to set the Start and End parameters in the Record dialog box

3. At the bottom of the Record dialog box, activate the Review Pre/Post-Roll option. Then enter the number of seconds you want Sound Forge to play, both before it begins recording and after it stops recording. This lets you get prepared before recording begins, and it lets you hear if there is a smooth transition after recording ends.

4. Click the Record button (or press R on your computer keyboard) to start recording. Depending on how many seconds you set for the Review Pre-Roll, you'll hear some of the material being played before recording begins.

5. Play along with the existing material as you did before when you first recorded the audio file. When Sound Forge reaches the time indicated by the Start parameter, the program automatically starts recording the new material over the old material.

6. When the Current Position has reached the time indicated by the End parameter, Sound Forge stops recording. Depending on how many seconds you set for the Review Post-Roll, you'll hear some of the material being played after recording stops. Sound Forge replaces any existing material between the times indicated

by the Start and End parameters with the new material that you just recorded. As long as no mistakes were made this time, your audio file is now fixed.

7. Listen to the new material by clicking the Play button (or pressing P on your computer keyboard). If you like what you hear, move on to the next step. Otherwise, go back to Step 4.

8. After you're satisfied with the new material, just click Close to leave the Record dialog box.

Remote Recording

The Remote Recording mode is a bit misleading because it is not really a recording mode like the ones mentioned earlier. And it doesn't allow you to control Sound Forge remotely. Instead, clicking the Remote button in the Record dialog box simply hides Sound Forge's main program window, leaving a small window on the screen that contains the essential controls from the Record dialog box (see Figure 6.10).

Figure 6.10
The Record Remote window is a condensed version of the Record dialog box

All of the controls in the Record Remote window work exactly the same way as in the Record dialog box. So why do you need a feature like this? Well, its main use is for running Sound Forge along with another program on your computer simultaneously. For example, let's say you want to make a stereo digital audio recording of a MIDI composition you created in your MIDI sequencer. You could do that by running your MIDI sequencer and Sound Forge on the same computer. With Sound Forge in Remote Recording mode, it's much easier to access your MIDI sequencer and control Sound Forge at the same time. By initiating playback in your MIDI sequencer and then starting the recording process in Sound Forge via the Record Remote window, you can easily record your MIDI compositions as stereo audio files.

Synchronization

Another aspect related to recording that you should know about is synchronization. This subject is very complicated and a bit beyond the scope of this book, but you might need to utilize synchronization in a couple of different situations. So, I cover a few of the basics and explain how to use synchronization when Sound Forge is syncing to an external device or an external device is syncing to Sound Forge.

CHAPTER 6

Basics

All music is based on time. Without time, there is no music. To record and play audio data, Sound Forge needs a timing reference. It uses this reference to keep track of the Current Position during recording and playback. When you work with Sound Forge alone, it uses the clock built into your sound card as a timing reference. So, the built-in clock on your sound card provides the timing for the Current Position during recording and playback. This is internal synchronization.

Sometimes, however, you might need to synchronize Sound Forge externally with another device. For example, if you have a videotape containing some footage to which you want to add narration or music, you could use Sound Forge for this task by syncing it to the videotape. In this situation, the VCR is known as the master device, and Sound Forge is the slave device. The master sends messages to the slave, telling it when to start and stop, and what timing to use so that they can stay in sync with one another. To accomplish this, you need to use what is called SMPTE/MIDI Time Code.

SMPTE/MIDI Time Code

You learned a little about SMPTE in Chapter 5, so you know that it is a timing reference that counts hours, minutes, seconds, and frames (as in video frames). But you didn't really learn how it works.

NOTE
In addition to video, SMPTE/MIDI Time Code is often used to synchronize digital audio software to an external multitrack tape recorder, or DAT (Digital Audio Tape) deck. The procedure for doing this (explained in the following section) is the same.

SMPTE is a complex audio signal that is recorded onto a tape track (in the case of video, it's recorded onto one of the stereo audio tracks) by using a Time Code generator. This signal represents the absolute amount of time over the length of the tape in hours, minutes, seconds, and frames. A program (such as Sound Forge) reading the code can be synchronized to any exact moment along the length of the entire tape recording. In our video example, the VCR is the master, and Sound Forge is the slave. When you play the tape in the VCR, Sound Forge records the current audio file to the exact hour, minute, second, and frame.

Reading the time code from tape requires a SMPTE converter, which translates the SMPTE code into MTC (MIDI Time Code). The MIDI Time Code is read by your MIDI interface and sent to Sound Forge via the MIDI input port that you set back in Chapter 3. MIDI Time Code is the equivalent of SMPTE, except that it exists as special MIDI messages rather than as an audio signal. As Sound Forge receives MTC, it calculates the exact Current Position that corresponds to the exact time reading. This means that you can start playback anywhere along the tape, and Sound Forge begins recording audio data at precisely the right point in the current file in perfect sync.

Sync with SMPTE (Recording)

As an example, suppose you want to add some narration to a video. This video might be your own or a video from a client. To synchronize Sound Forge to the video, you need to follow these steps:

1. If the video is your own, you need to add SMPTE Time Code to it by using a SMPTE generator. This process is called striping. I won't go into the details of doing that here. You'll need to purchase a SMPTE generator and read the instructions in the included manual on how to stripe SMPTE to tape. If the video is from a client, they will probably stripe the tape before sending it to you.

TIP

You also need a SMPTE converter to read the time code from the tape. If you have a professional MIDI interface attached to your computer, it might provide SMPTE generating and converting capabilities. Check the user's manual to be sure. You might be able to save yourself some money. I use a Music Quest 8Port/SE MIDI interface, which includes multiple MIDI ports as well as SMPTE capabilities. Unfortunately, the 8Port/SE is no longer available, but you can find similar products from a company called Midiman (www.midiman.com).

2. Create a new audio file by choosing File > New (or pressing Ctrl + N on your computer keyboard) to open the New Window dialog box.

3. Set the sampling rate, bit depth, and number of channels you want to use for your new file. Then click OK.

4. Select Options > Preferences to open the Preferences dialog box. Click the MIDI/Sync tab. Choose the appropriate MIDI input port from the Input drop-down list. I talk in detail about MIDI settings in Chapter 3.

5. Choose Special > Transport > Record (or press Ctrl + R on your computer keyboard) to open the Record dialog box.

6. Activate the DC Adjust option, and click the Calibrate button to compensate for any DC offset that may be present because of your audio hardware.

7. Select the recording device you want to use via the Device drop-down list. If you have more than one sound card or you have a sound card with multiple audio inputs, you can choose which input you want to use for recording.

8. Select the Automatic Retake recording mode via the Mode drop-down list.

9. Activate the Monitor option. You should see the recording meters display your current audio input signal level in decibels.

10. Set the audio input level for your sound card so that it's not too loud, but also not too soft. To do so, you have to use the software mixer that came with your sound card. In the Windows Taskbar, you should see a small, speaker icon. Double-click the speaker icon to open your sound card mixer. Then, choose

Options > Properties to open the sound card mixer Properties dialog box. In the Adjust Volume For section, select Recording, make sure all boxes below are checked, and click OK to display the recording controls for your sound card mixer.

11. For the set of controls labeled Line-In, deactivate the Mute option. For all other controls, keep the Mute option activated. This option tells your sound card that you want to record audio by using its line input connection. If you want to use a different connection (such as a microphone or internal CD player), use the set of controls associated with that connection.

12. When you have access to the input level controls for your sound card, begin playing the material you want to record. Be sure the material is played at the loudest level at which you plan to record. As the material plays, the recording meters in the Record dialog box light up, displaying the current audio input signal level. You should adjust the input level (by manipulating the Volume fader for the Line-In connection in your sound card mixer) so that when the loudest part of your material is playing, the recording meters do not turn red. If they turn red, you have overloaded the input, and if you record at that level, your audio signal will be distorted. If the recording meters light up at around –6dB during the loudest portion of your material, you have a good input level setting.

13. Click the Sync button to open the Record Synchronization dialog box (see Figure 6.11).

Figure 6.11
You can set the synchronization parameters via the Record Synchronization dialog box

14. Activate the Enable MTC/SMPTE Input Synchronization option.

15. If you want recording to start at a specific SMPTE time automatically, activate the Start option and then input a SMPTE time in hours, minutes, seconds, and frames. Otherwise, recording starts as soon as a time code from the external device is received.

16. If you want recording to end at a specific SMPTE time automatically, activate the End option and then input a SMPTE time in hours, minutes, seconds, and frames. Otherwise, you have to manually stop the recording process by clicking the Stop button.

17. Click Close to close the Record Synchronization dialog box.

18. Using the Input Format drop-down list, select the format of SMPTE sync (as in the frame rate) that you want to use. If you're adding audio to your own video, just use the SMPTE Non-Drop format. If you're adding audio for a client, they should let you know what format you need to use.

NOTE

Different types of video material use different tape speeds for recording. The frame rate corresponds to how many frames per second are used to record the video to tape. For film, 24 frames per second is used. For video, several different rates are used, depending on whether the video is recorded in color or black and white, and so on. For more information about frame rates, you should consult the user's guide for your SMPTE generating/reading device.

19. Click the Prepare button to tell Sound Forge to start "listening" for any incoming SMPTE/MTC data. Sound Forge flashes a green indicator light that says Prepared (see Figure 6.12).

Figure 6.12
After you click the Prepare button, Sound Forge flashes a green indicator light letting you know it is ready and waiting

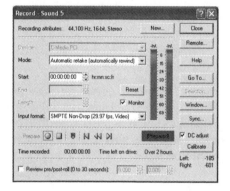

20. Start playback on your master device (in this case, start the tape playing in the VCR). It then sends SMPTE code to Sound Forge. If you entered a value into the Input Synchronization Start parameter, Sound Forge won't start recording until the appropriate SMPTE time is reached. Otherwise, it starts recording right away.

21. If you entered a value into the Input Synchronization End parameter, Sound Forge stops recording automatically at the appropriate SMPTE time. If you didn't enter a value for the End parameter, click the Stop button to stop recording when you're ready. Also, be sure to stop playback on your master device.

22. After you've finished recording, click Close to leave the Record dialog box.

Sync with SMPTE (Playback)

You may also run into a situation where you need an external device to synchronize to the playback of a file in Sound Forge. In that case, do the following:

1. Open an audio file in Sound Forge.

2. Choose Options > Preferences to open the Preferences dialog box. Click the MIDI/Sync tab. Choose the appropriate MIDI output port from the Output drop-down list. This is the MIDI port to which your external device is connected. I talk in detail about MIDI settings in Chapter 3.

3. Choose Options > MIDI In/Out > Generate MIDI Timecode (or press F7 on your computer keyboard) to activate MTC output from Sound Forge.

4. Set up your external device to receive SMPTE/MTC. Refer to the owner's manual for your device to find out how to do this.

5. You may need to enter a SMPTE/MTC offset in hours, minutes, seconds, and frames. For example, if you are syncing a tape deck to Sound Forge but the material on the tape doesn't start at the very beginning, you may need Sound Forge to output SMPTE/MTC starting at a different value than 00:00:00:00, which is its default starting value. To set a playback offset, choose Options > Preferences. Click the MIDI/Sync tab. Activate the Enable SMPTE Playback Offset option, and type in an offset in hours, minutes, seconds, and frames.

6. Start playback on the external device. Instead of playing, it should wait for an incoming SMPTE/MTC signal.

7. In Sound Forge, choose Special > Transport > Play (or press the space bar on your computer keyboard) to begin playback of the current audio file. At this time, Sound Forge starts playback of the file and simultaneously sends out SMPTE/MTC to the external device. The external device should also start playing in sync with the audio from Sound Forge.

A little confused? Well, as I said, synchronization is a complicated subject. You'll find some more information in the Sound Forge manual and the Help file, but it can still be difficult to understand. Your best bet is to experiment as much as possible with synchronization and get a good beginner's book on audio recording. Knowing how to utilize synchronization is worthwhile if a situation that requires it ever arises.

Playback

In the previous sections of this chapter, I touched upon some of the playback features that Sound Forge provides, but didn't really cover all the features in detail. Sound Forge includes many different playback methods and modes that each have their own special uses. First, let's talk about the basic playback functions.

Basics

You've already learned about some of the ways to play an audio file in Sound Forge. Just to refresh your memory, they are as follows:

▶ Choose Special > Transport > Play to start playback, and choose Special > Transport > Stop to stop playback. To pause playback, choose Special > Transport > Pause.

▶ Press the space bar on your computer keyboard to start playback, and press the space bar again to stop playback. To pause playback, press Enter.

▶ Click the Play buttons in either the Transport toolbar or the Data Window Playbar to start playback. Click the Stop buttons in either the Transport toolbar or the Data Window Playbar to stop playback. To pause playback, click the Pause button in the Transport toolbar. There is no Pause button available in the Data Window Playbar.

Play All

There is one additional method available to start playback called the Play All function. If you start playback using one of the previously mentioned methods, Sound Forge only plays the currently selected data. The Play All function plays the entire audio file no matter if there is a data selection or not. This can come in handy when doing editing or processing tasks and you want to keep your data selection intact but want to listen to the entire audio file.

To use the Play All function, choose Special > Transport > Play All (or press Shift + Space on your computer keyboard). You can also use the Play All button in the Transport toolbar. There is no Play All button available in the Data Window Playbar.

Loop Playback

When editing or processing an audio file (or selected area of an audio file), it can be useful to continuously hear the audio data played over and over as you make your changes. Sound Forge provides for this situation with its Loop Playback function. To toggle the Loop Playback function on/off, click the Loop Playback button in the Transport toolbar (or press Q on your computer keyboard). If you made a data selection in the audio file, the data in that selection is played over and over again when you activate playback. If there is no data selection, then the entire audio file is played repeatedly.

Playback Modes

All of the previously mentioned playback functions are known as Play Normal Mode functions, but Sound Forge actually provides four different playback modes. They are as follows:

▶ Play Normal Mode. To activate this mode, choose Special > Transport > Play Normal Mode. In Play Normal Mode, Sound Forge's playback functions work as previously mentioned in this chapter.

▶ Play Plug-In Chainer Mode. To activate this mode, choose Special > Transport > Play Plug-In Chainer Mode. The Audio Plug-In Chainer allows you to apply effects to an audio file nondestructively. Using this playback mode, Sound Forge processes the audio file through the Audio Plug-In Chainer. I talk more about the Audio Plug-In Chainer in Chapter 9.

▶ Play As Sample Mode. To activate this mode, choose Special > Transport > Play As Sample Mode. You can use Sound Forge to create your own digital audio sample loops. Using this playback mode, Sound Forge plays the audio file as a digital audio sample loop. I talk more about sampling and sample loops in Chapter 13.

▶ Play As Cutlist Mode. To activate this mode, choose Special > Transport > Play As Cutlist Mode. Using Sound Forge's Cutlist function, you can make edits to your audio files nondestructively. Using this playback mode, Sound Forge plays the audio file according to the cutlist that you have defined. I talk more about the Cutlist function in Chapter 7.

CHAPTER 6

Advanced Playback

In addition to all of the previously mentioned playback functions, Sound Forge includes an advanced playback function called the Playlist. With the Playlist, you can designate what sections of an audio file will play (along with how many times they will play) and what sections will not play. This can be useful for testing out how the audio file will sound with and without certain sections. It can also be useful in a performance situation for sound effect or musical passage playback.

For the Playlist function to work, you need to define Regions within your audio file. If you need to, please read Chapter 5 again to become familiar with Regions before reading the rest of this chapter.

Create a Playlist

To create a new Playlist, just do the following:

1. Separate your audio file into sections using Regions (see Chapter 5 for more information). For this example, just open the sample file included with Sound Forge called VOICEOVER.PCA. You'll notice that the sample file already has some Regions defined (see Figure 6.13).

Figure 6.13
Open the
VOICEOVER.PCA
sample file for this
Playlist example

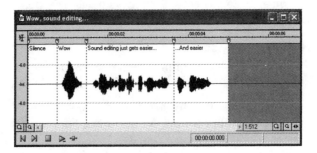

2. Choose View > Regions List (or press Alt + 1 on your computer keyboard) to open the Regions window.

3. Choose View > Playlist (or press Alt + 2 on your computer keyboard) to open the Playlist window.

4. Drag and drop the Region called Wow from the Regions window to the Playlist window. This creates an entry in the Playlist (see Figure 6.14).

Figure 6.14
Drag and drop Regions
from the Regions
window to the Playlist
window to create entries
in the Playlist

NOTE

You can also select a Region in the Regions window, and right-click in the
Playlist window. Then choose Add from the shortcut menu to create a Playlist
entry. But I find it much easier to use the drag-and-drop method.

5. Drag and drop the Region called Sound Editing Just Gets Easier from the Regions
    window to the Playlist window.

6. Drag and drop the Region called …And Easier to the Playlist window.

You now have a Playlist for the VOICEOVER.PCA audio file. To listen to the Playlist, click the
small Play button next to the first entry in the list (see Figure 6.15). You can also start playback
from any entry in the list by clicking the appropriate Play button.

Figure 6.15
Click the small Play
button next to a Playlist
entry to start playback
from that entry

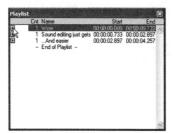

CHAPTER 6

Edit a Playlist

I'm sure you noticed that the Playlist we created in the previous example wasn't anything spectacular. The Playlist entries simply played the audio file Regions in their original order. To demonstrate the real power of the Playlist, you need to do a little editing. We continue on where we left off with the previous example. Here's how to edit a Playlist:

1. To move an entry to a different position within the Playlist, drag and drop the entry up or down within the list. For this example, let's move the Wow entry so that it appears second instead of first in the list (see Figure 6.16).

Figure 6.16
To move an entry in the Playlist, drag and drop the entry up or down within the list

2. You can also change the number of times an entry will be played. For this example, let's have the Wow entry play three times. Double-click the Wow entry to open the Edit Playlist dialog box (see Figure 6.17).

Figure 6.17
Double-click an entry to edit its properties using the Edit Playlist dialog box

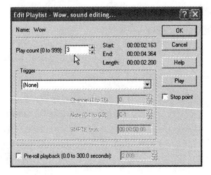

3. Enter three for the Play Count parameter, and click OK.

4. Start playback from the first entry. Sounds pretty good, eh? I think another Wow entry at the end would be cool though, so let's add one. Right-click the Wow entry and choose Replicate from the shortcut menu.

5. Move the new Wow entry to the end of the list, and change its Play Count to one. Start playback from the first entry.

6. Hmmm… on second thought, lets get rid of that last Wow entry. To delete an entry from the Playlist, right-click the entry and choose Delete from the shortcut menu.

If you want to use the Playlist function as a performance tool, there are two additional options that make this feasible—the Stop Point and MIDI Trigger options. In the Playlist, you can designate any entry as a Stop Point. This means when the list is played and it encounters an entry that has been labeled as a Stop Point, playback stops. Let me show you how it works with a brief example:

1. Continuing on from the last example, right-click the …And Easier entry and choose Stop Point from the shortcut menu. This designates that entry as a Stop Point in the Playlist (see Figure 6.18).

Figure 6.18
Right-click an entry and choose Stop Point to designate that entry as a Stop Point in the Playlist

2. Start playback from the first entry in the Playlist. You'll notice that the first two entries play, but the last one doesn't because it is a Stop Point. To play the rest of the entries in the Playlist, you need to start playback from the …And easier entry. Then, it and any entries that might be after it play.

3. If you want to remove a Stop Point from the list, right-click the entry and choose Stop Point from the shortcut menu.

The Stop Point option becomes even more powerful when you combine it with the MIDI Trigger option. I talk about MIDI Triggers in Chapter 3. MIDI Triggers can be used to start playback of a Region (or Playlist entry) using MIDI messages from your MIDI device. Combined with Stop Points, you can easily create a complex Playlist for use in a musical performance situation. You can also use it to trigger the playback of sound effects in a foley recording session for video, and more. To set up a MIDI Trigger for a Playlist entry, do the following:

1. Double-click the Playlist entry to open the Edit Playlist dialog box.

2. In the Trigger section, choose the type of trigger you want to use for that entry from the drop-down list (see Figure 6.19).

Figure 6.19
Use the Edit Playlist
dialog box to set up a
MIDI Trigger for a
Playlist entry

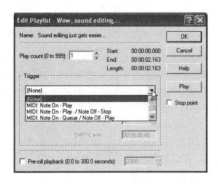

3. Depending on the type of trigger you choose, do the following: for a MIDI Trigger, enter a MIDI Channel and MIDI Note in the appropriate parameters; for a SMPTE Trigger, enter a time value for the SMPTE Time parameter. The MIDI Channel and Note that you designate are the ones that must be transmitted from your MIDI device to start playback of that entry. If you choose the SMPTE option, the entry will be played when a certain SMPTE time is reached if you are synchronizing Sound Forge to another device using SMPTE synchronization (I talk about synchronization earlier in this chapter).

4. Click OK.

Save and Open a Playlist

After you've created a Playlist for an audio file, you can save it as a separate Playlist file (which can also be opened for use at a later time). This means you can have multiple Playlists for the same audio file, if you want. To save a Playlist:

1. Right-click anywhere within the Playlist window and choose Save As from the shortcut menu to open the Save As Regions/Playlist dialog box (see Figure 6.20).

Figure 6.20
Use the Save As
Regions/Playlist dialog
box to save your Playlist

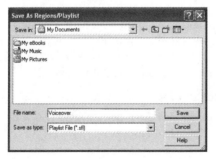

2. Choose a disk/folder location in which to save the file using the Save In drop-down list.

3. Type in a name for the file in the File Name field.

4.   Click Save.

To open an existing Playlist:

1.   Right-click anywhere within the Playlist window and choose Open from the shortcut menu to open the Open Regions/Playlist dialog box.

2.   Choose a disk/folder location in which the file is located using the Look In drop-down list.

3.   Select the file to open.

4.   Click Open.

Create a New Audio File

One final but very powerful Playlist feature is the ability to convert a Playlist into a new audio file. This feature renders all the entries in a Playlist and converts them into a real audio file. To do this, you simply right-click anywhere within the Playlist window and choose Convert To New from the shortcut menu. If we did this with the previous Playlist example, we would get what is shown in Figure 6.21.

Figure 6.21
Use the Convert To New function to create a new audio file from your Playlist

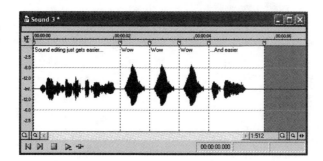

You'll notice that there are four Regions in the new audio file. The first Region represents the first entry in the Playlist. The next three Regions represent the second entry in the Playlist; remember that the second entry in the Playlist had a Play Count of three, which is why we get three Regions with the same data in the new audio file. And finally, the last Region is represented by the last entry in the Playlist.

The Convert To New function can actually be used as an editing tool. I talk more about this in Chapter 7.

CHAPTER 6

7

Editing Basics

After you've finished recording, it's time to do some editing. This is where Sound Forge shines. The program provides a vast array of editing, processing, and effects tools so that you can mold your audio data every which way imaginable. I talk about the processing tools in Chapter 8 and the effects tools in Chapter 9. In this chapter, however, you'll learn to:

▶ Work with the Data Window

▶ Select audio data

▶ Copy, cut, delete, crop, and paste audio data

▶ Use Undo/Redo and the Undo/Redo History

▶ Use the Edit, Magnify, and Pencil tools

CAUTION

Before you do any editing to your recently recorded material, I suggest that you make a backup of your audio file. This way, if you totally mess things up during the editing process, you still have your raw data to fall back on.

The Data Window

When you open an existing audio file or record a new one, Sound Forge displays a Data Window (see Figure 7.1).

Figure 7.1
Sound Forge displays your audio file in a Data Window

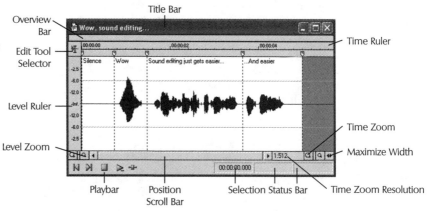

The Data Window gives you access to your audio data for viewing, editing, and processing. More than one Data Window can be open simultaneously so that you can edit more than one file at a time, if necessary. You already learned how to work with the Data Window in terms of navigating within Sound Forge and recording new audio files. However, you haven't learned how to actually manipulate the audio data within the Data Window. Manipulating includes selecting, copying, cutting, pasting, and so on.

Scrolling

As you already know, the Data Window displays the data from your file as a graphical representation of its audio waveform. If your file is monophonic (one channel), one waveform is shown. If your file is stereo (two channels), two waveforms are shown; the top waveform represents the left channel and the bottom waveform represents the right channel. The length of the audio waveform is shown horizontally from left (the beginning of the file) to right (the end of the file). More often than not, the data from the entire file does not fit within the Data Window. For situations like this, the Data Window provides a scroll bar (located just below the waveform display and just above the Playbar). This scroll bar works the same as scroll bars in any standard Windows application. You can either click the scroll bar arrows to move the display, or click and drag the scroll bar itself to move the display. As you scroll to the right, the values in the Time Ruler increase and you are able to view the data in the remaining part of the audio file. Scrolling doesn't change the Current Position cursor, though (as you learn in Chapter 5).

Zooming

The Data Window also provides zooming functions. Using these functions, you can magnify the audio waveform in case you want to do some really precise editing. If you take a look at the bottom of the Data Window, you'll notice two sets of buttons (one set to the left of the scroll bar and one set to the right of the scroll bar) that have little pictures of magnifying glasses on them. Using the buttons to the right of the scroll bar (the Time Zoom buttons), you can magnify the audio waveform horizontally in time. So, by clicking the Time Zoom In button (the one with the big magnifying glass on it), the audio waveform grows longer horizontally and gives you a more detailed look at the data. Clicking the Time Zoom Out button (the one with the small magnifying glass on it), of course, does the opposite. As you use the Time Zoom buttons, you'll also notice that the values in the Time Ruler change to reflect the more detailed view, and the Time Zoom Resolution display (located to the right of the scroll bar) also changes. The Time Zoom Resolution display shows the current zoom resolution as a ratio. A zoom resolution of 24:1 (24 screen pixels = 1 audio sample) gives you the most detailed (magnified) view of the audio waveform that's possible. The least detailed view you can achieve depends on the length of the audio waveform. By default, a ratio of 1:4,096 can be achieved.

TIP

You can change the default zoom out ratio, by choosing Options > Preferences, to open the Preferences dialog box. Then, click the Display tab and select a new ratio from the Normal Zoom Ratio drop-down list.

The buttons to the left of the scroll bar (the Level Zoom buttons) work in the same manner as the Time Zoom buttons, except that they affect the display vertically. Clicking the Level Zoom In button (the one with the big magnifying glass on it) magnifies the amplitude level of the audio waveform. Clicking the Level Zoom Out button (the one with the small magnifying glass on it) does the opposite. As you manipulate these buttons, the Level Ruler (located on the left side of the Data Window) changes to reflect the different amplitude levels shown for the audio waveform.

TIP

The Level Ruler can be made to show amplitude levels in decibels (dB) or as a percentage. Just right-click the Level Ruler and select the appropriate option: Label In dB or Label In Percent.

In addition to the Zoom buttons themselves, you'll notice a small vertical bar located in between each set of Zoom buttons. By clicking and dragging on this bar, you can quickly change the zoom values for either level or time. Click and drag to the left to decrease the values; click and drag to the right to increase the values.

TIP

For an even quicker way to change the zoom values, use the View > Zoom Level and View > Zoom Time menus. They are self-explanatory.

The Magnify Tool

In addition to the Zoom In and Zoom Out buttons, as well as the Zoom menu functions, Sound Forge provides the Magnify tool. You can use this tool to select a range of data and just zoom in on that selection. To use it, simply do the following:

1. Choose Edit > Tool > Magnify to activate the Magnify tool. You can also click the Magnify Tool button in the Standard Toolbar (see Chapter 3 for more information). Or, you can click on the Edit Tool Selector in the Data Window.

2. Move your mouse pointer within the waveform display of the Data Window, and it turns into a magnifying glass.

3. Click and drag anywhere within the area to draw a rectangle around the data that you want to zoom (see Figure 7.2).

Figure 7.2
You just click and drag
to draw a rectangle with
the Magnify tool

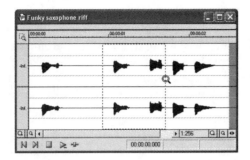

4.   Release the mouse button. Sound Forge then zooms in on the data within the
     rectangle.

The Magnify tool remains activated so that you can perform another zoom procedure if you
want. To reactivate the Edit tool (which I talk about shortly), choose Edit > Tool > Edit (or press
Ctrl + D on your computer keyboard). You can also click the Edit Tool button in the Standard
Toolbar, or you can click on the Edit Tool Selector in the Data Window.

Custom Time Zoom

Sound Forge also provides one last zoom function called Custom Zoom. This function allows
you to define two custom time zoom settings, which can then be accessed with simple keyboard
shortcuts. This lets you set up two of your most used time zoom settings and implement them
with ease. To define the Custom Zoom settings, do the following:

1.   Choose Options > Preferences to open the Preferences dialog box.

2.   Click the Display tab.

3.   To define the first custom time zoom setting, choose a value from the Custom
     Zoom Ratio 1 drop-down menu.

4.   To define the second custom time zoom setting, choose a value from the Custom
     Zoom Ratio 2 drop-down list.

5.   Click OK.

To access the first custom time zoom setting, press 1 on the number pad of your computer
keyboard. To access the second custom time zoom setting, press 2 on the number pad of your
computer keyboard.

Selecting and the Edit Tool

To manipulate your audio data in a file, you have to be able to select it. There are a number of
ways to do this in Sound Forge. The most common is by simply dragging your mouse within the
waveform display of the Data Window. Just activate the Edit tool (the tool used for selecting data
in Sound Forge) by choosing Edit > Tool > Edit (or pressing Ctrl + D on your computer
keyboard). You can also click the Edit Tool button in the Standard Toolbar, or you can click the
Edit Tool Selector in the Data Window. Then, just click and drag your mouse within the
waveform display in the Data Window to select a portion of the data.

CHAPTER 7

TIP
When working with stereo files, you can select data in the left and right channels independently, or in both channels at once. To select data in both channels, click and drag your mouse in the middle of the waveform display. To select data in the left channel, click and drag your mouse in the top portion of the waveform display. You'll notice a small letter L attached to your mouse cursor, which lets you know that only data in the left channel will be selected. To select data in the right channel, click and drag your mouse in the bottom portion of the waveform display. You'll notice a small letter R attached to your mouse cursor, which lets you know that only data in the right channel will be selected.

When you select a portion of data in the Data Window, you'll notice the values in the Selection Status Bar change. The first value shows the time at which the beginning of the selection resides. The second value shows the time at which the ending of the selection resides. The third value shows the length of the current selection. These values are shown in the same format as the Time Ruler. If you change the Time Ruler format (by right-clicking and choosing a different format from the shortcut menu), the format of the Selection Status Bar changes as well.

You can also select data in a number of other ways, including the following:

▶ To select all the data in a file, choose Edit > Select All or press Ctrl + A on your computer keyboard.

▶ To toggle the selection on and off, choose Special > Toggle Selection or press the Backspace key on your computer keyboard.

The Set Selection Dialog Box

If you want to be more precise, you can select data by entering exact numeric values for the start, end, and length of a selection by using the Set Selection dialog box. Here's how:

1. Choose Edit > Selection > Set (or press Ctrl + Shift + D on your computer keyboard) to open the Set Selection dialog box (see Figure 7.3).

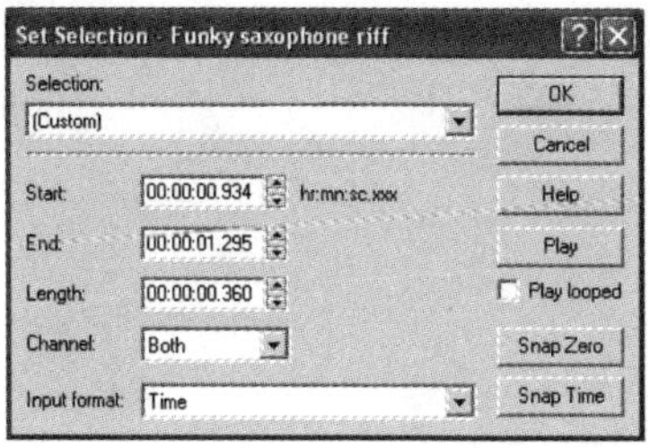

Figure 7.3
The Set Selection dialog box allows you to specify a selection using exact numerical values

2. Choose a value format via the Input Format drop-down list. For example, if you would rather specify your selection in measures and beats rather than in time, choose Measures & Beats from the drop-down list.

3. If you are editing a stereo audio file, use the Channel drop-down list to choose whether you want to make a selection in both channels or just in the left or right channel.

4. Enter a value for the Start parameter to define where in the file the selection will begin.

5. Enter a value for the End parameter to define where in the file the selection will end.

6. You can also enter a value to define how long the selection will be by using the Length parameter. Changing the Length parameter, however, also changes the End parameter.

7. To listen to the data within your selection, click the Play button.

8. When finished defining the selection, click OK.

Your new selection is set in the Data Window.

Adjust the Selection

After you've made your selection, you may find that it needs a little adjusting. This can be done easily with a quick click and drag of the mouse. To adjust your selection, do one of the following:

▶ To adjust the beginning or end of a selection, move your mouse over the start or end of the selection until your mouse cursor turns into a double-headed arrow. Then, click and drag either left or right to make the selection longer or shorter.

▶ You can also adjust the ends of a selection by simply holding down the Shift key on your computer keyboard and then clicking once anywhere before or after the defined selection to adjust the selection's beginning or end.

TIP
You can also set and adjust selections using nothing but your computer keyboard. There are twenty different keyboard combinations available that provide various selection functions. To see a list of these keyboard combinations, open the Sound Forge Help file by choosing Help > Contents and Index (or pressing F1 on your computer keyboard). Double-click on Shortcuts in the Contents list. Click on Keyboard Shortcuts. Click on Selecting Data. The list is displayed.

Snap the Selection

There may be occasions when you want the start and/or end of a selection to match up to the exact time values in the Time Ruler. This can be difficult to do with a mouse, but Sound Forge has some specific functions to remedy the situation:

▶ To snap both the start and end of a selection to the nearest rounded time values on the Time Ruler, choose Edit > Selection > Snap To Time (or press T on your computer keyboard).

▶ To snap just the start of a selection to the nearest rounded time value on the Time Ruler, move the Current Position cursor to the start of the selection by moving your mouse over the start of the selection until the mouse cursor turns into a double-headed arrow, and clicking the left mouse button once (or press the Home key on your computer keyboard). Then, choose Edit > Selection > Snap Edge To Time (or press Shift + T on your computer keyboard).

▶ To snap just the end of a selection to the nearest rounded time value on the Time Ruler, move the Current Position cursor to the end of the selection by moving your mouse over the end of the selection until the mouse cursor turns into a double-headed arrow, and clicking the left mouse button once (or press the End key on your computer keyboard). Then, choose Edit > Selection > Snap Edge To Time (or press Shift + T on your computer keyboard).

Even more important, however, is being able to snap the start and/or end of a selection to a zero crossing in the audio waveform.

NOTE

Remember the description of the zero axis from Chapter 6? Well, any point in an audio waveform that lands on the zero axis is called a zero crossing. It's called that because, as the waveform moves up and down, it crosses over the zero axis.

Why is it important that your selections line up with zero crossings? It's because a zero crossing is a point in the audio waveform at which no sound is being made. A zero crossing provides a perfect spot at which to edit the waveform—for example, when you're cutting and pasting pieces of audio. If you edit an audio waveform at a point where it's either above or below the zero axis, you might introduce glitches, which can come in the form of audible pops and clicks. You get these glitches because you cut at a moment when sound is being produced. You also get them because, when you're pasting pieces of audio together, you cannot guarantee that the ends of each waveform will line up perfectly (except, of course, if they both are at zero crossings).

To snap a selection to a zero crossing, do one of the following:

▶ To snap both the start and end of a selection to the nearest zero crossings, choose Edit > Selection > Snap To Zero (or press Z on your computer keyboard).

▶ To snap just the start of a selection to the nearest zero crossing, move the Current Position cursor to the start of the selection by moving your mouse over the start of the selection until the mouse cursor turns into a double-headed arrow, and clicking the left mouse button once (or press the Home key on your computer keyboard). Then, choose Edit > Selection > Snap Edge To Zero (or press Shift + Z on your computer keyboard).

▶ To snap just the end of a selection to the nearest zero crossing, move the Current Position cursor to the end of the selection by moving your mouse over the end of the selection until the mouse cursor turns into a double-headed arrow, and clicking the left mouse button once (or press the End key on your computer keyboard). Then, choose Edit > Selection > Snap Edge To Zero (or press Shift + Z on your computer keyboard).

TIP

If you want to have your selections snap automatically as you are making a selection, choose one of the following options: Options > Auto Snap To Time or Options > Auto Snap To Zero.

Copy, Cut, Paste, and More

After you've made a selection, you can do a variety of things to the selected data. Some of the more common ones include copying the data to the Clipboard (a temporary storage area), cutting and removing the data from the file to the Clipboard, deleting the data, trimming/cropping the data, and pasting the data. You can accomplish these tasks as follows:

▶ To delete the data, choose Edit > Delete (or press the Delete key on your computer keyboard).

▶ To delete all the data in the file, except for the data in the selection, choose Edit > Trim/Crop (or press Ctrl + T on your computer keyboard).

▶ To copy the data to the Clipboard, choose Edit > Copy (or press Ctrl + C on your computer keyboard). This simply makes a copy of the data and leaves the data in the selection intact.

▶ To cut the data from the file and store it in the Clipboard, choose Edit > Cut (or press Ctrl + X on your computer keyboard). This removes the selected data from the file and places it in the Clipboard. This is the same as copying the selected data and then deleting it.

▶ To paste any data from the Clipboard to an open audio file, move the Current Position cursor to the position within the audio file at which you want to paste the data. Then, choose Edit > Paste (or press Ctrl + V on your computer keyboard). The data is inserted into the file starting at the Current Position cursor. If there is data located after the cursor, that data is pushed back to make room for the new data.

TIP

After you have copied or cut data from a file, it is placed in the Clipboard. To view statistical information about the data being held in the Clipboard, choose View > Clipboard > Contents. This gives you the format, attributes, length, number of samples, and size in bytes of the audio data being held in the Clipboard. You can also listen to the data being held in the Clipboard by choosing View > Clipboard > Play.

Special Pasting Functions

There may be times when pasting (inserting) the data from the Clipboard into your audio file isn't exactly what you need. You may want to utilize the Clipboard data in a variety of ways, and Sound Forge provides five special paste functions for these purposes.

Overwrite

The Paste Overwrite function lets you paste the data from the Clipboard over a current data selection. For example, if you have a situation in which you are trying to piece together a great vocal audio recording from a couple of prerecorded files, you can copy a good section from one file and paste it into the other file, thereby replacing the bad part in the second file. Here's how the function works:

1. Select and copy the data you want to use for overwriting so that it is placed on the Clipboard.

2. Select the data to be replaced. The data to be replaced can reside either in the current file or in a different file.

3. Choose Edit > Paste Special > Overwrite.

Sound Forge replaces the selected data with the data on the Clipboard. There are two exceptions to this: If the selected data is longer than the data on the Clipboard, the data on the Clipboard replaces only the first part of the data in the selection. The remaining data in the selection is untouched. If the selected data is shorter than the data on the Clipboard, the data on the Clipboard replaces all of the data in the selection, but only for the length of the selection. In this instance, not all of the data from the Clipboard is used. More often than not, you'll want the length of the selected data and the length of the data on the Clipboard to match up.

Replicate

The Paste Replicate function lets you paste the data from the Clipboard repeatedly over a current data selection. For example, if you have a one-measure drum beat and you want to fill up four more measures in your audio file with the same drum beat, you can copy and paste that one measure into the next four measures quickly and easily using the Paste Replicate function. Here's how the function works:

1. Select and copy the data you want to use for replicating so that it is placed on the Clipboard.

2. Make a new selection in the current file or a selection in another open file, and be sure the length of the new selection matches up to the amount of data you want to replicate. So, if you copied one measure of data and you want to copy it four times, be sure to make the new selection four measures long.

3. Choose Edit > Paste Special > Replicate to open the Replicate dialog box (see Figure 7.4).

Figure 7.4

The Paste Replicate function lets you paste multiple copies of the data contained on the Clipboard

4. If the length of the new selection you made in Step 2 is not an exact multiple of the length of the data on the Clipboard, the new selection may or may not be filled entirely with data. In other words, if the data on the Clipboard is one measure long, but you only make the new selection three and a half measures long, that last half of a measure might be left empty. In the Replicate dialog box, if you choose the Whole Copies option, only whole copies of the Clipboard data are used to fill the selection, so in our example, only three measures are filled. If you choose the Copy Partials option, the entire selection is filled. The first three measures would contain whole copies of the Clipboard data and the last half of a measure would contain only the first half of the Clipboard data. Choose the option you want to use.

5. Click OK.

Sound Forge copies the data from the Clipboard as many times as it takes to fill the current data selection.

Paste To New

The Paste To New function is the simplest of the Paste functions. To use the Paste To New function, select and copy some data into the Clipboard. Then, choose Edit > Paste Special > Paste To New (or press Ctrl + E on your computer keyboard). Sound Forge takes the data from the Clipboard and places it into a new Data Window, ready and waiting to be edited and saved as an entirely separate audio file.

Mix

The Paste Mix function lets you mix the data from the Clipboard with the data in an open audio file. For example, if you have a vocal narration that you want to add to an already existing piece of background music, you can use the Paste Mix command to mix the two parts together into one audio file. Here's how the function works:

1. Select and copy the data you want to use for mixing so that it is placed on the Clipboard.

2. Set the Current Position cursor or set a selection in another open file to specify where the mixed audio will be placed.

3. Choose Edit > Paste Special > Mix (or press Ctrl + M on your computer keyboard) to open the Mix dialog box (see Figure 7.5).

Figure 7.5
The Paste Mix function lets you mix the contents of the Clipboard with the data in an open audio file

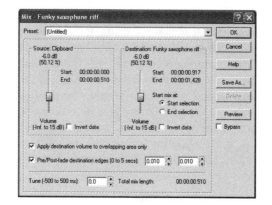

4. If you set a selection in the file rather than just setting the Current Position cursor, you can specify whether the mixing starts at the beginning or the end of the current selection. Choose either the Start Mix At Start Selection option or the Start Mix At End Selection option.

5. Adjust the Source Volume slider and the Destination Volume slider. These controls determine how loud the audio data from the Clipboard (Source) and the audio data in the file (Destination) will be after they are mixed together. You can test how the final mixed audio will sound by clicking the Preview button.

6. After setting the appropriate amplitudes for the Source and Destination, click the Preview button again. This time, listen to determine if the audio sounds "hollow." This usually happens due to phase cancellation, which occurs when one audio waveform increases in volume and the other decreases in volume at exactly the same time with the same amount. Because of this phenomenon, they cancel each other out, making the mixed audio sound hollow. If this occurs, try activating the Invert Data option for either the Source or the Destination, but not both. This option inverts the audio waveform and can usually fix the phase cancellation problem.

7. If the Invert Data options don't help with phase cancellation, you might be able to fix the problem using the Tune parameter. This parameter lets you slightly alter the mix start position in the destination file, meaning the data from the Clipboard will be mixed slightly before or after the current mixing point. This makes it so that the audio waveforms don't line up exactly, and thus won't be changing volumes at exactly the same time, so phase cancellation won't occur. To adjust the Tune parameter, simply enter a value in milliseconds anywhere from −500 to +500. You'll need to judge by ear how this affects the final mix by using the Preview button.

8. If you want the Destination Volume to be applied only in the part of the file where the two audio parts are being mixed, activate the Apply Destination Volume To Overlapping Area Only. Otherwise, the Destination Volume slider changes the amplitude of all the data in the file. More often than not, you'll want to have this option activated.

9. If you have the Apply Destination Volume To Overlapping Area Only option activated, you can also apply an automatic fade to the Destination Volume. This is a great way to mix a vocal narration with background music. When the vocal comes in, the background gets softer so that you can hear the vocal better. To accomplish a fade, activate the Pre/Post Fade Destination Edges option. Then, set the number of seconds you want it to take for the Destination Volume to get lower at the beginning of the mix (the level is set via the Destination Volume slider), and the number of seconds you want it to take for the Destination Volume to get back to its original level at the end of the mix. For an example, select the Fast Duck (-6 dB) Preset from the Preset drop-down list at the top of the dialog box.

NOTE

A fade is a gradual and smooth increase from a low volume to a higher volume (usually called a fade-in), or a gradual and smooth decrease from a high volume to a lower volume (usually called a fade-out). In the vocal example provided earlier, fading out a piece of background music during a mix and then fading the music back in after the mix is usually called ducking.

10. Click OK.

Sound Forge mixes the data together according to your parameter settings.

Crossfade

The Paste Crossfade function is similar to the Paste Mix function in that it lets you mix the data from the Clipboard with the data in an open audio file. However, the Paste Crossfade function goes a bit further. A crossfade is a special kind of mixing procedure that can come in handy when you want to make a smooth transition from one style of music to another or from one instrument to another. It is especially useful when you're adding audio to video; you can smoothly change from one type of background music to another as the scene changes. Of course, it has many other types of creative uses as well.

When you apply a crossfade to two pieces of audio, it usually works like this: As the final mixed audio is being played, one of the original pieces of audio fades in and the other piece of audio fades out. These fades can occur fast or slow, and at different levels that are independent of each other. It all depends on how you apply the crossfade. You can apply a crossfade as follows:

1. Select and copy the data you want to use for mixing so that it is placed on the Clipboard.

2. Set the Current Position cursor or set a selection in another open file to specify where the mixed audio will be placed.

3. Choose Edit > Paste Special > Crossfade (or press Ctrl + F on your computer keyboard) to open the Crossfade dialog box (see Figure 7.6).

Figure 7.6
The Paste Crossfade function is similar to the Paste Mix function, except that it allows you to apply fades to both pieces of audio data

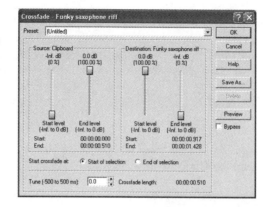

4. If you set a selection in the file rather than just setting the Current Position cursor, you can specify whether the mixing starts at the beginning or at the end of the current selection. Choose either the Start Crossfade At Start Of Selection option or the Start Crossfade At End Of Selection option.

5. Adjust the Source and Destination Start Level and End Level sliders. These controls determine what the amplitude of the Clipboard and audio file data will be both at the start and end of the crossfade. For example, if you want the Clipboard data to fade in and the audio file data to fade out, set the Source Start Level to –Inf dB, the Source End Level to 0 dB, the Destination Start Level to 0 dB, and the Destination End Level to –Inf dB.

6. If phase cancellation occurs, adjust the Tune parameter as I talked about earlier in the Paste Mix section of this chapter.

7. Click OK.

Sound Forge mixes and crossfades the data together according to your parameter settings.

Dealing with Editing Errors

Sound Forge provides an Undo function that enables you to reverse any action that you take while editing an audio file. You're probably familiar with this feature, because it can be found in most applications that enable you to manipulate data, such as word processing software and so on. So, if you ever make a mistake, just choose Edit > Undo (or press Ctrl + Z on your computer keyboard). If after you undo the action, you decide that you didn't really make a mistake after all, you can actually undo the Undo function by choosing Edit > Redo (or pressing Ctrl + Shift + Z on your computer keyboard).

Sound Forge goes even further to help you with editing errors, by providing an Undo/Redo History feature. This feature logs every step you take while working on an audio file and enables you to undo or redo each step, all the way back to the beginning or all the way forward to the end of your current editing session. Each open Data Window is provided with its own Undo/Redo History log, so that you can undo and redo steps independently for each audio file with which you are working.

CAUTION

The Undo/Redo History log for each Data Window is not saved, so as soon as you close a Data Window, you lose the ability to undo any changes you have made to that audio file.

To access the Undo/Redo History log, choose View > Undo/Redo History (or press Alt + 7 on your computer keyboard) to open the Undo/Redo window (see Figure 7.7).

Figure 7.7

You can reverse the actions that you take via the Undo/Redo History window

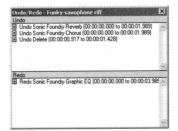

In the top half of the window, you can see all the actions that can be undone. In the bottom half of the window, you can see all the actions that can be redone. Each entry in each list has a description of the action that was performed along with a range of time (shown as hours, minutes, seconds, and milliseconds) that designates the part of the audio file that was processed. In addition, each entry has a small Play button next to it. This lets you hear what the audio sounds like at that particular point in the editing session. To go back to a certain point in the session, double-click an entry. If you want, you can keep the Undo/Redo window open while you work.

There are a number of other useful features associated with the Undo/Redo functions. They are as follows:

▶ If you want to undo all the editing actions for the current Data Window, choose Edit > Undo All.

▶ If you want to clear the Undo/Redo History lists for the current Data Window (thus losing the ability to reverse any mistakes, but clearing up some memory and disk space), choose Special > Undo/Redo History > Clear.

▶ If you want to clear the Undo/Redo History lists for all the open Data Windows, choose Special > Undo/Redo History > Clear All.

Nondestructive Editing

With the introduction of version 6, Sound Forge now employs nondestructive editing when you use the copy, cut, and paste functions. This means that although it looks like your data is being changed, it's really not. Instead, Sound Forge creates a list of pointers, which tell it what sections of audio have been copied, cut, or pasted. It then renders your audio data using the pointer list when you save the audio file. This makes editing changes instantaneous, even on large files.

In addition to this, Sound Forge provides an additional nondestructive editing feature called the Cutlist. I talk about this briefly in Chapter 6 while explaining the Playlist feature. Actually, the Cutlist works in a similar manner to the Playlist, except you make a list of the Regions you want to remove instead of the Regions you want to be played. Why would you want to use the Cutlist instead of the usual editing features? Well, at times you may find it more intuitive because you can actually see the data that has been removed. Let's work through an example, so I can show you what I mean:

1. Open the sample audio file that comes included with Sound Forge called VOICEOVER.PCA.

2. Choose Special > Playlist/Cutlist > Treat As Cutlist to turn off the Playlist function and turn on the Cutlist function.

3. Choose View > Regions List (or press Alt + 1 on your computer keyboard) to open the Regions window.

4. Choose View > Cutlist (or press Alt + 2 on your computer keyboard) to open the Cutlist window.

5. Adding Regions to the Cutlist works the same way as adding them to the Playlist. For this example, drag and drop the Sound Editing Just Gets Easier entry from the Regions window to the Cutlist window. You'll notice that Region has been shaded out in the Data Window (see Figure 7.8).

Figure 7.8
Regions in the Cutlist are shaded out from the audio file in the Data Window

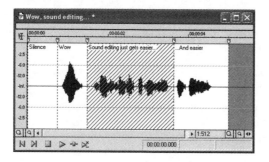

6. Choose Special > Transport > Play As Cutlist Mode. This sets the default play mode for the current audio file to Cutlist. Press the space bar on your computer keyboard. You'll notice that all the data except the Region on the Cutlist is played.

7. If you want to copy or delete an entry in the Cutlist, right-click the entry and choose Replicate or Delete (respectively) from the shortcut menu.

NOTE

Even though you still have access to the Stop Point and Edit options, they do not work in the Cutlist window. For more information about these options, please read the Advanced Playback section in Chapter 6.

8. After you've created a Cutlist, you can make its changes permanent in two different ways. You can right-click in the Cutlist window and choose Convert To New to create a new audio file in a new Data Window that only includes audio Regions not in the Cutlist. You can also right-click in the Cutlist window and choose Delete Cut Regions to remove all the Regions in the Cutlist from the current audio file in the current Data Window. Either way, this makes your editing changes permanent and allows you to save your new audio file.

NOTE

Just as with a Playlist, you can also save and open Cutlist files. For details, please read the Advanced Playback section in Chapter 6.

The Pencil Tool

One other basic editing tool that Sound Forge provides is the Pencil tool. This tool allows you to "draw" audio data into a file. That's a bit misleading, though. You can't actually use the Pencil tool to create new sounds or anything like that. Instead, its main purpose is for making precise changes or repairs to your audio data. For example, if you have a click or a pop in your audio that you want to remove, you may be able to take it out with the Pencil tool. Here's an example of how to use the Pencil tool:

1. Find the click or pop in the audio data either by ear or by using the Find tool as described in Chapter 5.

2. Zoom in on the area of the audio data containing the disturbance. The click or pop should look like a sharp disturbance in the audio waveform, similar to the one shown in Figure 7.9.

Figure 7.9
Clicks or pops are
usually fast noises that
look like spikes in the
normal curve of the
audio waveform

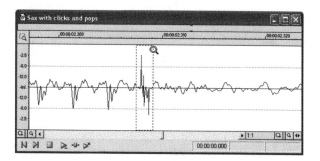

NOTE

The Pencil tool only works when you are using a zoom ratio of 1:32 or lower.
So be sure to use at least that ratio.

3. Activate the Pencil tool by choosing Edit > Tool > Pencil or by clicking the
    Pencil tool button in the Standard Toolbar.

4. Place the Pencil tool on the zero axis immediately before the location of the
    glitch in the audio waveform (see Figure 7.10).

Figure 7.10
When removing
glitches, start by placing
the Pencil tool on the
zero axis just before the
location of the glitch in
the audio waveform

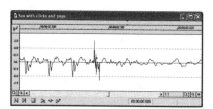

5. Click and hold the left mouse button while you drag the Pencil tool slowly over
    the waveform, so that the data you are drawing looks similar to the waveform
    data shown right before or after where the glitch is located (see Figure 7.11).

Figure 7.11
Fix the glitch in the
waveform by dragging
the Pencil tool over it

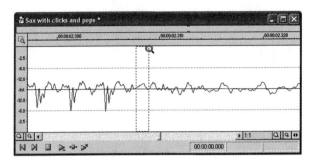

TIP

For more precise movement of the Pencil tool, use the arrow keys on your
computer keyboard as you hold down the left mouse button.

6. When you've finished "drawing," release the left mouse button to complete the
    editing task.

When you play the audio file, the glitch should be gone. If not, undo the work you did with the
Pencil tool and try again.

8

Exploring the Processing Functions

In Chapter 7, you learned about some of the essential editing features found in Sound Forge, including the Data Window (and the tools it provides), as well as how to manipulate your audio data via copy, cut, paste, delete, and so on. Although these features provide a lot of power, you might be asking yourself, "Is that all there is?" Not even close! In addition to its fundamental tools, Sound Forge provides a full arsenal of sophisticated editing features. These features can be used to change many of the different aspects of your audio, such as amplitude (volume), equalization (frequency content), length, and so on. In this chapter, you'll learn about:

▶ Presets and how to use the Preset Manager

▶ Dealing with silence in audio data

▶ Dealing with audio data quality

▶ Changing the loudness of audio data

▶ Equalization

▶ Various audio data manipulation features

Presets

While working with many of the editing functions in Sound Forge, you'll find yourself manipulating a multitude of parameter settings. At times, you may find a certain combination of settings that you want to save for future use. Sound Forge's Preset feature lets you do this. Presets let you store and later recall any parameter settings for a given function. You work with presets within the individual function dialog boxes, such as the Mix dialog box (see Figure 8.1), which I talk about in Chapter 7.

Figure 8.1
Presets are accessed
within individual
function dialog boxes,
such as the Mix dialog
box, shown here

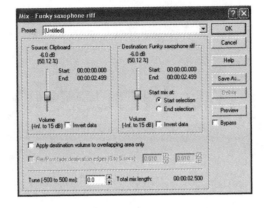

Load a Preset

At the top of the dialog box, you'll notice the Preset drop-down list. This parameter allows you
to load a preset into the current dialog box for the current function. To load a preset, just select it
from the Preset drop-down list (see Figure 8.2).

Figure 8.2
The Preset drop-down
list allows you to load a
preset

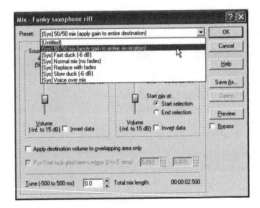

Save a Preset

If you want to save the current parameter settings as a new preset, do the following:

    1.   Click the Save As button to open the Save Preset dialog box (see Figure 8.3).

Figure 8.3
Use the Save Preset
dialog box to save the
current parameter
settings as a new preset

    2.   Type in a name for the new preset.

    3.   Click OK.

You'll notice that your new preset is now shown in the Preset drop-down list.

Delete a Preset

You can also delete presets from the Preset drop-down list. Just select a preset from the list to load the preset, and then click the Delete button.

NOTE

You can't delete any of the default presets that are included with Sound Forge.

The Preset Manager

After using Sound Forge on a regular basis, you'll build up your own collection of presets for many of the different editing and processing functions in the program. What if you want to share your presets with a fellow Sound Forge user? Or how about if you need to transfer your Sound Forge application to a different computer and you want to transfer your presets along with it? Keeping a backup of your presets collection is also a good idea. Well, Sound Forge's Preset Manager allows you to do all of these things.

The Preset Manager comes as a separate program on the Sound Forge CD and you need to install it manually. It is not automatically installed with Sound Forge. To install the Preset Manager, just put the Sound Forge CD into your CD-ROM drive, wait for the Setup screen, click on Install Preset Manager 1.0, and follow the instructions. After the Preset Manager is installed, you can access it in Windows by clicking Start ⊳ All Programs > Sonic Foundry > Preset Manager 1.0 > Preset Manager 1.0 (see Figure 8.4).

Figure 8.4
You can back up, share, and transfer your collection of presets using the Preset Manager

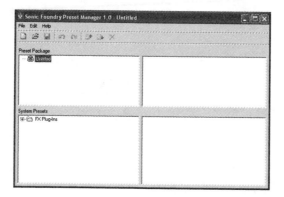

In the bottom half of the window is the System Presets pane, which lists all of the available presets in your current Sound Forge installation. Initially, the System Presets pane shows a single plug-in folder called FX Plug-Ins. Click the plus sign next to the FX Plug-Ins folder, and a list of functions that have user presets available is displayed. Click on one of the function names, and a list of presets available from that function is displayed (see Figure 8.5).

Figure 8.5
The System Presets pane displays a list of available presets

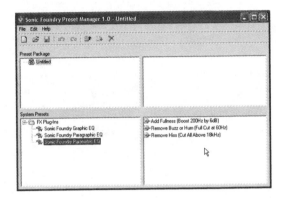

In the top half of the window is the Preset Package pane, which shows a list of the presets that you want to save. Initially, the Preset Package pane is blank, but you can easily add some presets to the list and then save them as a file for backup or sharing purposes.

Save a Preset Package File

To save a list of presets, do the following:

1. Select a preset from the System Presets pane, by clicking it.

2. Add the preset to the Preset Package pane, by clicking the Copy To File button (see Figure 8.6).

Figure 8.6
The Copy To File button allows you to add a preset to the Preset Package pane

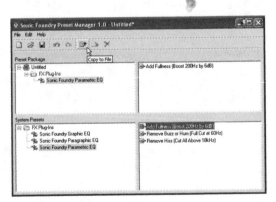

3. To remove a preset from the Preset Package pane, select the preset and then click the Delete button (see Figure 8.7).

Figure 8.7
Click the Delete button
to remove a preset from
the Preset Package pane

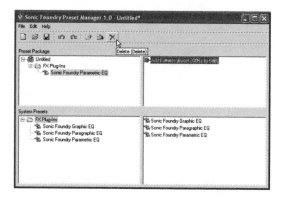

CAUTION

The Delete button can also be used to delete presets in the System Presets
pane. If you do this, it removes the preset from your computer entirely. So be
careful when selecting presets to delete. If you make a mistake and delete the
wrong preset, use the Edit > Undo function immediately to retrieve the
deleted preset.

4.   Repeat Steps 1 through 3 until you have all the presets you want to save listed in
     the Preset Package pane.

5.   Choose File > Save As to open the Save Preset Package dialog box (see Figure
     8.8).

Figure 8.8
Save your presets using
the Save Preset Package
dialog box

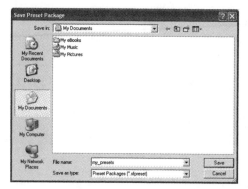

6.   Select a location in which to save the Preset Package file using the Save In drop-
     down list.

7.   Type in a name for the Preset Package file in the File Name field.

8.   Click Save.

CHAPTER 8

Your selected presets are saved as a Preset Package file (.sfpreset) in the location you specified. Now, you can use this file as a backup or even share it with another Sound Forge user. Of course, you also need to be able to open the file for future use.

Open a Preset Package File

The Preset Manager allows you to open the Preset Package files as well. To do so, follow these steps:

1.   In the Preset Manager, choose File > Open to display the Open Preset Package dialog box (see Figure 8.9).

Figure 8.9
Open a Preset Package File using the Open Preset Package dialog box

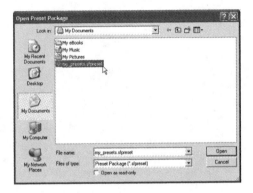

2.   Choose the Preset Package file that you want to open, and click the Open button. You'll see your Preset Package file displayed in the Preset Package pane (see Figure 8.10).

Figure 8.10
Your Preset Package file is shown in the Preset Package pane

3.   Click the plus sign next to your Preset Package file to display the presets it holds. Then select the presets you want to transfer to your computer, and click the Copy To System button (see Figure 8.11).

Figure 8.11
Click the Copy To System button to transfer presets from a Preset Package file to your computer

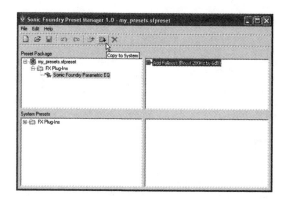

4.   When you are finished with the Preset Manager, choose File > Exit to close it.

The presets that you selected from the Preset Package File are added to your current Sound Forge installation. The next time you use the function to which those presets pertained, you will see the presets listed in the function's Preset drop-down list.

Prepare Audio Data for Editing

Back in Chapter 6, I talked about how to remove DC offset, set the bit depth, and set the sampling rate for a new audio file that you're about to record. But what if you have an existing audio file that needs to have DC offset removed, or needs to have its bit depth or sampling rate changed? Sound Forge provides three different functions specifically for these purposes.

Remove DC Offset

To recap a bit of what I talked about in Chapter 6, depending on the quality of your sound card, your audio may not get recorded as accurately as it should. Many times (especially with less expensive sound cards, such as the Sound Blaster), an electrical mismatch may occur between a sound card and the input device. When this happens, an excess of current is added to the incoming signal and the resulting audio waveform is offset from the zero axis. This is known as DC offset. To remove DC offset from an existing sound file, do the following:

1.   Select the data in your audio file from which you want to remove the DC offset. If you want to process the entire file, don't select any data, or select it all by choosing Edit > Select All (or pressing Ctrl + A on your computer keyboard).

2.   Choose Process > DC Offset to open the DC Offset dialog box (see Figure 8.12).

Figure 8.12
Remove DC offset from
audio data via the DC
Offset dialog box

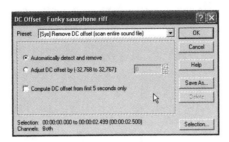

3. To have Sound Forge automatically detect and remove any DC offset in your
    data, choose the Automatically Detect And Remove option.

4. If you already know the amount of DC offset in your file and you want to remove
    it manually, choose the Adjust DC Offset By option. Then, enter a number of
    samples by which to adjust the position of the audio waveform around the zero
    axis. For example, if your file has a DC offset of 95, then enter a value of –95 so
    that the addition of the two numbers results in 0, or no DC offset.

TIP

To manually find out the amount of DC offset in an audio file, choose Tools >
Statistics to open the Statistics dialog box. This dialog box tells you a number
of different things about the current audio file, including the amount of DC
offset it contains.

5. If you are processing a very long audio file, activate the Compute DC Offset From
    First 5 Seconds Only option. This instructs Sound Forge to only look at the first
    five seconds of a file when determining how much DC offset it contains.

CAUTION

Activating the Compute DC Offset From First 5 Seconds Only option usually
provides accurate results. However, if your audio file starts off with a long
period of silence or the volume of the file is gradually faded in, you should
deactivate this option. In these circumstances, with the option activated,
Sound Forge does not accurately detect the amount of DC offset.

6. Click OK.

The DC offset in your selected audio data (or entire audio file) is then removed.

TIP

If you have an existing audio file and are not sure whether it contains DC offset, you should always process the file with the DC Offset function before you do any other kind of editing or processing. If you don't, the editing or processing can introduce noise and other anomalies into your data.

Convert to a New Bit Depth

There may be times when you want to change the bit depth of an existing audio file. For example, if you initially record and edit your file using 24 bits, but you want to later burn that file to CD, you need to change the bit depth to 16 bits. An audio CD can only use audio data with 16 bits. To change the bit depth of an audio file, do the following:

1. Choose Process > Bit-Depth Converter to open the Bit-Depth Converter dialog box (see Figure 8.13).

Figure 8.13
The Bit-Depth Converter function allows you to change the bit depth of an audio file

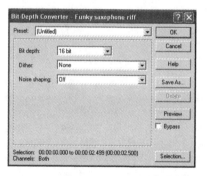

2. Set the new bit depth for your audio file by using the Bit Depth drop-down list.

TIP

If you have a file with a low bit depth and you convert the file to a higher bit depth, this does not raise the audio quality. For example, if you have an 8-bit audio file and you change it to a 16-bit audio file, it still sounds like an 8-bit file because that is how it was originally recorded. There is at least one advantage to raising the bit depth of a file: It gives the file a higher resolution, so that any editing or processing done to the file does not add additional noise. For example, if you want to edit an 8-bit audio file, it's a good idea to first raise the bit depth of the file. On the other hand, if you lower the bit depth of an audio file, this *does* lower the audio quality, so be sure to keep a copy of the original file before you process it. For example, if you have a 24-bit audio file and you want to lower the bit depth to 16 so that you can burn the file to CD, be sure to keep a copy of the 24-bit version for any future editing or processing.

CHAPTER 8

3. Set the Dither parameter. This parameter lets you specify how much dither noise you want to add to your file so as to mask any quantization noise (see the following note) that occurs because of the bit-depth conversion. When converting from a low bit depth to a higher bit depth, you probably want to keep this parameter set to None. When converting from a high bit depth to a lower bit depth, you need to experiment with the parameter to see which setting sounds best. As a starting point, however, I like to use the Highpass Triangular setting. I find it usually gives the best results in most situations.

NOTE

When you convert an analog audio waveform to digital, the waveform is defined using a finite range of numbers. As the bit depth of an audio file gets lower, there are fewer numbers to represent the audio waveform, which results in more noise. When you convert an audio file from a higher bit depth to a lower bit depth, the process can introduce what is known as quantization noise. Quantization noise occurs because the numbers in a higher bit depth file have to be mathematically rounded down to fit in a lower bit depth file. To mask the quantization noise, you can add dither noise to the data. It may seem strange to add noise to a file in order to actually lower the amount of noise that you might hear, but by adding dither noise, it helps to smooth out the rough edges (so to speak) in the audio waveform because of quantization noise.

Quantization noise is only audible at low levels of audio that is 16-bit or higher—it isn't really perceptible except in fade outs and reverb tails when the audio level gets to the point where, because of the lack of resolution, a normally complex waveform oscillates between one or two quantization values and thus it becomes a square wave instead of a complex waveform. The square wave adds harmonics to the signal that never existed in the original and, therefore, is undesirable. The dither noise fixes this problem by adding enough low-level noise that the signal doesn't just simply oscillate between the lowest values. You get a low level hiss, but it is generally more natural sounding than the quantization noise. Add good noise shaping and you can almost eliminate (perceptually) the dither noise.

4. Set the Noise Shaping parameter. This parameter lets you move any noise that may occur in your file up into the higher frequencies where humans have more trouble hearing. You have to experiment with this parameter to find the best setting for your audio file. As a starting point, however, I like to use the High-Pass Contour setting.

TIP

If your audio file has a low sampling rate (i.e., lower than 44,100 Hz), you should leave the Noise Shaping parameter set to Off. This is because files with low sampling rates also have a lower frequency range. If you use the Noise Shaping parameter with these types of files, you can actually make the noise content of the file worse.

5. Click the Preview button to hear how your file will sound before you have Sound Forge make any actual changes to the data.

TIP

By default, the Preview feature plays only the first four seconds of the selected data. You can adjust the Preview time by choosing Options > Preferences to open the Preferences dialog box. Under the Previews tab, set the Limit Previews To option to the number of seconds (1 to 600) that you want to use for the Preview feature. You can also set whether you want the Preview to loop continuously, fade out at the end, or react to any parameter changes you make during playback, as well as play some of the audio data unprocessed before or after your selection so you can hear the difference between the two. Just activate the appropriate options. They are pretty self-explanatory.

6. Click OK.

The bit depth of the current audio file is then changed according to your parameter settings.

Resample to a New Sampling Rate

As with bit depth, there may be times when you want to change the sampling rate of an existing audio file. Again, the example of burning the audio data to CD comes to mind. An audio CD can only use audio data with a sampling rate of 44.1 kHz (44,100 Hz). To change the sampling rate of an audio file, do the following:

1. Choose Process > Resample to open the Resample dialog box (see Figure 8.14).

Figure 8.14
The Resample function allows you to change the sampling rate of an audio file

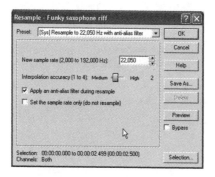

CHAPTER 8

2.   Set the new sampling rate for your audio file by using the New Sample Rate parameter.

TIP

If you have a file with a low sampling rate and you resample the file to a higher sampling rate, this does not raise the audio quality. For example, if you have a file with a 22 kHz sampling rate and you change the sampling rate to 44.1 kHz (so that you can burn the file to CD), it still sounds like a 22 kHz file because that is how it was originally recorded. There is at least one advantage to raising the sampling rate of a file: Raising the sampling rate gives the file a higher resolution, so that any editing or processing done to the file does not degrade it. For example, if you want to edit a 22 kHz audio file, it's a good idea to first raise the sampling rate of the file. On the other hand, if you lower the sampling rate of an audio file, this *does* lower the audio quality, so be sure to keep a copy of the original file before you process it. For example, if you have a 48 kHz audio file and you want to lower the sampling rate to 44.1 kHz so that you can burn the file to CD, be sure to keep a copy of the 48 kHz version for any future editing or processing.

3.   Set the Interpolation Accuracy parameter. This parameter lets you specify the accuracy of the resampling process. A lower setting provides faster but less accurate processing. A higher setting provides slower but more accurate processing. Unless you have a really long audio file, you probably want to keep this parameter set to 4.

4.   If you are converting from a higher sampling rate to a lower sampling rate, be sure to activate the Apply An Anti-Alias Filter During Resample option. This prevents any high frequency content from the file with a higher sampling rate from becoming noise in the converted file.

5.   If you just want to set a new playback rate for your file rather than changing the actual data, activate the Set The Sample Rate Only option. By using this option, the data in your file is not changed, it is only played back at a different rate. This also results in the pitch of the audio sounding different. The only time you would probably want to use this option is if someone gives you a file with the wrong playback sampling rate.

6.   Click the Preview button to hear how your file will sound before you have Sound Forge make any actual changes to the data.

7.   Click OK.

The sampling rate of the current audio file is then changed according to your parameter settings.

NOTE

When you convert to a lower bit depth or sampling rate, your audio loses some of its high-frequency content. This can make the audio sound dull. To compensate for this side effect, try processing the audio with Sound Forge's Smooth/Enhance function. Just select the audio data you want to process, and choose Process > Smooth/Enhance to open the Smooth/Enhance dialog box. Then, adjust the Operation parameter slider. You have to experiment here, but a good setting to start with is 3 (Enhance). Use the Preview button to test how your audio sounds before you actually apply the processing. When you like what you hear, click OK.

Dealing with Silence

Sound Forge provides a number of functions that allow you to manipulate the silent passages in your audio data. There may be times when you want to remove the silent sections from your data, such as awkward pauses between vocal phrases or dialogue. There may also be times when you want to add silence to your data, such as a delay between different musical sections. The Auto Trim/Crop, Insert Silence, and Mute functions let you tackle these tasks with ease.

Getting Rid of Silence

The Auto Trim/Crop function automatically removes silence from an audio file by scanning the data for certain characteristics that you specify. To detect these characteristics, the Auto Trim/Crop function uses a digital noise gate. Depending on your parameter settings, this noise gate opens up when the Auto Trim/Crop function comes upon a section in your audio that has an amplitude (volume) level greater than the one you set. It identifies this part of the audio as acceptable sound and lets it pass through. When the level of audio dips below a certain amplitude level that you set, the noise gate identifies that part of the audio as the end of the section (or the beginning of silence), and it closes to stop it from passing through. At that point, the Auto Trim/Crop function scans for the next section of audio and then deletes any silence in between the sections. This happens until your selected data is processed or the entire audio file is processed.

To automatically remove silence using the Auto Trim/Crop function, do the following:

1. Select the data in your audio file from which you want to remove any silence. If you want to process the entire file, don't select any data or select it all by choosing Edit > Select All (or pressing Ctrl + A on your computer keyboard).

2. Choose Process > Auto Trim/Crop to open the Auto Trim/Crop dialog box (see Figure 8.15).

Figure 8.15
The Auto Trim/Crop
function allows you to
remove silence from
your audio file

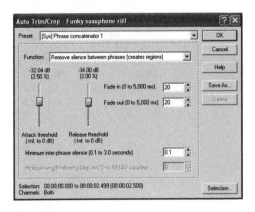

3. Choose the type of processing you want by using the Function drop-down list. Use the Keep Edges Outside Of The Selection option to remove the silence inside a selection of audio but leave any data outside the selection alone. Use the Remove Edges Outside Of The Selection option to remove the silence inside a selection of audio and delete any data (even data other than silence) that is outside of the selection. This option is useful for keeping only a good section of the file and discarding the rest. Use the Remove Silence Between Phrases option to remove the silence between phrases (such as vocal dialogue) inside a selection or entire file. This option also automatically creates Regions separating each phrase in the file (I talk about Regions in Chapter 5). Use the Remove Data Beyond Loop Points option to remove all data (not just silence) after a selected loop in an audio file (I talk more about loops in Chapter 13). Use the Remove Data From Start And Limit File Length option to remove any silence at the start of an audio file and also to "chop off" the end of a file at a specified number of seconds, thus limiting the length of the file.

4. Set the Attack Threshold parameter by dragging its slider up or down. This parameter determines how loud the audio data has to be to make the noise gate open, thus identifying the data as acceptable sound and the start of a trim/crop start point. The only time you don't need to set this parameter is when using the Remove Data Beyond Loop Points option.

5. Set the Release Threshold parameter by dragging its slider up or down. This parameter determines how soft the audio data has to be to make the noise gate close, thus identifying a trim/crop end point. The only time you don't need to set this parameter is when using the Remove Data Beyond Loop Points option.

6. If you want the segments of audio in your file to sound smooth after silence has been removed, it's a good idea to apply a slight fade-in and fade-out to the start and end points. To do this, just enter a number of milliseconds for the Fade In and Fade Out parameters. The default number of 20 milliseconds usually works quite well. When using the Remove Data Beyond Loop Points option, you don't need to set these parameters.

7. If you choose the Remove Silence Between Phrases option, you also need to set the Minimum Inter-Phrase Silence parameter. This tells the Auto Trim/Crop function how many seconds (from 0.1 to 3) of silence must exist between phrases in order for a new Region to be created. For example, if you're removing the silence between sentences from a vocal dictation, set this parameter to a higher setting so that the function doesn't detect the silence between individual words by mistake. It takes some trial and error to get the right setting. For the vocal example, a good setting is probably around 0.5.

8. If you choose the Remove Data Beyond Loop Points option, you also need to set the Minimum Length Following Loop End parameter. This tells the Auto Trim/Crop function to leave a certain number of samples of data after the loop end point. This is to prevent some sample players from malfunctioning, because not all sample players use exact loop points. (I talk more about loops and sample players in Chapter 13).

9. If you choose the Remove Data From Start And Limit File Length option, you also need to set the Auto Delete From Start and Maximum Output Size parameters. The Auto Delete From Start parameter tells the Auto Trim/Crop function to remove a certain amount of data (measured in seconds) from the beginning of the file no matter if it is silence or not. The Maximum Output Size parameter tells the Auto Trim/Crop function to limit the entire size of the file to a certain length (measured in seconds).

10. Click OK.

Sound Forge scans your data selection or entire audio file and removes any silence according to your Auto Trim/Crop parameter settings.

Inserting Silence

There may be times when instead of removing silence, you actually need to add silence to your audio file. The Insert Silence function allows you to do this, and here is how it works:

1. If you want to insert silence at a specific point in your audio file, set the Current Position cursor to that point in the file.

2. Choose Process > Insert Silence to open the Insert Silence dialog box (see Figure 8.16).

Figure 8.16
The Insert Silence function allows you to add silence to your audio file

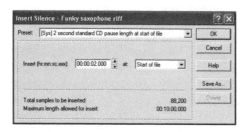

3. Enter the amount of silence (measured in hours, minutes, seconds, and frames) that you want to add to your file using the Insert parameter.

4. Choose an option from the At drop-down list to determine where in the file the silence will be added. If you want to insert silence at a specific point in your audio file, choose the Cursor option. If you want to add silence to the beginning or end of the file, choose the Start Of File or End Of File options, respectively.

5. Click OK.

Silence is inserted into your audio file according to your parameter settings. If you inserted silence at a specific point in the file, any data occurring after that point is pushed back toward the end of the file, and the length of the file is increased.

Muting Audio

The Mute function is similar to the Insert Silence function because it lets you introduce silence into your audio file. But unlike the Insert Silence function, the Mute function doesn't insert silence. Instead, the Mute function simply erases any selected data, thus turning it into silence. To use the Mute function, simply make a selection in your audio file and choose Process > Mute. Any audio data in the selection is then overwritten and turned to silence.

Adjust Audio Volume

One of most fundamental ways of working with audio data is changing its amplitude (volume). There are countless reasons why you might want to change the amplitude of your audio data, and Sound Forge provides a number of different functions that allow you to do this. These functions are called Volume, Fade, and Normalize.

The Volume Function

To simply increase or decrease the amplitude of a data selection or entire audio file, you need to use the Volume function. Here is how the Volume function works:

1. Select the data in your audio file to which you want to apply amplitude changes. If you want to process the entire file, don't select any data or select it all by choosing Edit > Select All (or pressing Ctrl + A on your computer keyboard).

2. Choose Process > Volume to open the Volume dialog box (see Figure 8.17).

Figure 8.17
The Volume function allows you to adjust the amplitude of your audio data

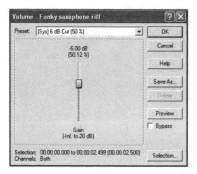

3. To adjust the amplitude of your data, set the Gain parameter. Move the slider up to increase amplitude. Move the slider down to decrease amplitude. This does not provide an absolute setting. Instead, the amplitude is either boosted or cut from its current value by the amount that you specify.

CAUTION
Remember the description about setting your input level during the recording process in Chapter 6? I mentioned that you have to be careful not to set the level too high because it can overload the input and cause your audio to be distorted. Well, when you're raising the volume of your audio data, you also have to watch out not to raise it too high. Raising it too high can cause "clipping." Clipping occurs when Sound Forge attempts to raise the amplitude of the audio data higher than 100 percent (according to the amplitude ruler in the Data Window). The top and bottom of the waveform become clipped, and when you play the audio, it sounds distorted. So, be careful when using the Volume function. Be sure to keep an eye on the amplitude levels of your audio waveforms, and also be sure to listen to your data to see if it sounds OK. If you hear distortion, use Undo to remove the volume change.

4. Click the Preview button to hear how your file will sound before you have Sound Forge make any actual changes to the data.
5. Click OK.

Sound Forge increases or decreases the amplitude of your audio data according to the parameter settings you specified.

Fade Audio

In addition to basic volume changes, Sound Forge allows you to apply a fade-in or fade-out to your audio data.

NOTE

A fade-in is a gradual and smooth increase from a lower volume to a higher volume. This increase in volume is also called a *crescendo* in musical terms. A fade-out is the exact opposite—a gradual and smooth decrease from a higher volume to a lower volume. In musical terms, this decrease in volume is called a *decrescendo.*

To apply a fade-in or fade-out to your audio data, follow these steps:

1. Select the data in your audio file to which you want to apply a fade. If you want to process the entire file, don't select any data or select it all by choosing Edit > Select All (or pressing Ctrl + A on your computer keyboard).

2. To apply a fade-in, choose Process > Fade > In.

3. To apply a fade-out, choose Process > Fade > Out.

Sound Forge applies a fade to your data selection according to your choice.

Complex Fading

Although the Fade In and Fade Out functions allow you to apply fades to your audio, they are just basic linear fades. This means that the volume of the audio increases or decreases in a uniform fashion. If you want to get a little more creative with your volume changes, you can build much more complex fades by using the Graphic Fade function as follows:

1. Select the data in your audio file to which you want to apply a fade. If you want to process the entire file, don't select any data or select it all by choosing Edit > Select All (or pressing Ctrl + A on your computer keyboard).

2. Choose Process > Fade > Graphic to open the Graphic Fade dialog box (see Figure 8.18). The dialog box displays a graph. The left side of the graph shows amplitude values, which can range from 0 to 400 percent (according to the Maximum Gain option located just below the graph). Inside the graph is a line, which represents the fade that will be applied to your selected audio data. If you look at the line from left to right, the left end of the line represents the beginning of your audio data selection, and the right end of the line represents the end of your audio data selection. If the line was set so that the left end was at the bottom of the graph and the right end was at the top, a straight linear fade-in would be applied to your audio data, because as you look at the graph, the left end of the line is set at 0 percent, and the right end of the line is set at 100 percent. So, the volume of the audio data would begin at 0 percent and fade-in all the way up to 100 percent. See how it works?

Figure 8.18
You can use the Graphic Fade function to apply complex fades to your audio data

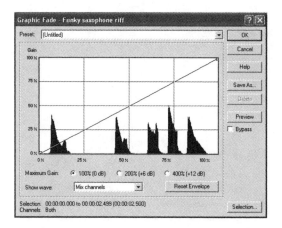

TIP

If you are applying a fade to a stereo file, you can choose to have your audio data displayed in the background of the graph by activating the Show Wave option. You can also choose to show just the data from the left or right channels, or from both channels mixed, by choosing an option from the Show Wave drop-down list. This does not affect how the fade is applied to your data. If you only want to apply a fade to one of the stereo channels, you need to select only the data from that channel before you open the Graphic Fade dialog box.

3. You can change the shape of the fade line in one of two ways: You can simply choose one of the available presets from the Preset drop-down list, or you can change the fade line graphically by clicking and dragging the small squares at the ends of the line. These squares are called Envelope Points.

4. If you want to create some really complex fades, you can add more Envelope Points by clicking anywhere on the fade line. The more Envelope Points you add (the allowed maximum being 16), the more flexibility you have in changing the shape of the line (see Figure 8.19).

CHAPTER 8

Figure 8.19
You can create some really complex fades by adding more Envelope Points

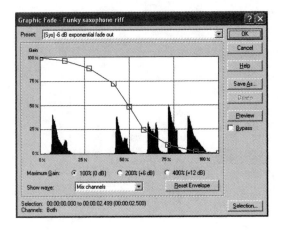

5. Click the Preview button to hear how your file will sound before you have Sound Forge make any actual changes to the data.

6. Click OK.

Sound Forge changes the volume of your audio data selection according to the fade that you defined in the Graphic Fade dialog box.

Normalize Audio

Like the Volume function, the Normalize function also raises the volume of audio, but in a different way. Instead of simply raising the volume, the Normalize function first scans the audio waveform to find its highest amplitude level. It subtracts that amplitude level from the maximum level, which is 100 percent (or a maximum level that you set). The Normalize function then takes that value and uses it to increase the volume of the audio data. So, when all is said and done, the highest amplitude in the waveform is 100 percent (or a maximum level that you set), and all the other amplitude values are increased.

In other words, if an audio waveform has its highest amplitude value at 80 percent, and you set a normalize level of 100 percent, the Normalize function subtracts that value from 100 percent to get 20 percent. It then increases the volume of the audio data by 20 percent so that the highest amplitude value is 100 percent, and all the other amplitude values are 20 percent higher. Basically, you can use the Normalize function to raise the volume of your audio data to the highest it can be without causing any clipping.

To use the Normalize function, do the following:

1. Select the data in your audio file that you want to normalize. If you want to process the entire file, don't select any data or select it all by choosing Edit > Select All (or pressing Ctrl + A on your computer keyboard).

2. Choose Process > Normalize to open the Normalize dialog box (see Figure 8.20).

Figure 8.20
You can normalize the
amplitude of your audio
data using the
Normalize function

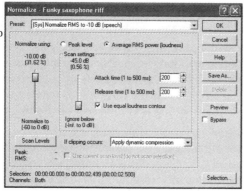

3. For the Normalize Using parameter, choose the Peak Level option. (I talk about the Average RMS Power option later.)

4. Click the Scan Levels button to find the highest amplitude level in your audio data.

5. Adjust the Normalize To parameter by dragging its slider up or down. This sets the highest amplitude level to which you want your audio to be normalized. More often than not, you want to set this to 100 percent, but if you plan to do any additional editing or processing to your data, you should set this parameter to a lower level, such as 50 percent or –6 dB because additional processing can raise the amplitude and cause clipping.

6. Click the Preview button to hear how your file will sound before you have Sound Forge make any actual changes to the data.

7. Click OK.

Sound Forge normalizes the amplitude of your audio data according to your parameter settings.

Root Mean Square

In addition to the basic peak normalizing, the Normalize function provides more advanced processing in the form of average RMS (Root Mean Square) power. In this mode, the Normalize function doesn't simply find the highest amplitude in an audio file. Instead, it measures the loudness of the file, as a listener would hear it over a period of time. This is also known as perceived loudness. Even though the volume of audio may be set at a certain level, it can sometimes be perceived to be louder because of the way human hearing works. The subject is a bit complicated to explain in detail here, but normalizing via average RMS power usually gives better results than peak normalizing when matching the loudness of different audio files.

When scanning an audio file, the Normalize function with RMS uses a digital noise gate like the Auto Trim/Crop function (discussed earlier in this chapter). To use the Normalize function with RMS, do the following:

1. Select the data in your audio file that you want to normalize. If you want to process the entire file, don't select any data or select it all by choosing Edit > Select All (or pressing Ctrl + A on your computer keyboard).

2. Choose Process > Normalize to open the Normalize dialog box.

3. For the Normalize Using parameter, choose the Average RMS Power option.

4. Adjust the Ignore Below parameter slider to specify the threshold above which the Normalize function will judge material as acceptable sound. In other words, you should set this parameter a few dB above what you consider to be silence in your audio data. Anything below the threshold is ignored when calculating the RMS for the data. A good setting is around –45 dB, but it depends on your audio data.

5. Set the Attack Time parameter. This parameter determines how fast the digital noise gate opens to let through acceptable sound material during the scan. If you have fast occurring sounds in your audio (like drum beats), set the attack to a lower amount. Higher amounts cause fast-occurring sounds to be ignored. A good setting is around 200 ms, but it depends on your audio data.

6. Set the Release Time parameter. This parameter determines how fast the digital noise gate closes to stop sound material from being scanned and included in the RMS calculation. If you want more material included in the scan, you should set a slow release time. A fast release time includes less material in the scan. A good setting is around 200 ms, but, again, it depends on your audio data.

7. Because of the limitations of human hearing, very low and very high frequencies are more difficult to hear than mid-range frequencies. To compensate for this, the Normalize function provides the Use Equal Loudness Contour option. You'll usually want to keep this option activated.

8. Click the Scan Levels button to find the RMS of the audio data.

9. Set the Normalize To parameter to specify the new average RMS power for your audio data.

CAUTION

Because the Average RMS Power mode works with perceived sound rather than with actual sound levels, you need to be careful when setting the Normalize To parameter. If you set it too high, you get distorted and/or clipped audio data. The best rule of thumb is to never set the Normalize To parameter any higher than –6 dB when using the Average RMS Power mode.

10. For a bit of extra protection against clipping, be sure to set the If Clipping Occurs parameter. You usually want to keep this parameter set to the Apply Dynamic Compression option, unless you actually want your audio data to be distorted or clipped (such as when processing an electric guitar performance).

11. Click the Preview button to hear how your file will sound before you have Sound Forge make any actual changes to the data.

12. Click OK.

Sound Forge normalizes the amplitude of your audio data according to your parameter settings.

Play with the Stereo Image

When working with stereo audio files, Sound Forge provides a number of different ways to process the left and right channels. For example, you can convert stereo files to mono files, or vice versa. You can also move sounds around the stereo field for different types of effects. The Channel Converter and Pan/Expand functions allow you to tackle these (and other) tasks.

Change Channels

If you ever need to convert a stereo file to a mono file, or vice versa, you need the Channel Converter function. To use the Channel Converter function, do the following:

1. Choose Process > Channel Converter to open the Channel Converter dialog box (see Figure 8.21).

Figure 8.21
The Channel Converter function allows you to convert stereo files to mono files, and vice versa

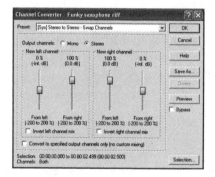

2. Set the Output Channels parameter. If you want to convert your file to mono, choose the Mono option. If you want to convert your file to stereo, choose the Stereo option.

3. If you just want to do a simple, straight conversion, activate the Convert To Specified Output Channels Only option. Then click OK, and skip the remaining steps.

4. If you want to adjust the levels of the left and right channels, and specify how much of each will end up in the final file, leave the Convert To Specified Output Channels Only option deactivated.

5. In the New Left Channel section, adjust the From Left and From Right parameter sliders. If you are converting to mono, only the From Left parameter is available. The From Left parameter determines how much of the left channel from the original audio file will be added to the left channel of the converted file. The From Right parameter determines how much of the right channel from the original audio file will be added to the left channel of the converted file.

6. In the New Right Channel section, adjust the From Left and From Right parameter sliders. If you are converting to mono, only the From Left parameter is available. The From Left parameter determines how much of the left channel from the original audio file will be added to the right channel of the converted

CHAPTER 8

file. The From Right parameter determines how much of the right channel from the original audio file will be added to the right channel of the converted file.

7. Click the Preview button to hear how your file will sound before you have Sound Forge make any actual changes to the data. If you don't like what you hear, adjust the levels in each section.

8. After adjusting the levels in the New Left Channel and New Right Channel sections, click the Preview button again. This time, listen to determine if the audio sounds "hollow." This usually happens due to phase cancellation, which occurs when one audio waveform increases in volume and the other decreases in volume at exactly the same time with the same amount. Because of this phenomenon, they cancel each other out, making the mixed audio sound hollow. If this occurs, try activating the Invert Left Channel Mix option or the Invert Right Channel Mix option, but not both. This option inverts the audio waveform and can usually fix the phase cancellation problem.

9. Click OK.

Sound Forge converts your audio file according to the parameter settings that you specified. You can also achieve some cool effects with the Channel Converter function, such as creating a pseudo-stereo signal from a mono signal. Be sure to check out some of the presets to test some of the other capabilities of this function.

TIP
The Channel Converter function can be used somewhat successfully to remove the lead vocal from a prerecorded song, leaving just the background music. This can be useful if you're trying to create some karaoke tracks or add your own vocal to existing background music. For step-by-step instructions on how to do this, check out Issue 10 of my DigiFreq music technology newsletter. You can download the issue for free at:

http://www.digifreq.com/digifreq/issues.asp.

Panning Around

The Pan/Expand function allows you to determine where a sound will be heard in the sound field between two stereo speakers. You can make it so that the sound will play out of the left speaker, the right speaker, or anywhere in between. That is called *panning*. The Pan/Expand function also provides a few other features, which I talk about shortly. To use the Pan/Expand function for panning, do the following:

1. Select the data in your audio file that you want to process. If you want to process the entire file, don't select any data or select it all by choosing Edit > Select All (or pressing Ctrl + A on your computer keyboard).

2. Choose Process > Pan/Expand to open the Pan/Expand dialog box (see Figure 8.22).

Figure 8.22

You can pan the sound in a stereo audio file to any position in the sound field using the Pan/Expand function

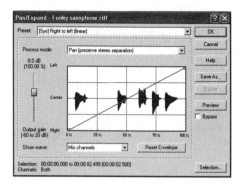

3. Set the Process Mode parameter. Use the Pan (Preserve Stereo Separation) option to perform panning without mixing the left and right channels of the stereo audio together. This option is useful if you have a stereo signal (such as the recording of a background vocal group), and you want to keep the stereo signal intact but you also want to pan the group of voices to a specific location in the stereo field. Use the Pan (Mix Channels Before Panning) option to perform panning while also mixing the left and right channels of stereo audio together. This option is useful for changing the entire stereo field rather than a specific sound within the stereo field.

4. In addition to the Process mode parameter, you'll notice a graph. The left side of the graph shows stereo positioning, which ranges from Right to Center to Left, representing the stereo field. Inside the graph is a line, which represents the panning that will be applied to your selected audio data. If you look at the line from left to right, the left end of the line represents the beginning of your audio data selection, and the right end of the line represents the end of your audio data selection. If the line was set so that the left end was at the bottom of the graph and the right end was at the top, a straight linear pan from right to left would be applied to your audio data, because as you look at the graph, the left end of the line is set at the Right side of the stereo field, and the right end of the line is set at the Left side of the stereo field. So, the sound would begin in the right speaker and move all the way across the stereo field to the left speaker. See how it works?

TIP

Because you are working with a stereo audio file, you can choose to have your audio data displayed in the background of the graph by activating the Show Wave option. You can also choose to show just the data from the left or right channels, or from both channels mixed, by choosing an option from the Show Wave drop-down list. This does not affect how the panning is applied to your data.

5. You can change the pan line graphically by clicking and dragging the small squares at the ends of the line. These squares are called Envelope Points.

6. If you want to create some really complex panning, you can add more Envelope Points by clicking anywhere on the pan line. The more Envelope Points you add (the allowed maximum being 16), the more flexibility you have in changing the shape of the line (see Figure 8.23).

Figure 8.23
You can create some really complex panning by adding more Envelope Points

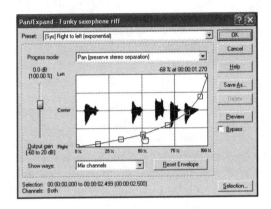

7. Adjust the Output Gain parameter slider to specify the volume of the file after it is processed. You can use this to boost or cut the volume of the audio if you want.

8. Click the Preview button to hear how your file will sound before you have Sound Forge make any actual changes to the data.

9. Click OK.

Sound Forge applies the panning to your audio data selection according to the pan line that you defined in the Pan/Expand dialog box.

Stereo Compress/Expand

In addition to panning, the Pan/Expand function allows you to compress or expand the entire stereo field. In other words, you can compress your stereo audio so that the stereo field sounds smaller (the left and right sides of the field are compressed closer to the center between the two speakers). You can also expand your stereo audio so that the stereo field sounds bigger (the left and right sides of the field are expanded to give the illusion of being beyond the two speakers). You need to hear it to truly understand what I mean. To compress or expand your audio, do the following:

1. Select the data in your audio file that you want to process. If you want to process the entire file, don't select any data or select it all by choosing Edit > Select All (or pressing Ctrl + A on your computer keyboard).

2. Choose Process > Pan/Expand to open the Pan/Expand dialog box.

3. Set the Process Mode parameter to Stereo Expand.

4. You'll notice that the left side of the graph (explained in the last section) now

shows stereo field measurements, which range from Center to Normal to Wide. As you adjust the line on the graph, the closer the line gets to the bottom of the graph, the more your audio is compressed toward the center of the stereo field. The closer the line gets to the top of the graph, the more your audio is expanded outward beyond the stereo field. Again, as in the last section, the left end of the line represents the beginning of your audio data selection, and the right end of the line represents the end of your audio data selection.

5. Adjust the compression or expansion by clicking and dragging the Envelope Points at the ends of the line.

6. If you want to create some really complex panning, you can add more Envelope Points by clicking anywhere on the pan line. The more Envelope Points you add (the allowed maximum being 16), the more flexibility you have in changing the shape of the line.

7. Adjust the Output Gain parameter slider to specify the volume of the file after it is processed. You can use this to boost or cut the volume of the audio if you want.

8. Click the Preview button to hear how your file will sound before you have Sound Forge make any actual changes to the data.

9. Click OK.

Sound Forge applies the compression or expansion to your audio data selection according to the line that you defined in the Pan/Expand dialog box.

Mid-Side Processing

One last use for the Pan/Expand function is in processing Mid-Side recordings.

NOTE

A Mid-Side recording is a special type of recording in which one microphone is pointed directly at the performer(s) to record the middle (center) channel, and another microphone is pointed 90 degrees away from the performer(s) to record the side (stereo) channel.

To convert a Mid-Side recording using the Pan/Expand function, do the following:

1. Select the data in your audio file that you want to process. If you want to process the entire file, don't select any data or select it all by choosing Edit > Select All (or pressing Ctrl + A on your computer keyboard).

2. Choose Process > Pan/Expand to open the Pan/Expand dialog box.

3. Set the Process Mode parameter to Mix Mid-Side (MS) Recording To Left And Right Channels.

4. Place the graph line in the center of the graph so that it is lined up with the Normal measurement on the left side of the graph (see Figure 8.24).

Figure 8.24
Place the line in the
center of the graph to
convert a Mid-Side
recording

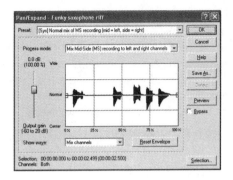

5. Adjust the Output Gain parameter slider to specify the volume of the file after it is processed. You can use this to boost or cut the volume of the audio if you want.

6. Click the Preview button to hear how your file will sound before you have Sound Forge make any actual changes to the data.

7. Click OK.

Sound Forge converts your Mid-Side recording to a regular stereo recording.

TIP

The Pan/Expand function can be used somewhat successfully to extract the lead vocal from a prerecorded song. This can be useful if you want to create your own backing tracks to a song but still want to use the original vocal performance. For step-by-step instructions on how to do this, check out Issue 11 of my DigiFreq music technology newsletter. You can download the issue for free at:

http://www.digifreq.com/digifreq/issues.asp.

Equalization (EQ)

You have a radio in your car, right? Maybe even a cassette or CD player, too? If so, then you've probably used equalization without even knowing it. Adjusting the bass and treble controls on your car radio is a form of equalization. Equalization (EQ) enables you to adjust the tonal characteristics of an audio signal by increasing (boosting) or decreasing (cutting) the amplitude of different frequencies in the audio spectrum.

NOTE

When a musical object (such as a string) vibrates, it emits a sound. The speed at which the object vibrates is called the *frequency*, which is measured in vibrations (or cycles) per second. This measurement is also called *Hertz* (Hz). If an object vibrates 60 times per second, the frequency is 60 Hz. The tricky point to remember here, though, is that most objects vibrate at a number of different frequencies at the same time. The combination of all these different vibrations makes up the distinct sound (or *timbre*) of a vibrating object. That's why a bell sounds like a bell, a horn sounds like a horn, and so on with all other types of sounds.

Of course, we humans can't perceive some very slow and very fast vibrations. Technically, the range of human hearing resides between the frequencies of 20 Hz and 20 KHz (1 KHz is equal to 1000 Hz). This range is known as the *audio spectrum*.

Equalization enables you to manipulate the frequencies of the audio spectrum, and because sounds contain many of these frequencies, you can change their tonal characteristics (or timbre).

In other words, using EQ, you can bump up the bass, add more presence, reduce rumble, and sometimes eliminate noise in your audio material. Not only that, but you can also use EQ as an effect. You know how in some of the modern dance tunes the vocals sound like they're coming out of a telephone receiver or an old radio? That's an effect done with EQ.

Sound Forge provides three different types of EQ: Graphic, Parametric, and Paragraphic. There's also a special Smooth/Enhance function, which I talk about later. All of these functions have their strengths and weaknesses.

Graphic EQ

You may already be familiar with graphic equalizers because they are sometimes included on boom boxes and home stereo systems. Sound Forge's Graphic EQ function simulates a hardware-based graphic equalizer (although it also provides an advanced mode of operation that I talk more about later). It even looks similar (see Figure 8.25).

Figure 8.25
The Graphic EQ function resembles a real graphic equalizer

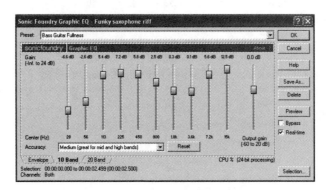

CHAPTER 8

In its most basic mode of operation, the Graphic EQ function provides ten different frequencies (called *bands*) that you can adjust. Each band can either be boosted by 24 dB or cut by –inf (or minus infinity, which is the same as cutting the frequency out of the spectrum altogether). You simply drag the appropriate slider up (boost) or down (cut) to increase or decrease the amplitude of that frequency. But herein lies the weakness of graphic equalization. Although it's very easy to use, you are limited by the frequencies that you can manipulate. You can't change any of the frequencies below, above, or in between the ones provided. Still, the Graphic EQ function is very useful if you want to make quick equalization changes, and its advanced mode lets you get around this limitation somewhat. Here's how the Graphic EQ function works:

1. Select the data in your audio file that you want to process. If you want to process the entire file, don't select any data or select it all by choosing Edit > Select All (or pressing Ctrl + A on your computer keyboard).

2. Choose Process > EQ > Graphic to open the Graphic EQ dialog box. Then choose the 10 Band mode by clicking on the 10 Band tab near the bottom of the box.

3. Adjust the sliders for the frequencies that you want to cut or boost.

TIP

For a quick way to return a slider to 0 dB, double-click on the slider's handle.

CAUTION

Be careful when you're boosting frequencies, because doing so also increases the overall volume of the audio data. If you raise the volume too high, you can introduce clipping into the data.

4. If all you want to do is make basic EQ adjustments to your audio, skip to Step 10. Otherwise, click the 20 Band tab to switch to the 20 Band mode (see Figure 8.26).

Figure 8.26
Make even finer frequency adjustments using the 20 Band mode

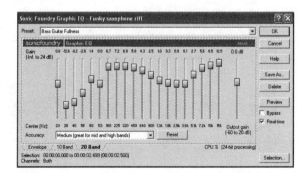

5. You'll notice that your adjustments in the 10 Band mode have been carried over to the 20 Band mode. Now, make more adjustments to fine tune the equalization of your audio even further.

6. If using the 20 Band mode is sufficient for your EQ adjustments, skip to Step 10. Otherwise, click the Envelope tab to switch to Envelope mode (see Figure 8.27).

Figure 8.27
In Envelope mode, the Graphic EQ function allows you to do adjustments using an actual graph

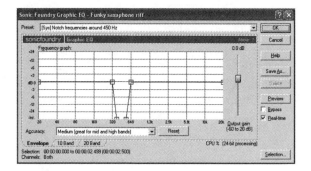

7. In Envelope mode, the Graphic EQ function takes on a whole new look. Instead of sliders, you'll see a graph. The bottom of the graph shows the frequencies being adjusted, which range from 20 Hz to 20 KHz. The left side of the graph shows the amplitude of each frequency, which ranges from –inf to +24 dB. Inside the graph is a line, which represents the equalization curve to be applied to your audio data. Any part of the line above 0 dB represents frequencies that are being boosted. Any part of the line below 0 dB represents frequencies that are being cut.

8. You can adjust the line by clicking and dragging the Envelope Points. As you drag a point, you'll notice the frequency and amplitude values being displayed on top of the upper-right corner of the graph.

9. If you want to create a really complex EQ curve, you can add more Envelope Points by clicking anywhere on the line. The more Envelope Points you add, the more flexibility you have in changing the shape of the line (see Figure 8.28).

Figure 8.28
You can create a more complex EQ curve by adding more Envelope Points

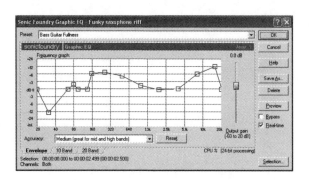

CHAPTER 8

10. Set the Accuracy parameter to specify the quality of the EQ processing you want to use. The higher the quality, the slower the processing. But unless you have a really large audio file, you can usually keep this set to the best option, which is High.

11. Click the Preview button to hear how your file will sound before you have Sound Forge make any actual changes to the data. If you hear any clipping, adjust the Output Gain parameter so that the overall volume of the EQ processing is reduced. Try bringing it down to –1 dB and use trial and error from there.

12. Click OK.

Sound Forge applies the equalization to your audio data according to the EQ curve that you defined in the Graphic EQ dialog box.

Parametric EQ

Parametric equalization is a bit more powerful and flexible than graphic equalization. With the Parametric EQ function, you're not limited to set frequencies. You can specify an exact frequency to adjust. Yes, by using Graphic EQ Envelope mode you can specify frequencies, but not exactly. You are limited by the resolution of the graph. The Parametric EQ function isn't difficult to use, and I can explain it best by showing you how it works:

1. Select the data in your audio file that you want to process. If you want to process the entire file, don't select any data or select it all by choosing Edit > Select All (or pressing Ctrl + A on your computer keyboard).

2. Choose Process > EQ > Parametric to open the Parametric EQ dialog box (see Figure 8.29).

Figure 8.29
The Parametric EQ function allows you to adjust very specific frequencies

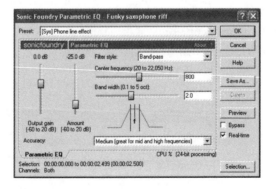

3. Choose an option from the Filter Style parameter drop-down list: Low-Frequency Shelf, High-Frequency Shelf, Band-Pass, or Band-Notch/Boost.

4. Set the Center Frequency parameter. If you choose the Low-Frequency Shelf filter style, any frequencies below the Center Frequency are either cut or boosted. If you choose the High-Frequency Shelf filter style, any frequencies above the Center Frequency are either cut or boosted. If you choose the Band-Pass filter style, frequencies above or below the Center Frequency are cut or boosted. If you choose the Band-Notch/Boost filter style, the Center Frequency is cut or boosted.

5. If you choose the Low-Frequency Shelf or High-Frequency Shelf filter styles, you need to adjust the Transition Width parameter. This parameter determines how much the frequencies above or below the Center Frequency are affected. The lower the value, the sharper the EQ curve is at the Center Frequency. The higher the value, the smoother the EQ curve.

6. If you choose the Band-Pass or Band-Notch/Boost filter styles, you need to adjust the Band Width parameter. This parameter determines how many frequencies are affected around the Center Frequency. The lower the value, the fewer frequencies that are affected. The higher the value, the more frequencies that are affected.

7. Adjust the Amount Parameter. This parameter determines how much the specified frequencies are cut or boosted. It ranges from –60 dB to +20 dB.

8. Set the Accuracy parameter to specify the quality of the EQ processing you want to use. The higher the quality, the slower the processing. But unless you have a really large audio file, you can usually keep this set to the best option, which is High.

9. Click the Preview button to hear how your file will sound before you have Sound Forge make any actual changes to the data. If you hear any clipping, adjust the Output Gain parameter so that the overall volume of the EQ processing is reduced. Try bringing it down to –1 dB and use trial and error from there.

10. Click OK.

Sound Forge applies the equalization to your audio data according to the parameters you specified in the Parametric EQ dialog box.

Paragraphic EQ

Sound Forge's most advanced EQ function is the Paragraphic EQ. The Paragraphic EQ combines many of the features from the different EQ functions I've already discussed. If you take a look at the Paragraphic EQ dialog box (see Figure 8.30), you'll notice a frequency graph in the upper-right portion of the dialog box.

CHAPTER 8

Figure 8.30

The Paragraphic EQ function is a combination of multiple EQ functions

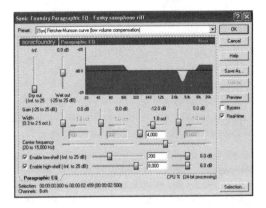

This graph displays the EQ curve (like in the Graphic EQ function), but this graph is not adjustable directly. Instead, it shows the EQ curve according to the other parameter settings. The Paragraphic EQ also contains four independent Parametric EQs, each complete with Gain, Width, and Center Frequency controls. All of these controls work the same as described earlier. The only difference is that if the Gain of an EQ is set to 0 dB, that means the EQ is deactivated. To activate an EQ, adjust the Gain. The other controls then become available. In addition, the Paragraphic EQ contains low-shelf and high-shelf EQs, each with adjustable Gain and Center Frequency controls. One final difference between the Paragraphic EQ and the other EQ functions is that instead of a master Gain control, the Paragraphic EQ provides the Dry Out and Wet Out controls. This allows you to mix the original audio data with the equalized audio data and determine how much of each will end up in the processed audio. The Dry Out parameter controls the level of the original audio, and the Wet Out parameter controls the level of the equalized audio.

So, basically, the Paragraphic EQ is a combination of four full-band Parametric EQs as well as a low-shelf and a high-shelf EQ. The combination of all these functions together provides the means to create some very complex equalization processing. To get an idea of how powerful the Paragraphic EQ funtion is, be sure to try out some of the presets by using the Preset drop-down list.

Some EQ Applications

Right about now, you might be saying to yourself, "Okay, EQ sounds pretty cool, but what can I do with it?" Well, you can use EQ in many different ways to process your audio. To begin with, you might want to try some of the presets that come included with Sound Forge. After that, you might want to try experimenting with some of the settings described in the following sections.

Fullness

To make your audio sound a little fuller, try boosting the range of frequencies around 200 Hz by 6 dB. To do so, use the Parametric EQ function with Band-Pass filter style and set the filter parameters to the following: Center Frequency = 200, Band Width = 2.0, and Amount = 6.0 dB (see Figure 8.31).

Figure 8.31
Use the Parametric EQ
function to add fullness
to your audio

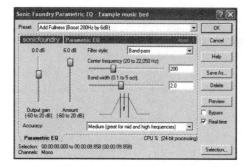

Punch

To add a little more punch to your audio, try boosting the range of frequencies between and around 800 Hz and 2 kHz by 6 dB. To do so, use the Paragraphic EQ function with the first band set to the following: Center Frequency = 800, Width = 2.0, and Gain = 6.0 dB. And set the second band parameters to: Center Frequency = 2000, Width = 2.0, and Gain = 6.0 dB (see Figure 8.32).

Figure 8.32
Use the Paragraphic EQ
function to add punch
to your audio

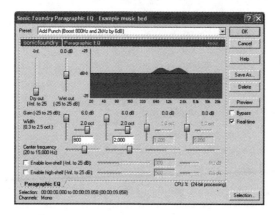

Noise Reduction

EQ can also be used as a simple means of reducing noise in your audio. This is especially true for high frequency hiss. Use the Parametric EQ function with the High-Frequency Shelf filter style and the set the filter parameters to the following: Cutoff Frequency = 18000, Transition Width = 2.0, Amount = -60.0 dB (see Figure 8.33).

CHAPTER 8

Figure 8.33
Use the Parametric EQ
function to remove high
frequency hiss from
your audio

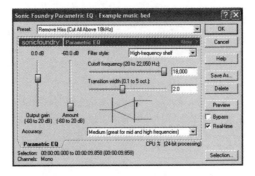

To get rid of buzzing or humming noises with EQ, use the Parametric EQ function with the
Band-Notch/Boost filter style and set the filter parameters to the following: Center Frequency =
60, Band Width = 1.0, Amount = -60.0 dB (see Figure 8.34).

Figure 8.34
Use the Parametric EQ
function to remove hum
or buzz from your audio

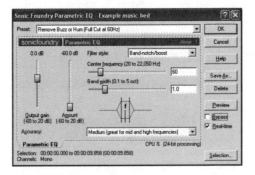

TIP
I'll talk about more applications using equalization in future issues of my
DigiFreq music technology newsletter. To sign up for a free subscription, go to:

http://www.digifreq.com/digifreq/.

Play It Backward

Assuming you're old enough to remember vinyl recordings, did you ever take a record and play it backward to see whether your favorite band had left some satanic messages in their songs or perhaps a recipe for their favorite lentil soup? Well, guess what? You can do the same thing with your audio data. Sound Forge enables you to "turn around" the data in a file (or selection) so that it plays in reverse.

This feature doesn't have much practical use, but combined with some other processing, it can render some cool effects. To use it, simply select the data that you want to change, and choose Process > Reverse. Now the data plays backward. If you don't make a data selection, all the data in the file is processed.

Flip It Over

Back in Chapter 7, I talked about the Paste Mix function and about how when you mix certain sound files together, phase cancellation can occur. Phase cancellation occurs when one audio waveform increases in volume and the other decreases in volume at exactly the same time with the same amount. Because of this phenomenon, they cancel each other out, making the mixed audio sound "hollow." The Paste Mix function provides an invert option, which inverts the audio waveform around the zero axis. This can sometimes help eliminate phase cancellation.

Sound Forge allows you to manually invert the data in an audio file using the Invert/Flip function. To use it, simply select the data that you want to change, and choose Process > Invert/Flip. The data is inverted. If you don't make a data selection, all the data in the file is inverted.

Change the Length

Usually, when you change the length of audio data, the pitch also changes. Shorten the data and the pitch rises. Lengthen the data and the pitch falls. More often than not, you want to avoid pitch changes. Luckily, Sound Forge provides a function that lets you change the length of your audio data without affecting the pitch. This function is called Time Stretch, and here is how it works:

1. Select the data in your audio file that you want to process. If you want to process the entire file, don't select any data or select it all by choosing Edit > Select All (or pressing Ctrl + A on your computer keyboard).

2. Choose Process > Time Stretch to open the Time Stretch dialog box (see Figure 8.35).

CHAPTER 8

Figure 8.35

The Time Stretch
function lets you change
the length of audio
without changing its
pitch

3. Set the Mode parameter. To provide the best type of processing, the Time Stretch function takes into account the type of audio data you are processing. You should select the appropriate option in the drop-down list according to the type of data you want to process. For instance, if you are processing unpitched percussion instruments, you might want to use the Drums, Unpitched option.

4. Set the Input Format parameter. You can choose to specify a new length for your audio as a percentage, a tempo, or a specific length in time.

5. Whichever option you choose for the Input Format parameter, the appropriate control appears that allows you to specify the length for your audio. If you choose Percentage, the Final Percentage parameter is available. If you choose Tempo, the Final Tempo parameter is available. If you choose Time, the Final Time parameter is available. Adjust the available parameter to specify the new length of your audio data.

6. Click the Preview button to hear how your file will sound before you have Sound Forge make any actual changes to the data.

7. Click OK.

Sound Forge changes the length of your audio data according to the parameter settings you specified in the Time Compress/Expand dialog box.

9

Exploring Effects

Just as adding spices to a recipe makes it taste better, adding effects to your audio data makes it sound better. Effects can make the difference between a dull, lifeless recording and a recording that really rocks. For example, you can apply echoes and background ambiance to give the illusion that your audio was recorded in a particular environment, such as a concert hall. You can also use effects to make your vocal recordings sound rich and full. And the list goes on. Sound Forge provides a number of different effects functions that you can use to spice up your audio data. Although applying these effects to your data isn't overly complicated, understanding what they do and how to use them can sometimes be confusing. In this chapter, you'll learn to use:

▶ Reverberation and the Acoustic Mirror

▶ Delay, Chorus, and Flanging

▶ Pitch bending and pitch shifting

▶ Compression and limiting

▶ Various other types of effects

▶ Plug-ins and the DirectX menu

▶ The Plug-In Manager and the Audio Plug-In Chainer

Echo Effects

You know what an echo is, right? It's a repeating sound that mimics an initial sound. For example, if you yell the word *hello* in a large, enclosed area (such as a concert hall or a canyon), you hear that word repeated (or echoed) back over and over until it fades away. This effect is also known as *delay*. Delay can be used to create many different kinds of effects; not just echoes. Sound Forge provides a number of functions that allow you to create these effects. I talk about them one by one in this section.

Simple Delay

The Simple Delay function lets you apply basic echo effects to your audio data. To use this function, do the following:

1. Select the data in your audio file that you want to process. If you want to process the entire file, don't select any data or select it all by choosing Edit > Select All (or pressing Ctrl + A on your computer keyboard).

CHAPTER 9

2. Choose Effects > Delay/Echo > Simple to open the Simple Delay dialog box (see Figure 9.1).

Figure 9.1
Use the Simple Delay function to add basic echoes to your audio

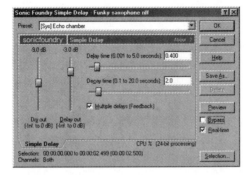

3. Set the Delay Time parameter. This parameter determines how much time (in seconds) occurs between each echo. You can set the Delay Time from 0.001 to 5 seconds.

TIP

Many professional musicians use delay to synchronize the echoes with the music. For instance, you can have the echoes play in time with each quarter note, eighth note, sixteenth note, and so on, if you are applying echoes to some recorded music. All that's required for this cool trick is a little simple math.

Begin by figuring the Delay Time needed to synchronize the echoes to each quarter note. To do so, just divide 60,000 (the number of milliseconds in one minute) by the current tempo (measured in beats per minute) of your recorded music. So, for a tempo of 120 bpm, you get 500 milliseconds (which is 0.500 seconds). If you set the Delay Time to 0.500, the resulting echoes sound at the same time as each quarter note in your music.

To figure out the Delay Time for other note values, you just need to divide or multiply. Because an eighth note is half the value of a quarter note, you simply divide 500 by 2 to get 250 milliseconds (or 0.250 seconds). A sixteenth note is half the value of an eighth note, so 250 divided by 2 is 125 milliseconds (or 0.125 seconds). See how it works? If you want to find out larger note values, just multiply by 2. Because a half note is twice as long as a quarter note, you multiply 500 by 2 to get 1000 milliseconds (or 1 second), and so on.

4. Set the Dry Out and Delay Out parameters. When you apply an effect to your original data, you can determine how much of the effect and how much of the original data ends up in the final sound. This way, you can add a certain amount of effect without drowning out the entire original data. The Dry Out parameter determines how much of the original data you will hear in the processed audio,

and the Delay Out parameter determines how much of the effect you will hear in the processed audio.

5. Set the Multiple Delays option and the Decay Time parameter. With some effects, you can take their resulting signals and send them back through to have the effect applied multiple times. This is called *feedback*. The resulting sound can be different depending on the effect. For the Simple Delay function, the Multiple Delays option and the Decay Time parameter control how many echoes occur. If you activate the Multiple Delays option, more than one echo will occur. The Decay Time parameter determines how many echoes there will be. The lower the Decay Time, the fewer number of echoes. The higher the Decay Time, the more echoes.

6. Click the Preview button to hear how your file will sound before you have Sound Forge make any actual changes to the data.

7. Click OK.

Sound Forge applies the Simple Delay function to your audio data according to your parameter settings.

Multi-Tap Delay

The Multi-Tap Delay function allows you to create very complex echo effects by letting you set up multiple delays at once, such as setting up multiple Simple Delay effects at the same time to process your audio data. Here is how the Multi-Tap Delay function works:

1. Select the data in your audio file that you want to process. If you want to process the entire file, don't select any data or select it all by choosing Edit > Select All (or pressing Ctrl + A on your computer keyboard).

2. Choose Effects > Delay/Echo > Multi-Tap to open the Multi-Tap Delay dialog box (see Figure 9.2).

Figure 9.2
The Multi-Tap Delay function lets you create very complex echo effects

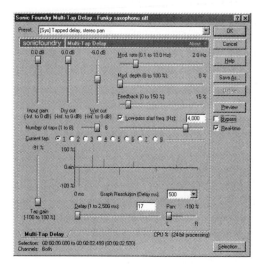

3. Set the Dry Out and Wet Out parameters. These parameters work exactly the same as the Dry Out and Delay Out parameters of the Simple Delay function.

4. Set the Input Gain parameter. This parameter determines how much of the original audio is allowed to be processed. More often than not, you want to leave this set to 0 dB.

5. Set the Mod Rate and Mod Depth parameters. These parameters are a bit difficult to describe. They enable you to add a "warble" type of effect to your audio data along with the echoes. The sound is also similar to that of the tremolo you hear on an electronic organ. The Mod Rate determines the speed (in Hz or cycles per second) of the "warble," and the Mod Depth determines how much your audio data will be affected by it.

6. Set the Feedback parameter. This parameter works just the like the combination of the Multiple Delays option and the Decay Time parameter of the Simple Delay function.

7. If you want to apply some low-pass EQ to your delay effect, activate and set the Low-Pass Start Freq parameter. This allows you to filter out some of the high frequencies so that you can simulate more dense echo environments, such as echoes in a small room. For an example, check out the preset called Small Room 2.

8. Set the Number Of Taps parameter. This parameter determines how many different taps (delays) you want to set up in your effect. You can have up to eight different taps. As you adjust the Number Of Taps parameter, you'll notice the Current Tap options (1-8) become available.

9. Each tap comes with its own Tap Gain, Delay, and Pan parameters. This means that you can control the initial volume, echo time, and panning in the stereo field of each delay. To adjust the parameters for a certain tap, choose the number of the tap via the Current Tap options. Then, adjust the Tap Gain, Delay, and Pan parameters for that tap. You can do this for all eight taps individually.

10. As you adjust the parameters for each tap, you'll notice changes on the graph displayed just below the Current Tap options. This graph (called the Echogram) gives you a visual display of the echoes that will occur because of the parameter settings you have chosen. Each line represents an echo. The length of the line corresponds to the volume of the echo, measured as a percentage (the left side of the graph) of the original audio. The distance of the line from the left side of the graph represents the time at which the echo will sound after the original audio. The red line represents the currently selected tap. The black lines are other available taps. And the blue lines are echoes resulting from the Feedback parameter. To adjust how much time the Echogram shows, select an option from the Graph Resolution drop-down list.

11. Click the Preview button to hear how your file will sound before you have Sound Forge make any actual changes to the data.

12. Click OK.

Sound Forge applies the Multi-Tap Delay function to your audio data according to your parameter settings. Be sure to check out some of the presets for the Multi-Tap Delay function that come with Sound Forge. They can demonstrate the true power of this function.

Chorus

Believe it or not, Sound Forge's Chorus function has many of the same parameters as the Simple Delay and Multi-Tap Delay functions. Why? Because technically, chorus is a form of delay. Chorus uses delay and detuning to achieve its results. You don't hear echoes when using chorus, though, because the delay is extremely short. Instead, chorus makes your audio data sound "fatter" or "fuller." The name *chorus* comes from the fact that people singing in a chorus produce a full sound because each person sings slightly out of tune and out of time—not enough to make the music sound bad, but actually better. You can use Sound Forge's Chorus function to achieve similar results with your audio data. To use the Chorus function, do the following:

1. Select the data in your audio file that you want to process. If you want to process the entire file, don't select any data or select it all by choosing Edit > Select All (or pressing Ctrl + A on your computer keyboard).

2. Choose Effects > Chorus to open the Chorus dialog box (see Figure 9.3).

Figure 9.3
Make your audio sound "fatter" or "fuller" with the Chorus function

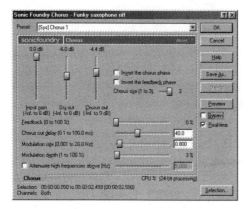

3. Set the Chorus Out Delay parameter. This parameter works just like the Delay Time parameter of the Simple Delay function. The only difference is that the Chorus Out Delay parameter is limited to 100 milliseconds. If you set this parameter high enough, you can actually get some quick repeating echoes out of it. For adding chorus to your audio, though, you should keep it set somewhere between 20 and 40.

4. Set the Dry Out, Chorus Out, and Input Gain parameters. The Chorus Out parameter is the same as the Delay Out parameter of the Simple Delay function. I explained the Dry Out and Input Gain parameters in the last section.

5. Set the Feedback parameter. Instead of setting the number of echoes to occur (as in the Multi-Tap Delay function), this parameter determines the "fullness" of the

chorus. The higher the value, the "fuller" the chorus. For an example, check out the preset called Chorus 5.

6. Set the Modulation Rate and Modulation Depth parameters. Instead of adding a "warble" to your audio (as in the Multi-Tap Delay function), these parameters determine how detuning is added to the chorus. The Modulation Rate determines how quickly the detuning occurs, and Modulation Depth determines the amount of detuning. A high Modulation Depth setting makes your audio sound really out of tune (which isn't usually desirable), but a lower setting produces a nice chorus effect.

7. Set the Attenuate High Frequencies parameter. This parameter works the same as the Low-Pass Start Freq parameter of the Multi-Tap Delay function.

8. Set the Chorus Size parameter. This parameter allows you to determine how many times your audio is processed with the Chorus function. You can have the function applied up to three times in succession, which gives a very deep chorus effect. For an example, check out the preset called Chorus 1. Try changing the Chorus Size parameter to hear how each setting sounds.

9. Set the Invert The Chorus Phase and Invert The Feedback Phase options. Back in Chapter 7, I talked about the Paste Mix function and about how when you mix certain sound files together, phase cancellation can occur. Phase cancellation occurs when one audio waveform increases in volume and the other decreases in volume at exactly the same time with the same amount. Because of this phenomenon, they cancel each other out, making the mixed audio sound "hollow." By adjusting the Invert The Chorus Phase or Invert The Feedback Phase options, you can eliminate phase cancellation if the need arises.

10. Click the Preview button to hear how your file will sound before you have Sound Forge make any actual changes to the data.

11. Click OK.

Sound Forge applies the Chorus function to your audio data according to your parameter settings.

Flange/Wah-Wah

Although the Flange/Wah-wah function doesn't have the same parameters as the Simple Delay function, flanging is nevertheless a form of delay. So are phasing and wah-wah, which can also be achieved with the Flange/Wah-wah function. These effects produce very strange "spacey," "whooshy," or "warble" types of sounds by mixing a slightly delayed version of the original audio with itself. As with chorus, you don't hear echoes because the delay occurs so quickly. It's difficult to describe what these effects sound like, so you'll have to hear them for yourself. To use the Flange/Wah-wah function, do the following:

1. Select the data in your audio file that you want to process. If you want to process the entire file, don't select any data or select it all by choosing Edit > Select All (or pressing Ctrl + A on your computer keyboard).

2. Choose Effects > Flange/Wah-Wah to open the Flange/Wah-wah dialog box (see Figure 9.4).

Figure 9.4
Give your audio a really
strange sound using the
Flange/Wah-wah
function

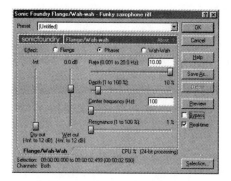

3. Choose an option for the Effect parameter. Your choices are Flange, Phaser, or Wah-wah.

4. Set the Dry Out and Wet Out parameters. These parameters work the same as the Dry Out and Chorus Out of the Chorus function.

5. Set the Rate parameter. This parameter controls the speed of the effect in all three modes of operation: Flange, Phaser, or Wah-wah.

6. Set the Depth parameter. If you choose the Flange mode, the Depth parameter controls how much of the flanging effect is applied to your audio data. If you choose the Phaser mode, the Depth parameter controls the range of frequencies that are affected by the phasing effect. If you choose the Wah-wah mode, the Depth parameter controls the range of frequencies that are affected by the Wah-wah effect.

7. If you choose the Flange mode, you can skip to Step 9. Otherwise, set the Center Frequency parameter. In both the Phaser and Wah-wah modes, the Center Frequency parameter controls the frequency at which phasing or wah-wah effect is most pronounced. For example, if you are processing a tenor vocal recording, you could set the Center Frequency to about 261 Hz to center the effect with the range of the tenor voice (the tenor range is about 130 to 493 Hz).

8. Set the Resonance parameter. For both the Phaser and Wah-wah modes, the Resonance parameter controls how pronounced the phasing and wah-wah effects are on your audio data. The lower the Resonance, the less pronounced the effect. The higher the Resonance, the more pronounced the effect.

9. Click the Preview button to hear how your file will sound before you have Sound Forge make any actual changes to the data.

10. Click OK.

Sound Forge applies the Flange/Wah-wah function to your audio data according to your parameter settings.

Pitch Effects

There may be times when you want to change the pitch of your audio data. Maybe you need to make corrections to an out-of-tune vocal or instrument part. Or, perhaps you want to create a tune in the style of Alvin & the Chipmunks. Sound Forge includes three different functions that allow you to alter the pitch of your data in a variety of ways. These functions include Pitch Bend, Pitch Shift, and Vibrato. I explain them one by one in this section.

Pitch Bend

The Pitch Bend function allows you to change the pitch of your audio data over a period of time. For example, with this function, you could have your audio data slowly rise in pitch from beginning to end, if that's the effect you desire. The Pitch Bend function is quite versatile. Here is how it works:

1. Select the data in your audio file that you want to process. If you want to process the entire file, don't select any data or select it all by choosing Edit > Select All (or pressing Ctrl + A on your computer keyboard).

2. Choose Effects > Pitch > Bend to open the Pitch Bend dialog box (see Figure 9.5). The dialog box displays a graph. The left side of the graph shows pitch values, which can range from –24 to +24 semitones (according to the Range parameter located just to the left of the graph). Inside the graph is a line, which represents the pitch bend that will be applied to your selected audio data. If you look at the line from left to right, the left end of the line represents the beginning of your audio data selection, and the right end of the line represents the end of your audio data selection. If the line was set so that the left end was at the bottom of the graph and the right end was at the top, a quick drop, and then a gradual rise in pitch would be applied to your audio data. This occurs because, as you look at the graph, the left end of the line is set at a pitch lower than normal (represented by zero in the middle of the graph), and the right end of the line is set at a pitch higher than normal. So, the pitch would quickly begin at a lower value and then gradually rise to normal, and then upwards to a higher value. See how it works?

Figure 9.5
Use the Pitch Bend function to change the pitch of your audio data gradually over time

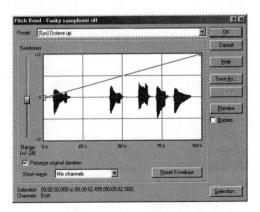

TIP

If you are applying a pitch bend to a stereo file, you can choose to have your audio data displayed in the background of the graph by activating the Show Wave option. You can choose to show just the data from the left or right channels, or both channels mixed by choosing an option from the Show Wave drop-down list. This does not affect how the pitch bend is applied to your data, though. If you only want to apply a pitch bend to one of the stereo channels, you need to select only the data from that channel before you open the Pitch Bend dialog box.

3. You can change the shape of the pitch bend line in one of two ways. You can simply choose one of the available presets from the Preset drop-down list. Alternatively, you can change the pitch bend line graphically by clicking and dragging the small squares at the ends of the line. These squares are called Envelope Points.

4. If you want to create some really complex pitch bends, you can add more Envelope Points by clicking anywhere on the pitch bend line. The more Envelope Points you add (the allowed maximum being 16), the more flexibility you have in changing the shape of the line (see Figure 9.6).

Figure 9.6
You can create some really complex pitch bends by adding more Envelope Points

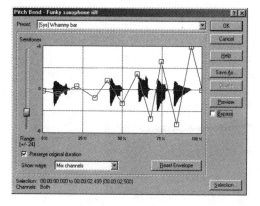

5. If you want to adjust the range of the pitch bend (along with the pitch resolution of the graph), use the Range parameter that I mentioned earlier. For subtle pitch bends, use small values. For more prominent pitch bends, use large values.

CHAPTER 9

TIP

Normally, when you change the pitch of audio data, the length is altered, too. Raise the pitch and the data gets shorter; lower the pitch and the data gets longer. This can be a problem if you need your audio to remain at a certain length but a pitch change is required. In this case, be sure to activate the Preserve Original Duration option. This allows you to change the pitch without altering the length of the audio.

6. Click the Preview button to hear how your file will sound before you have Sound Forge make any actual changes to the data.

7. Click OK.

Sound Forge applies the Pitch Bend function to your audio data according to your parameter settings.

Pitch Shift

As I mentioned in the previous section, when you change the pitch of audio data, the length is also altered. As with the Pitch Bend function, Sound Forge's Pitch Shift function allows you to change the pitch without changing the length of the audio data. But the Pitch Shift function is applied all at once and can't be applied gradually over time as with the Pitch Bend function. Here is how the Pitch Shift function works:

1. Select the data in your audio file to which you want to apply a pitch change. If you want to process the entire file, don't select any data or select it all by choosing Edit > Select All (or pressing Ctrl + A on your computer keyboard).

2. Choose Effects > Pitch > Shift to open the Pitch Shift dialog box (see Figure 9.7).

Figure 9.7
Use the Pitch Shift function to change the pitch of your audio data all at once instead of gradually over time

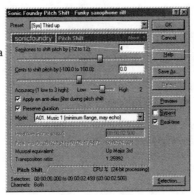

3. Set the Semitones To Shift Pitch By and Cents To Shift Pitch By parameters. These parameters control how much the pitch will be shifted up or down. For large changes, use the Semitones To Shift Pitch By parameter. For finer control,

use the Cents To Shift Pitch By parameter. There are 100 cents to each semitone in terms of pitch.

TIP

The only problem to be wary of is that pitch shifting can produce unwanted artifacts if you use too large an interval. The famous Alvin & the Chipmunks was a product of this problem. It's best to stay within an interval of a major third (four semitones) up or down if possible.

4. Set the Accuracy parameter to specify the quality of the pitch shift processing you want to use. The higher the quality, the slower the processing. But unless you have a really large audio file, you can usually keep this set to the best option, which is High.

5. When raising the pitch of audio, distortion can be introduced into the data. To remedy this problem, be sure to activate the Apply An Anti-Alias Filter During Pitch Shift option. If you're lowering the pitch of your audio data, you don't need to worry about this.

6. If you don't want the length of your audio data to change when you apply a pitch shift, activate the Preserve Duration option. Then, choose an option from the Mode drop-down list. You should select the appropriate option in the drop-down list according to the type of data you want to process. For instance, if you are processing unpitched percussion instruments, you might want to use the Drums, Unpitched option.

7. Click the Preview button to hear how your file will sound before you have Sound Forge make any actual changes to the data.

8. Click OK.

Sound Forge applies the Pitch Shift function to your audio data according to your parameter settings.

Vibrato

The Vibrato function is similar to the Pitch Bend function, but instead of bending the pitch, it modulates (or "vibrates") the pitch up and down continuously. This gives a sort of warble effect when you apply it subtly. If you apply it in large amounts, you can also produce some very strange pitch variation effects. Here is how the Vibrato function works:

1. Select the data in your audio file that you want to process. If you want to process the entire file, don't select any data or select it all by choosing Edit > Select All (or pressing Ctrl + A on your computer keyboard).

2. Choose Effects > Vibrato to open the Vibrato dialog box (see Figure 9.8). The dialog box displays a graph. The left side of the graph shows pitch values, which can range from –24 to +24 semitones (according to the Semitones parameter located just to the left of the graph). Inside the graph is a line, which represents

the vibrato that will be applied to your selected audio data over time. The line constitutes one cycle (or vibration). This vibration is repeated over and over at a certain rate until it has been applied to your entire audio data selection.

Figure 9.8
Use the Vibrato function to add pitch variation effects to your audio data

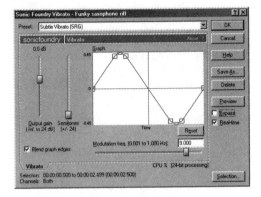

3. You can change the shape of the vibrato line in one of two ways: You can simply choose one of the available presets from the Preset drop-down list. Alternatively, you can change the vibrato line graphically by clicking and dragging the small squares (Envelope Points) at the ends of the line.

4. If you want to create some really complex vibratos, you can add more Envelope Points by clicking anywhere on the vibrato line. The more Envelope Points you add, the more flexibility you have in changing the shape of the line.

TIP

Because the vibrato line represents one frequency cycle (or vibration), the left and right ends of the line should end up at the same vertical position on the graph. For example, they might both rest on the zero line in the middle of the graph. This makes for smooth vibrato effects. If the ends of the line are not in the same vertical position, you might get clicks or pops in your audio. To help with this problem, you can try activating the Blend Graph Edges option to see if it helps to eliminate the clicks or pops.

5. If you want to adjust the range of the vibrato (along with the pitch resolution of the graph), use the Semitones parameter that I mentioned earlier. For subtle vibratos, use small values. For more prominent vibratos, use large values.

6. Set the Modulation Freq parameter. This parameter controls the speed of the vibrato. High values give you a warble effect. Low values give you more of a pitch bending effect.

TIP

For a very subtle vibrato effect, choose the Vibrato 2 preset. Then, change the Semitones parameter so that the range becomes –0.45 to +0.45 semitones. Finally, set the Modulation Freq parameter to 9.000. These are the settings I use for my Subtle Vibrato preset.

7. Adjust the Output Gain parameter slider to specify the volume of the file after it is processed. You can use this to boost or cut the volume of the audio if you want.

8. Click the Preview button to hear how your file will sound before you have Sound Forge make any actual changes to the data.

9. Click OK.

Sound Forge applies the Vibrato function to your audio data according to your parameter settings.

Volume Effects

In addition to all the volume processing functions that I talked about in Chapter 8, Sound Forge provides a number of other functions that manipulate volume for the purpose of producing effects. With these functions, you can apply amplitude modulation, distortion, compression, and many other types of processing to your audio data. I explain all of the functions one by one in this section.

Amplitude Modulation

The Amplitude Modulation function works almost identically to the Vibrato function, except that instead of modulating (or "vibrating") frequencies, the Amplitude Modulation function modulates amplitudes (or the volume) of your audio data. With this function, you can achieve effects such as the tremolo on an electronic organ. Here is how the Amplitude Modulation function works:

1. Select the data in your audio file that you want to process. If you want to process the entire file, don't select any data or select it all by choosing Edit > Select All (or pressing Ctrl + A on your computer keyboard).

2. Choose Effects > Amplitude Modulation to open the Amplitude Modulation dialog box (see Figure 9.9). The dialog box displays a graph. The left side of the graph shows amplitude values, which can range from –inf to 0 dB (according to the Amplitude parameter located just to the left of the graph). Inside the graph is a line, which represents the volume changes that will be applied to your selected audio data over time. The line constitutes one cycle (or vibration). This vibration is repeated over and over at a certain rate until it has been applied to your entire audio data selection.

Figure 9.9
Use the Amplitude
Modulation function to
add volume variation
effects to your audio
data

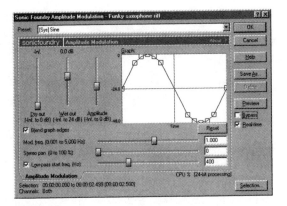

3. You can change the shape of the amplitude line in one of two ways: You can simply choose one of the available presets from the Preset drop-down list. Alternatively, you can change the amplitude line graphically by clicking and dragging the small squares (Envelope Points) at the ends of the line.

4. If you want to create some really complex volume changes, you can add more Envelope Points by clicking anywhere on the amplitude line. The more Envelope Points you add, the more flexibility you have in changing the shape of the line.

TIP

Because the amplitude line represents one frequency cycle (or vibration), the left and right ends of the line should end up at the same vertical position on the graph. For example, they might both rest on the line in the middle of the graph. This makes for smooth volume change effects. If the ends of the line are not in the same vertical position, you might get clicks or pops in your audio. To help with this problem, you can try activating the Blend Graph Edges option to see if it helps to eliminate the clicks or pops.

5. If you want to adjust the range of the volume changes (along with the amplitude resolution of the graph), use the Amplitude parameter that I mentioned earlier. For subtle changes, use small values. For more prominent changes, use large values.

6. Set the Mod Freq parameter. This parameter controls the speed of the volume changes. High values give you a tremolo effect. Low values give you more of a slow but smooth change in volume effect.

TIP

For a very subtle tremolo effect, choose the Sine Preset. Then, change the Amplitude parameter so that the range becomes 0 to –2.9 to –5.9. Finally, set the Mod Freq parameter to 10. These are the settings I use for my Subtle Tremolo preset.

7. Set the Low-Pass Start Freq parameter. This parameter works the same as the Low-Pass Start Freq parameter of the Multi-Tap Delay function. Basically, it allows you to filter out some of the high frequencies in your audio data.

8. Adjust the Dry Out and Wet Out parameters. I explained these earlier in the chapter.

9. Click the Preview button to hear how your file will sound before you have Sound Forge make any actual changes to the data.

10. Click OK.

Sound Forge applies the Amplitude Modulation function to your audio data according to your parameter settings.

TIP

If you're applying the Amplitude Modulation function to a stereo file, you can create some cool automated panning effects by adjusting the Stereo Pan parameter in the Amplitude Modulation dialog box. Set the parameter low for a subtle panning effect and set it high for really fast movement in the stereo field.

Distortion

Most of the time, bad sounding audio isn't something that you want. Distortion is something you usually try to avoid when recording audio data. But sometimes distortion can be a good thing. For example, if you want to dress up a guitar part for a rock song, adding a bit of distortion can make it sound really cool. Or maybe you want to add a bit of "grit" to a vocal part. Using distortion as an effect can come in handy here. This is where Sound Forge's Distortion function comes in, and here is how it works:

1. Select the data in your audio file that you want to process. If you want to process the entire file, don't select any data or select it all by choosing Edit > Select All (or pressing Ctrl + A on your computer keyboard).

2. Choose Effects > Distortion to open the Distortion dialog box (see Figure 9.10). The dialog box displays a graph. The left side of the graph shows output amplitude. The bottom of the graph shows input amplitude. Inside the graph is a line representing the input amplitude and output amplitude as they relate to each other. Initially, the line is drawn diagonally, and you "read" it from left to

right. This shows a 1:1 ratio between input and output amplitudes, meaning that as the input level goes up 1 dB, the output level also goes up 1 dB.

Figure 9.10
Use the Distortion function to add distortion effects to your audio data

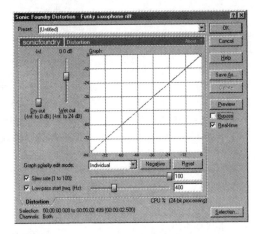

3. You can change the shape of the line graphically by clicking and dragging the small squares (Envelope Points) at the ends of the line. The real purpose of the Distortion function comes in when you add more Envelope Points by clicking anywhere on the line. When you add more points and change the shape of the line, the amplitude of your audio data is affected. If you adjust the Envelope Points toward the top of the graph, the amplitude is raised. If you adjust the Envelope Points toward the bottom of the graph, the amplitude is lowered. Lowering the amplitude doesn't really do much, but by raising the amplitude, you can cause distortion effects in your audio. For example, if you add an Envelope Point to the graph where the input and output levels intersect at –48 dB, and then raise the point so that the input stays at –48 dB but the output is raised to –24 dB, you will hear slight distortion in your audio. This is because as the input amplitude gets to –48 dB, the output amplitude is boosted by 24 dB.

4. The Distortion function goes even further by allowing you to adjust the amplitude of different parts of your audio data. An audio waveform has positive and negative parts. The positive parts are the parts of the waveform that are above the zero axis. The negative parts are the parts of the waveform below the zero axis. By setting the Graph Polarity Edit Mode and using the Positive/Negative button, you can create two lines in the graph that control how the Distortion function affects the different parts of your audio waveform. If you select the Individual mode, you can create two independent lines on the graph for the positive and negative audio data. Use the Positive/Negative button to switch between the line you want to edit. If you select the Synchronize mode, both the positive and negative data are controlled by one line. If you select the Mirror Y mode, the positive and negative lines are mirrored on the Y axis of the graph. If you select the Mirror X mode, the positive and negative lines are mirrored on the X axis of the graph. If you select the Mirror X/Y mode, the

positive and negative lines are mirrored on both the X and Y axes of the graph. Check out some of the presets to see how they use each mode.

5. If you want to control how much your audio data is allowed to change over time, activate the Slew Rate parameter. The lower the value, the less change. The higher the value, the more change. A low setting can sometimes be useful in stopping a signal from clipping while still keeping the distortion effect intact.

6. Set the Low-Pass Start Freq parameter to filter out some of the high frequencies of your audio data. This parameter can be useful if you have a really strong distortion effect going, but you get some unwanted buzzing in the higher frequencies of your audio. You can use this parameter to remove the buzzing.

7. Set the Dry Out and Wet Out parameters. These parameters work the same as all the other Dry Out and Wet Out parameters explained earlier in the chapter.

8. Click the Preview button to hear how your file will sound before you have Sound Forge make any actual changes to the data.

9. Click OK.

Sound Forge applies the Distortion function to your audio data according to your parameter settings.

Graphic Dynamics

The Graphic Dynamics function allows you to apply compression and limiting to your audio data. What exactly does that mean? Well, one way to explain it is to talk about taming vocal recordings. Let's say you recorded this vocalist who can really belt out a tune but doesn't have very good microphone technique. When he sings, he just stays in one place in front of the microphone. Professional singers know that during the quiet parts of the song, they need to sing up close to the microphone and during the loud parts, they need to back away so that an even amplitude level is recorded. If a singer doesn't do this, the amplitude of your recorded audio is very uneven. That's where compression and limiting comes in. Compression allows you to "squash" the audio signal so that the amplitude levels are more even. Limiting allows you to stop the amplitude of the audio signal from rising past a certain level to prevent clipping. This can happen if the performer sings too loudly. To use the Graphic Dynamics function, do the following:

1. Select the data in your audio file that you want to process. If you want to process the entire file, don't select any data or select it all by choosing Edit > Select All (or pressing Ctrl + A on your computer keyboard).

2. Choose Effects > Dynamics > Graphic to open the Graphic Dynamics dialog box (see Figure 9.11). The dialog displays a graph similar to the one found in the Distortion function. The left side of the graph shows output amplitude and the bottom of the graph shows input amplitude. Inside the graph is a line representing the input amplitude and output amplitude as they relate to each other. Initially, the line is drawn diagonally, and you "read" it from left to right. This shows a 1:1 ratio between input and output amplitudes, meaning as the input level goes up 1 dB, the output level also goes up 1 dB. Even though you can add Envelope Points to this graph, like with the Distortion function, you don't need to in order to create compression and limiting effects.

Figure 9.11

Use the Graphic
Dynamics function to
apply compression and
limiting to your audio
data

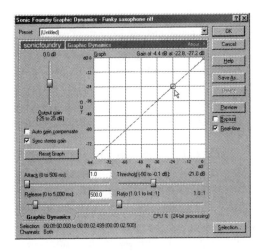

3. Set the Threshold parameter. The Graphic Dynamics function uses a digital
    noise gate to identify the parts of your audio data that should be processed. The
    Threshold parameter determines at what amplitude level your audio data will
    start being compressed or limited. When the amplitude of your audio data
    reaches the threshold level, processing begins.

4. Set the Ratio parameter. This parameter determines how much processing is
    done to your audio data. A ratio of 1:1 means no processing is done. A ratio of
    2:1 means that for every 2 dB increase in input amplitude, there is only a 1 dB
    increase in output amplitude. Thus, the amplitude is being compressed. If you
    set the Ratio parameter to its highest value (Inf:1), that causes limiting, so no
    matter how loud the input amplitude gets, it is limited to the level set by the
    Threshold parameter.

5. Set the Attack parameter. This parameter determines how quickly after the input
    level has reached the threshold that processing is applied. For example, if the
    input level reaches the threshold, it doesn't have to be compressed right away. A
    slow attack means the signal won't be compressed unless it lasts for a while.
    This is a good way to make sure fast, percussive parts are left alone, but long,
    drawn out parts are compressed. If you want to limit a signal though, a really
    fast attack (like 1 ms) is better.

6. Set the Release parameter. This parameter determines how quickly after the
    input level goes below the threshold that processing is stopped (or the digital
    noise gate is closed). If you set the Release parameter too low, your audio could
    get cut off. A longer release allows processing to sound more natural.

7. Set the Sync Stereo Gain option. If you are processing stereo audio, you more
    than likely want to have this option activated. It makes sure that both channels
    in the stereo audio are processed the same.

8. Set the Auto Gain Compensate option. In the singing example mentioned earlier,
    I talked about smoothing out the amplitude levels in a recorded vocal
    performance. When you compress the signal, its high amplitude levels are

reduced, but its low amplitude levels remain the same. To make the amplitude levels even, the low levels need to be raised. Activating the Auto Gain Compensate option raises the low amplitude levels in your audio so you get a smoother sound when you apply compression.

9. Set the Output Gain parameter. This parameter allows you to adjust the overall amplitude of your audio after it is processed.

10. Click the Preview button to hear how your file will sound before you have Sound Forge make any actual changes to the data.

11. Click OK.

Sound Forge applies the Graphic Dynamics function to your audio data according to your parameter settings.

Multi-Band Dynamics

Like the Graphic Dynamics function, the Multi-Band Dynamics function allows you to apply compression and limiting to your audio data. This function has one important difference, though; it allows you to process different frequency ranges in your audio independently. Why is that important? Well, one way to explain it is to talk about *de-essing*. You may have noticed while doing vocal recordings that some singers produce a sort of "hissing" sound whenever they pronounce words with the letter "s" in them. That "hissing" sound is called *sibilance*, and you usually don't want it in your audio. The process of removing sibilance is called de-essing, which is done by compressing certain frequencies in the audio spectrum. To use the Multi-Band Dynamics function, do the following:

1. Select the data in your audio file that you want to process. If you want to process the entire file, don't select any data or select it all by choosing Edit > Select All (or pressing Ctrl + A on your computer keyboard).

2. Choose Effects > Dynamics > Multi-Band to open the Multi-Band Dynamics dialog box (see Figure 9.12).

Figure 9.12
Use the Multi-Band Dynamics function to apply compression and limiting to specific frequency ranges in your audio data

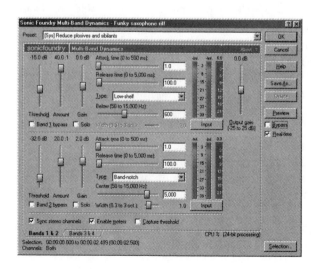

3. The Multi-Band Dynamics function actually provides four compression/limiting functions in one. You'll find four sets of controls called Bands. Each Band can be turned on or off by using the Band # Bypass option. The first two Bands are under the Bands 1 & 2 tab (located at the bottom of the dialog box). The second set of Bands are under the Bands 3 & 4 tab. All the Bands are identical. You can activate a Band by turning off its Band # Bypass option.

4. Set the Threshold parameter. This parameter works the same as the Threshold parameter of the Graphic Dynamics function.

TIP

The Multi-Band Dynamics function also provides an automatic threshold detection feature. When activated, the threshold level is detected automatically when you use the Preview button to listen to your audio before actually processing it. To turn this feature on, activate the Capture Threshold option at the bottom of the dialog box. The Capture Threshold feature can be useful for finding an initial setting for the Threshold parameter. You can then deactivate Capture Threshold to make additional adjustments to the Threshold parameter before processing.

5. Set the Amount parameter. This parameter works the same as the Ratio parameter of the Graphic Dynamics function.

6. Set the Gain parameter. This parameter controls the output amplitude of the current Band that you are working with. You can use the Gain parameters to determine how much processing from each Band is present in the final output of the Multi-Band Dynamics function.

7. Set the Attack Time parameter. This parameter works the same as the Attack parameter of the Graphic Dynamics function.

8. Set the Release Time parameter. This parameter works the same as the Release parameter of the Graphic Dynamics function.

9. Choose an option for the Type parameter. This parameter determines the type of EQ that you want to use to process your audio. I talked about these EQ types in the Parametric EQ section of Chapter 8. Low-Shelf lets you filter out low frequencies. High-shelf lets you filter out high frequencies. Band-Notch lets you filter out a specific frequency. For example, if you want to remove sibilance from your audio, you would probably use the Band-Notch option.

10. Set the Center/Above/Below parameter. This parameter determines the frequency above which, below which, or at which your audio content will be compressed. I also talked about this in the Parametric EQ section of Chapter 8. In regard to the sibilance example, a good setting for this parameter is about 5,000 Hz.

11. If you choose the Band-Notch option, you also need to set the Width parameter. This parameter determines how many of the frequencies around the Center

frequency will be affected. A low value makes it so that the focus is mainly on the one frequency that you specified for the Center parameter. A high value makes it so that a range of frequencies centered around the Center frequency are processed. In regard to the sibilance example, it's good to go with a lower value such as 1.0.

12. Go back through Steps 3 to 11 for each of the Bands that you want to use.

13. Set the Sync Stereo Channels option. If you are processing stereo audio, you more than likely want to have this option activated. It makes sure that both channels in the stereo audio are processed the same.

14. Set the Output Gain parameter. This parameter allows you to adjust the overall amplitude from all the Bands in the Multi-Band Dynamics function.

15. Click the Preview button to hear how your file will sound before you have Sound Forge make any actual changes to the data.

TIP

As you preview your audio, you can use the level meters in each Band to keep track of the input, output, and compression levels. Just make sure the Enable Meters option (located at the bottom of the dialog box) is activated. You can switch from monitoring the input or output levels by clicking on the Input/Output button (located just below each set of meters). In addition, if you want to hear your audio processed by only one Band to make sure you have the right parameter settings, just activate the Solo option for that Band. Deactivating the Solo option turns processing back on for all other available Bands.

16.   Click OK.

Sound Forge applies the Multi-Band Dynamics function to your audio data according to your parameter settings.

Envelope

Believe it or not, the Envelope function works virtually the same as the Graphic Fade function, which I talk about in Chapter 8. The Sound Forge documentation says the Envelope function is different, stating that "unlike the Graphic Fade command, which simply fades a waveform by a specific amount over time, with the Envelope feature the gain at each point is dynamically calculated to achieve the exact specified envelope." For example, if you take a sine wave (the most basic type of audio waveform—see the Sound Synthesis section in Chapter 10 for more information) that has an amplitude of –12 dB and you apply the Envelope function to it with the graph (explained shortly) set to raise the amplitude to –6 dB, the result is the sine wave with an amplitude of –6 dB. If you do the same this with the Graphic Fade function, the sine wave has an amplitude of –18 dB because 6 plus 12 is 18. The Envelope function sets amplitude in an absolute manner and the Graphic Fade function sets amplitude in a relative manner.

1. Select the data in your audio file that you want to process. If you want to process the entire file, don't select any data or select it all by choosing Edit > Select All (or pressing Ctrl + A on your computer keyboard).

2. Choose Effects > Envelope to open the Envelope dialog box (see Figure 9.13). The dialog box displays a graph. The left side of the graph shows amplitude values, which range from 0 to 100 percent. Inside the graph is a line, which represents the amplitude envelope that will be applied to your selected audio data. If you look at the line from left to right, the left end of the line represents the beginning of your audio data selection, and the right end of the line represents the end of your audio data selection. If the line was set so that the left end was at the bottom of the graph and the right end was at the top, a straight linear rise in amplitude would be applied to your audio data because as you look at the graph, the left end of the line is set at 0 percent, and the right end of the line is set at 100 percent. So, the volume of the audio data would begin at 0 percent and rise to 100 percent. See how it works?

Figure 9.13
The Envelope function is almost exactly the same as the Graphic Fade function

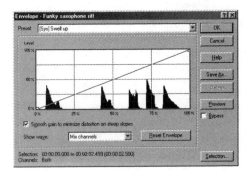

TIP

If you apply an envelope to a stereo file, you can choose to have your audio data displayed in the background of the graph by activating the Show Wave option. You can also choose to show just the data from the left or right channels, or both channels mixed by choosing an option from the Show Wave drop-down list. This does not affect how the envelope is applied to your data. If you only want to apply an envelope to one of the stereo channels, you need to select only the data from that channel before you open the Envelope dialog box.

3. You can change the shape of the envelope in one of two ways: You can simply choose one of the available presets from the Preset drop-down list, or you can change the envelope graphically by clicking and dragging the small squares (Envelope Points) at the ends of the line.

4. If you want to create some really complex envelopes, you can add more Envelope Points by clicking anywhere on the line. The more Envelope Points you add (the allowed maximum being 16), the more flexibility you have in changing the shape of the line.

5. Set the Smooth Gain To Minimize Distortion On Steep Slopes option. This option makes it so that amplitude changes aren't applied too quickly, which can sometimes result in distortion. You usually want to keep this option activated.

6. Click the Preview button to hear how your file will sound before you have Sound Forge make any actual changes to the data.

7. Click OK.

Sound Forge changes the volume of your audio data selection according to the envelope that you defined in the Envelope dialog box.

Gapper/Snipper

The Gapper/Snipper function is a bit odd, not because of the effects it can produce, but because of the way it produces them. By adding or cutting pieces of data to or from your audio, the Gapper/Snipper function allows you to produce tremolo, warble, and stuttering effects. The pieces of data applied to or removed from your audio are so small that they don't ruin it, but rather produce some interesting sounds. The problem with the Gapper/Snipper function is that by adding or cutting data from your audio, it also makes your audio longer or shorter, which in some cases may not be desirable. Then again, after you apply the Gapper/Snipper function, you could always use the Time Compress/Expand function to fix the length of your audio. In any case, here is how the Gapper/Snipper function works:

1. Select the data in your audio file that you want to process. If you want to process the entire file, don't select any data or select it all by choosing Edit > Select All (or pressing Ctrl + A on your computer keyboard).

2. Choose Effects > Gapper/Snipper to open the Gapper/Snipper dialog box (see Figure 9.14).

Figure 9.14
Use the Gapper/Snipper function to apply tremolo, warble, and stuttering effects to your audio

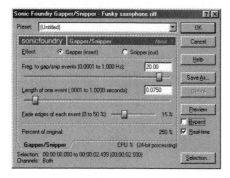

3. Choose an option for the Effect parameter. If you choose the Gapper option, small sections of silence are added to your audio and also make your file longer.

If you choose the Snipper option, small sections of data are cut from your audio and also make your file shorter.

4. Set the Freq To Gap/Snip Events parameter. This parameter determines how many gaps or snips are applied to your audio. The lower the setting, the fewer gaps or snips. The higher the value, the more gaps or snips. High values can give you "buzzing" effects when using the Snipper mode, and stuttering effects when using the Gapper mode.

5. Set the Length Of One Event parameter. This parameter determines the length of each gap or snip (in seconds) that is applied to your audio. The lower the setting, the smaller the gap or snip. The higher the setting, the larger the gap or snip. Use low values for subtle effects and high values to really alter the original form of your audio data.

6. If you find that the gapping or snipping done to your audio causes glitches in your audio, adjust the Fade Edges Of Each Event parameter to smooth out the edges of each gap or snip. This should allow you to get rid of any glitches that may occur.

7. Click the Preview button to hear how your file will sound before you have Sound Forge make any actual changes to the data.

8. Click OK.

Sound Forge applies the Gapper/Snipper function to your audio data according to your parameter settings.

Noise Gate

I've talked about digital noise gates before as they pertain to other functions, such as compression and limiting. You can also use digital noise gates independently to remove parts of your audio data. For example, if you want the quiet sections (such as the space between sentences or phrases) in a vocal dialogue recording to be perfectly silent, you can use a noise gate for that purpose. The Noise Gate function provides this type of effect, and here is how it works:

1. Select the data in your audio file that you want to process. If you want to process the entire file, don't select any data or select it all by choosing Edit > Select All (or pressing Ctrl + A on your computer keyboard).

2. Choose Effects > Noise Gate to open the Noise Gate dialog box (see Figure 9.15).

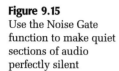

Figure 9.15
Use the Noise Gate
function to make quiet
sections of audio
perfectly silent

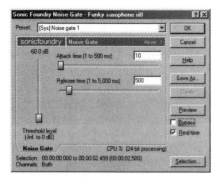

3. Set the Threshold Level parameter. The Threshold Level parameter determines at what amplitude audio is allowed to pass through the noise gate unaffected. Anything below the Threshold Level is not allowed to pass through and is thus turned into silence.

4. Set the Attack Time parameter. This parameter determines how quickly after the input level has reached the threshold level that the noise gate opens and allows audio through. A low setting keeps any quick, percussive sounds intact. A high setting makes the noise gate open more slowly, thus letting less audio data through.

5. Set the Release Time parameter. This parameter determines how quickly after the input level goes below the threshold level that the noise gate is closed. A low setting makes the noise gate close quickly. Again, this is good for percussive sounds. A high setting makes the noise gate close slowly. This is good for sounds that have a long decay, like a long piano note or anything with a lot of reverberation.

6. Click the Preview button to hear how your file will sound before you have Sound Forge make any actual changes to the data.

7. Click OK.

Sound Forge applies the Noise Gate function to your audio data according to your parameter settings.

Reverberation

Like some of the functions mentioned earlier, reverb (short for reverberation) is also a form of delay, but it's special because, instead of distinct echoes, reverb adds a complex series of very small echoes that simulate artificial ambiance. In other words, reverb produces a dense collection of echoes that are so close together that they create a wash of sound, making the original audio data sound like it's being played in another environment, such as a large concert hall. Using Sound Forge's reverb effects, you can make your music sound like it's being played in all kinds of different places, such as in an arena, a club, or even live on stage. Sound Forge includes two reverb effects: Reverb and Acoustic Mirror.

Reverb

For basic reverb effects, Sound Forge provides the Reverb function. To apply the Reverb function to your audio data, follow these steps:

1. Select the data in your audio file that you want to process. If you want to process the entire file, don't select any data or select it all by choosing Edit > Select All (or pressing Ctrl + A on your computer keyboard).

2. Choose Effects > Reverb to open the Reverb dialog box (see Figure 9.16).

Figure 9.16
Use the Reverb function to apply basic reverberation effects to your audio data

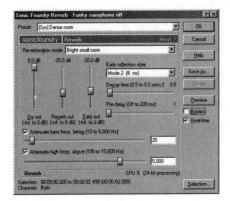

3. Choose an option for the Reverberation Mode parameter. This parameter determines the type of environment you are trying to simulate. The available options are self-explanatory. For example, to simulate a small environment, choose the Bright Small Room option. To simulate a large environment, choose the Cavernous Space option.

4. Set the Dry Out and Reverb Out parameters. I explained these parameters earlier in the chapter. They are similar to the Dry Out and Wet Out parameters used in other functions. One point you should note, however, is that in the case of reverb, the Dry Out and Reverb Out parameters also make a difference on how the effect sounds. If you set the Dry Out high and the Reverb Out low, your audio data sounds like it's positioned closer to the "front" of the imaginary environment. If you set the Dry Out low and Reverb Out high, your audio data sounds like it's positioned farther away. For example, if you want to simulate what it sounds like to be seated in the very back row of a music concert, you can set the Dry Out low and the Reverb Out high.

5. Choose an option for the Early Reflection Style parameter. When you make a sound in any enclosed environment, some very quick echoes always occur because of the reflective surfaces (such as walls) that you are standing next to. These echoes are known as *early reflections*. To make your reverb simulations sound more authentic, Sound Forge provides this parameter so that you can control the early reflection content in your reverb effect. The option you select depends on the environment you're trying to simulate. For small environments,

choose a mode with a faster time (measured in milliseconds), such as Mode 2 (8 milliseconds). For larger environments, choose a mode with a slower time, such as Mode 6 (36 milliseconds).

6. Set the Early Out parameter. This parameter determines how loud the early reflections will be in the reverb effect. The smaller the environment, the fewer early reflections are heard, and vice versa.

7. Set the Decay Time parameter. When you're applying reverb to your data, you should imagine what type of environment you want to create. Doing so helps you set the parameters. Technically, the Decay Time determines how long it takes for the reverberation to fade away, but you can think of it as controlling how big the artificial environment will be. The lower the Decay Time, the smaller the environment, and vice versa. So, if you want to make your audio sound like it's playing in a small room, a good Decay Time might be about 0.5 seconds. If you want to make your audio sound like it's playing in a large area, a good Decay Time might be about 3 seconds.

8. Set the Pre-Delay parameter. This parameter is similar to the Decay Time parameter, except that the Pre-Delay determines the time between when your audio is first heard and when the reverb effect begins. This gives you even more control in determining your artificial environment. For small spaces, use a low setting (such as 1 millisecond). For large spaces, use a high setting (such as 70 milliseconds).

9. Set the Attenuate Bass Freqs Below and the Attenuate High Freqs Above parameters. If you think these parameters look like equalization settings, you're right. Using these parameters also helps to create more authentic environment simulations because smaller, closed environments tend to stifle some frequencies of the audio spectrum, and larger environments usually sound brighter, meaning they promote more of the frequencies.

   The Attenuate Bass and Attenuate High parameters work just like the High-Pass and Low-Pass equalization functions that I've described before. If you activate the Attenuate Bass parameter and set its frequency (in Hz), any frequencies above that are allowed to pass and are included in the effect, and any frequencies below that are cut. If you activate the Attenuate High parameter, and set its frequency, any frequencies below that are allowed to pass, and any frequencies above that are cut. For examples on how to set these parameters, be sure to take a look at some of the included presets.

10. Click the Preview button to hear how your file will sound before you have Sound Forge make any actual changes to the data.

11. Click OK.

Sound Forge applies the Reverb function to your audio data according to your parameter settings.

CHAPTER 9

Acoustic Mirror

The Acoustic Mirror function also lets you simulate environments, but it is much more sophisticated than the Reverb function. The Acoustic Mirror simulations are based on actual real-life environments. Here is how it works:

1.   Select the data in your audio file that you want to process. If you want to process the entire file, don't select any data or select it all by choosing Edit > Select All (or pressing Ctrl + A on your computer keyboard).

2.   Choose Effects > Acoustic Mirror to open the Acoustic Mirror dialog box (see Figure 9.17).

Figure 9.17
Use the Acoustic Mirror function to apply complex environment simulation effects to your audio data

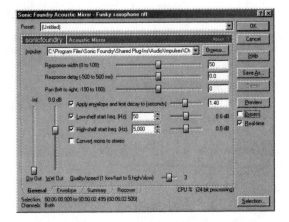

3.   Choose an option for the Impulse parameter. The Acoustic Mirror function bases its environment simulations on real-life environments by using what Sonic Foundry calls *Impulse* files. An Impulse file is similar to an actual recording of an acoustic space or acoustic signature. It models the characteristics of a real environment, such as a concert hall or even a kitchen in someone's home. Sound Forge ships with a large collection of Impulse files that you can use to make it seem as if your audio is playing in a variety of real environments. If you don't see any files listed in the Impulse parameter drop-down list, click the Browse button to display the Open Impulse File dialog box and choose a file that way. Impulse files have an .SFI extension.

TIP

In addition to environments, Impulse files can be used to model the characteristics of different audio equipment. This includes microphones. What this means is that you can make it sound as if your audio was recorded with a certain type of microphone using Acoustic Mirror, even if you don't own that particular microphone. Sound Forge ships with a number of microphone-based Impulse files that you can use. The effect is pretty cool.

In addition, the Acoustic Mirror function lets you use any ordinary WAV file that is less that twelve seconds long as the basis for its processing. You can get some really weird effects using the function in this manner. Just choose a WAV file instead of an Impulse file when you are choosing an option for the Impulse parameter. Sound effects work really good here. For example, try using a quick car horn sound and processing your audio data with it. Your audio data takes on the characteristics of the car horn. Weird, huh? You can also use Sound Forge's synthesis functions to create WAV files for use with Acoustic Mirror. I talk about the synthesis functions in Chapter 10.

4. Set the Dry Out and Wet Out parameters. These parameters work the same as the Dry Out and Reverb Out parameters of the Reverb function.

5. Set the Response Width parameter. This parameter allows you to control the width of the stereo field. This is similar to the Pan/Expand function, which I talk about in Chapter 8. When set at 50, you get a normal stereo image. The closer you set the Response Width to 0, the narrower the stereo field. This means that the audio sounds more like it's being compressed between your stereo speakers. If you set the Response Width to 0, you are basically converting the stereo signal to mono. The closer you set the Response Width to 100, the wider the stereo field. This means that the audio sounds like it's being expanded beyond your stereo speakers.

6. Set the Response Delay parameter. This parameter is similar to the Pre-Delay parameter of the Reverb function. A positive setting (in milliseconds) makes the processed audio sound later than the original audio. You can use this to simulate a larger space. For some strange effects, you can use a negative setting, which makes the processed audio actually sound before the original audio. This is something like hearing reverberation before hearing the sound that actually caused the reverberation.

7. Set the Pan parameter. This parameter works like any other panning parameter that I've mentioned before. It lets you pan the processed audio to any position in the stereo field.

8. Previously, I explained how the Reverb function provides a Decay Time parameter, which controls how long it takes for the reverberation to fade away (or lets you control how big your artificial environment will be). The Apply Envelope And Limit Decay To parameter of the Acoustic Mirror function is similar to Decay Time. The Apply Envelope parameter lets you control the length of your selected impulse file, which in turn controls the length of the environmental processing. This means you can use it to control the size of the

CHAPTER 9

room you are simulating. For example, if you choose an Impulse file that simulates the kitchen area inside a home, using the Apply Envelope parameter, you can control the size of the kitchen. Just activate the parameter and input a number of seconds (which is limited to the length of the Impulse file you are using). Enter a small value to simulate a small space. Enter a large value to simulate a large space.

The Apply Envelope parameter provides even more control, though, if you need it. Click the Envelope tab at the bottom of the Acoustic Mirror dialog box. You will see a graph that represents the amplitude (left side) of the Impulse file over time (bottom). This graph works just like the one for the Envelope function that I talked about earlier. The only difference is that this graph controls the amplitude of the Impulse file being applied to your audio, rather than the amplitude of your entire audio data selection.

9.   Back under the General tab, set the Low-Shelf Start Freq and the High-Shelf Start Freq parameters. These parameters work just like the Attenuate Bass Freqs Below and the Attenuate High Freqs Above parameters of the Reverb function, respectively.

10. If you are working with mono audio data rather than stereo, you can still simulate a stereo environment with the Acoustic Mirror. Just activate the Convert Mono To Stereo option and your audio is converted to stereo when you apply the Acoustic Mirror to it.

11. Set the Quality/Speed option to specify the quality of the Acoustic Mirror processing you want to use. The higher the quality, the slower the processing. But unless you have a really large audio file, you can usually keep this set to the best option, which is 5 (or High/Slow).

12. Click the Preview button to hear how your file will sound before you have Sound Forge make any actual changes to the data.

13. Click OK.

Sound Forge applies the Acoustic Mirror function to your audio data according to your parameter settings.

NOTE

While working with the Acoustic Mirror, you may have noticed two additional tabs at the bottom of the dialog box: Summary and Recover. The Summary tab provides you with information about the Impulse file you are using, such as its attributes, author, copyright, and any comments the author may have included about the file. Sometimes, you can even see a picture of the environment that was used to create the Impulse file, if the author has included one.

The Recover tab is used for creating your own Impulse files. Unfortunately, this is a very advanced topic that is beyond the scope of this book. If you feel adventurous, you might want to check out the Sound Forge Help files for more information about creating Impulse files. A word of warning, though: The procedure is pretty lengthy and not very easy to follow.

Wave Hammer

The Wave Hammer function is a combination of effects. It contains a Compressor and Volume Maximizer rolled into one. The Wave Hammer's main use is as a mastering tool. After you have edited and processed your audio data, you usually put it through a final mastering process before it gets put onto CD. The Wave Hammer allows you to apply processing to prepare your files for their final destination, and it works as follows:

1. Select the data in your audio file that you want to process. If you want to process the entire file, don't select any data or select it all by choosing Edit > Select All (or pressing Ctrl + A on your computer keyboard).

2. Choose Effects > Wave Hammer to open the Wave Hammer dialog box (see Figure 9.18).

Figure 9.18
Use the Wave Hammer for mastering your audio files

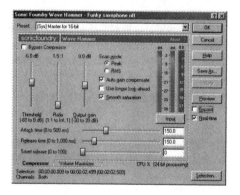

3. If you want to apply compression to your audio, deactivate the Bypass Compressor option under the Compressor tab.

4. Set the Threshold parameter. The Threshold parameter determines at what amplitude level your audio data will start being compressed or limited. When the amplitude of your audio data reaches the threshold level, processing begins.

5. Set the Ratio parameter. This parameter determines how much processing is done to your audio data. A ratio of 1:1 means no processing is done. A ratio of 2:1 means that for every 2 dB increase in input amplitude, there is only a 1 dB increase in output amplitude. Thus, the amplitude is being compressed. If you set the Ratio parameter to its highest value (Inf:1), it causes limiting, so no matter how loud the input amplitude gets, it is limited to the level set by the Threshold parameter.

6. Set the Attack Time parameter. This parameter determines how quickly after the input level has reached the threshold that processing is applied. For example, if the input level reaches the threshold, it doesn't have to be compressed right away. A slow attack means the signal won't be compressed unless it lasts for a while. This is a good way to make sure fast, percussive parts are left alone, but long, drawn-out parts are compressed. If you want to limit a signal though, a really fast attack (like 1 ms) is better.

CHAPTER 9

7. Set the Release Time parameter. This parameter determines how quickly after the input level goes below the threshold that processing is stopped. If you set the Release parameter too low, your audio could get cut off. A longer release allows processing to sound more natural.

8. You can also have Sound Forge vary the Release Time dynamically by setting the Smart Release parameter. If you set the Smart Release parameter to anything higher than zero, the Wave Hammer analyzes your audio material during processing and automatically varies the Release Time to match the dynamics of your material. The higher the Smart Release setting, the more your initial Release Time setting is varied. This parameter can be helpful if you have material that has a lot of both short and long sustaining parts.

9. Set the Scan Mode parameter. As the Wave Hammer processes your audio, it scans the data to determine its initial loudness so that it can figure out when to start compressing the data. You have two choices on how it scans the data: Peak and RMS. If you choose Peak, the Wave Hammer looks for the highest amplitude in the audio data. If you choose RMS, an average of the loudness over time is used. The option you choose depends on the audio material you are compressing. Check out the presets using the Preset drop-down list for examples of how the Scan Mode parameter should be set.

10. Set the Auto Gain Compensate option. When you compress the audio signal, its high amplitude levels are reduced, but its low amplitude levels remain the same. To make the amplitude levels even, the low levels need to be raised. Activating the Auto Gain Compensate option raises the low amplitude levels in your audio so you get a smoother sound when you apply compression.

11. Set the Use Longer Look-Ahead option. This option tells the Wave Hammer to scan further into the audio file during processing to determine how much the data should be compressed. There's not really any advantage to using this option, and sometimes it can even cause the compression to sound unnatural. So I recommend that you leave this option deactivated.

12. Set the Smooth Saturation option. If you apply really heavy compression to your audio, it can sometimes result in distortion. To reduce or even remove the distortion that may occur, activate the Smooth Saturation option. When you're only using light compression, leave the Smooth Saturation option deactivated.

13. Click the Volume Maximizer tab at the bottom of the Wave Hammer dialog box to access the Volume Maximizer parameters (see Figure 9.19). The Volume Maximizer allows you to raise the volume of your audio data to make it sound as loud as possible without clipping or distortion.

Figure 9.19
Click the Volume
Maximizer tab to access
the Volume Maximizer
parameters

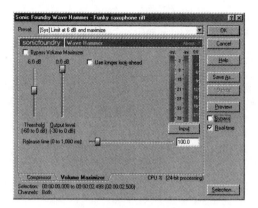

14. If you want to apply the Volume Maximizer to your audio, deactivate the Bypass Volume Maximizer option.

15. Set the Threshold parameter. This parameter works a bit differently here than it does under the Compressor tab. In the Volume Maximizer, the Threshold parameter works in conjunction with the Output Level parameter. Any audio amplitude levels that go above the threshold level are boosted or cut depending on how the Output Level parameter is set.

16. Set the Output Level parameter. To maximize the volume of your audio data, you usually want to set this parameter higher than the Threshold parameter. For an example, check out the preset called Limit At 6 dB And Maximize. With the Threshold set to – 6dB and the Output Level set to 0 dB, it means that the audio data is boosted by 6 dB so that any amplitude levels that go above the threshold level will reach 0 dB.

17. Set the Release Time parameter. This parameter works the same as it does under the Compressor tab.

18. Set the Use Longer Look-Ahead option. This option works the same as it does under the Compressor tab.

19. Click the Preview button to hear how your file will sound before you have Sound Forge make any actual changes to the data.

20. Click OK.

Sound Forge applies the Wave Hammer function to your audio data according to your parameter settings.

TIP

The Wave Hammer's main use is for mastering audio data. Mastering is the procedure during which the final mixed down stereo audio for a song is processed with various effects (such as EQ, compression, and limiting) to give the song that final professional touch before it is burned to CD. There have been entire books written on the topic of mastering, but you can also find some good information on the Internet at these sites:

- http://www.izotope.com/products/ozone/ozoneguide.html

- http://www.prorec.com/prorec/articles.nsf/files/F717F79532C9067386256688001A7623

- http://www.digido.com/cdmastering.html

Also, be sure to sign up for my free DigiFreq music technology newsletter so you don't miss the mastering information I will be providing in future issues. To sign up, go to: **http://www.digifreq.com/digifreq/**.

Plug-Ins and DirectX

In addition to all of the effects I've described so far, Sound Forge gives you access to third-party effects in the form of DirectX plug-ins.

NOTE

In basic terms, a *plug-in* is a small computer program that by itself does nothing, but when used together with a larger application provides added functionality to the larger program. You, therefore, can use plug-ins to easily add new features to a program. In Sound Forge's case, plug-ins provide you with additional ways to process your audio data. As a matter of fact, Sonic Foundry offers additional plug-in products for sale (XFX 1, XFX 2, XFX 3, and Noise Reduction), although all except Noise Reduction are already included with Sound Forge 6.

What's more, Sonic Foundry isn't the only vendor that sells plug-ins for Sound Forge. You can use plug-ins from a number of different third-party vendors because many plug-ins are programmed using standard computer code. Sound Forge enables you to use any audio plug-ins that are DirectX-compatible. DirectX is a special computer code built into Windows that controls all its multimedia functions, such as playing audio and video. So, if you are looking for new plug-ins to add to Sound Forge, just make sure they are DirectX-compatible (it will say so on the package), and you can be sure they will work.

TIP

For a great source of DirectX plug-ins that you can download and use for free, check out **http://www.directxfiles.com/**.

The DX Favorites Menu

All DirectX plug-ins are accessed via the DX Favorites menu in Sound Forge. Just select some audio data, and choose DX Favorites > Name Of Plug-in to access the DirectX plug-ins that you have installed on your computer system. To find out how to use any specific plug-in, you have to read the documentation that came with the plug-in.

When you first install Sound Forge, however, the DX Favorites menu is empty. This is because the menu can be customized to your own liking. In other words, you can organize your DirectX plug-ins within the menu. You can add all or only some of your plug-ins to the menu and even group them into submenus for better organization. You can customize the DX Favorites menu as follows:

1. Choose DX Favorites > Organize to open the Organize Favorites dialog box (see Figure 9.20). This box is divided into two panes. The left pane shows a directory of folders and the right pane shows the contents of a selected folder.

Figure 9.20
Use the Organize Favorites dialog box to customize the DX Favorites menu

2. Click the DirectX folder to select it and display a list of all the DirectX plug-ins that are installed on your computer system (see Figure 9.21).

Figure 9.21
The DirectX folder holds a list of all the DirectX plug-ins installed on your computer

3. The DX Favorites folder represents the DX Favorites menu. Any plug-ins that you add to the folder show up in the menu. To add a plug-in to the folder, drag and drop the plug-in onto the folder.

4. To delete a plug-in from the DX Favorites folder/menu, click the folder to select it and display a list of the plug-ins it contains. Then, right-click the plug-in you want to remove and choose Delete from the shortcut menu (see Figure 9.22).

Figure 9.22
Right-click on a plug-in and choose Delete to remove it from the DX Favorites folder

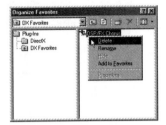

5. You can also change the name of any plug-in. This means that you are no longer limited to how your plug-ins are listed in the menu. You can give them any name you want. Just right-click the plug-in and choose Rename from the shortcut menu. Then, type in a new name.

6. You can also organize your plug-ins into subfolders/submenus. This is great when you have a bunch of plug-ins that are all from the same manufacturer and you want to group them together. It can also be used to set up special submenus of plug-ins that are used for specific tasks. Right-click the DX Favorites menu and choose New Folder to add a subfolder/menu. Then, type in a name for the folder/menu. Plug-ins can be added to subfolders the same way they are added to the DX Favorites menu.

7. When you are finished, close the Organize Favorites dialog box.

Now when you access the DX Favorites menu, you see all the plug-ins and submenus you added (see Figure 9.23) and your plug-ins are also accessible from the menu.

Figure 9.23
The DX Favorites menu displays all the changes you made via the Organize Favorites dialog box

TIP

You can also have Sound Forge customize the DX Favorites menu for you automatically. Choose DX Favorites > Recreate By Plug-In Name. This feature scans for all the plug-ins that are installed on your computer and organizes them according to their names. Plug-ins from the same manufacturer are grouped into their own submenus automatically as well. Be aware though that this procedure erases any of the changes you may have made via the Organize Favorites dialog box.

Plug-In Manager

Another way to organize the DX Favorites menu is to use the Plug-In Manager (see Figure 9.24).

Figure 9.24
You can also use the Plug-In Manager to organize the DX Favorites menu

You're probably saying to yourself, "Hey, this looks just like the Organize Favorites dialog box." Yes, you're right except for one thing—the Plug-In Manager is displayed in a window instead of a dialog box. This means that you can keep it open and still have access to the rest of the Sound Forge application. You can't do that with the Organize Favorites dialog box. Why would you want to? Well, in addition to organizing the DX Favorites menu, the Plug-In Manager allows you to organize the plug-ins themselves as well as any plug-in chains you may have created. (I discuss plug-in chains in a moment.)

If you open the DirectX menu in the left pane of the Plug-In Manager, you see a list of all the plug-ins installed on your computer. If you right-click a plug-in, you can change its name by choosing Rename from the shortcut menu. You can also display its properties, and you can also hide the plug-in.

Hide a Plug-In

Hiding a plug-in allows you to remove it from Sound Forge's plug-in registry and keep the plug-in installed on your computer for use within other applications. This means that although Sound Forge no longer "sees" the plug-in, it is still available in other applications. Why do this? Well, there are times when a program can accidentally be designated as a plug-in under Windows, which means it is listed in your DirectX folder but isn't accessible as a plug-in. Other times, some DirectX plug-ins that run under one host application won't run under another. Some manufacturers "lock" the DirectX plug-ins that ship with their host applications so they can't be used with other host applications. Hiding these from Sound Forge can remove some of the clutter from your DirectX folder and ensure that you don't accidentally try to use a plug-in that won't work within Sound Forge.

To hide a plug-in, simply right-click the plug-in and choose Hide from the shortcut menu. Sound Forge asks you if you want to permanently hide the plug-in.

CAUTION

You can make a plug-in visible again, but not easily. So be careful when hiding plug-ins and be certain you really want to do it.

If you choose Yes, Sound Forge hides the plug-in and it is no longer visible in the DirectX folder. Unfortunately, there is no way to make an individual plug-in visible again. You can, however, make all hidden plug-ins visible, but you need to do a little tweaking in the Windows Registry, as follows:

1. In Windows, choose Start > Run to open the Run dialog box.

2. Type REGEDIT and click OK to open the Registry Editor.

3. In the left pane of the Editor, double-click the folder named HKEY_LOCAL_MACHINE.

4. Under the HKEY_LOCAL_MACHINE folder, double-click the folder named Software.

5. Under the Software folder, double-click the folder named Sonic Foundry.

6. Under the Sonic Foundry folder, double-click the folder named Sound Forge.

7. Under the Sound Forge menu, double-click the folder named 6.0.

8. Under the 6.0 folder, right-click the folder named DXCache and choose Delete from the shortcut menu (see Figure 9.25).

Figure 9.25
Delete the DXCache folder in the Windows Registry to unhide any hidden plug-ins

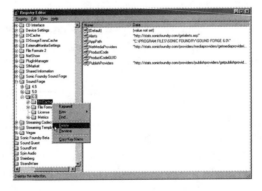

9. Click Yes in the Confirm Key Delete dialog box.

10. Choose Registry > Exit to automatically save your changes and close the Registry Editor.

Now, the next time you open Sound Forge, it scans your system for all installed DirectX plug-ins and any plug-ins that were previously hidden are visible again.

Apply a Plug-In

In addition to organizing plug-ins, the Plug-In Manager allows you to apply them to your audio files with a simple drag and drop of the mouse. If you want to apply a plug-in or plug-in chain (located in the DirectX Chains folder) to an audio file, just drag and drop it from the Plug-In Manager into the audio file's Data Window (see Figure 9.26).

Figure 9.26
Use the Plug-In Manager to apply plug-ins to your audio data

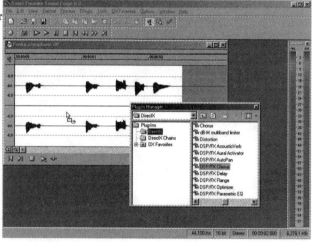

Dragging and dropping a plug-in onto a Data Window won't apply the plug-in in the normal way (as described earlier in the chapter). Instead, this opens the Audio Plug-In Chainer.

Audio Plug-In Chainer

Sound Forge includes a very powerful feature called the Audio Plug-In Chainer, which allows you to create what I like to call *Master Presets*, but Sonic Foundry calls them *Plug-In Chains*. As I mentioned in Chapter 8, Sound Forge enables you to save the settings for most of its functions as presets. This way, you can easily use the same editing parameters that you created by simply calling them up by name, instead of having to figure out the settings every time you use a function. Presets are a real time-saver, but, unfortunately, you can save presets for each of the individual functions only. What if you want to combine a few of the functions to create a certain editing process? For example, what if you want to add a bit of EQ before you process your audio with reverberation? To do so, you need to select your audio data, use one of the EQ functions, and then use the Reverb function to process your data. For each function, you have to make the appropriate parameter adjustments. If you chain the functions together, all you need to do is select your data and apply the plug-in chain. This is where the Audio Plug-In Chainer comes in. The Audio Plug-In Chainer allows you to daisy-chain some of Sound Forge's functions together (as well as any DirectX plug-ins you have installed) so that you can process your audio data with multiple functions (complete with specific parameter settings) in one fell swoop. In addition, the Audio Plug-In Chainer allows you to apply plug-in chains to your data in real-time instead of offline.

Offline Processing

You already know what offline processing is because you performed it while using Sound Forge's effects functions earlier in this chapter. With offline processing, the audio data in your files is permanently changed. Therefore, offline processing is also called *destructive processing* because it "destroys" the original data by modifying (or overwriting) it according to any processing that you apply.

NOTE
As you know, you can remove any offline processing done to your data by using Sound Forge's Undo and Undo History features. You can also load a saved copy of your audio file containing the original data. But neither of these restoration methods is as convenient as using real-time processing.

Real-Time Processing

On the other hand, real-time processing doesn't change the actual data in your audio files. Instead, the effects plug-ins are applied only during playback, letting you hear the results while leaving your original data intact. Therefore, real-time processing is also called *nondestructive*, because it doesn't apply any permanent changes to your data. By simply bypassing (or turning off) the effects plug-ins, you can listen to your data as it was originally recorded.

Create a Plug-In Chain

Using the Audio Plug-In Chainer, you can create plug-in chains and save them as chain presets for later use. To create a plug-in chain, do the following:

1.   You don't need to have an audio file open when creating a plug-in chain, but it's actually better if you do because you can test your settings as you go along. So go ahead and open a file in Sound Forge by choosing File > Open (or pressing Ctrl + O on your computer keyboard).

2.   Choose View > Audio Plug-In Chainer (or press Alt + 9 on your computer keyboard) to open the Audio Plug-In Chainer (see Figure 9.27).

Figure 9.27
Use the Audio Plug-In
Chainer to create a
chain preset

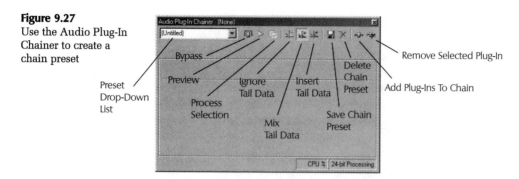

3. Click the Add Plug-Ins To Chain button to open the Plug-In Chooser dialog box (see Figure 9.28).

Figure 9.28
Use the Plug-In Chooser
dialog box to add plug-
ins to a plug-in chain

4. Click the DirectX folder to display a list of all the DirectX plug-ins installed on your system.

5. Select a plug-in from the list and click the Add button to add it to the plug-in chain (see Figure 9.29). You'll notice that the plug-in is shown along the top of the dialog box.

Figure 9.29
Select a plug-in and
click Add to insert the
plug-in into the chain

6. Continue adding plug-ins until you have all the plug-ins you need for the chain. Then click OK. The Audio Plug-In Chainer now displays all the plug-ins you added along the top of the dialog box and the parameters of the currently selected plug-in in the bottom portion of the box (see Figure 9.30).

CHAPTER 9

Figure 9.30
The Audio Plug-In
Chainer displays your
new plug-in chain along
with the parameter
settings of the currently
selected plug-in

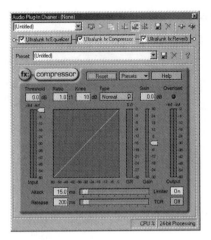

7.   Select each plug-in one at a time and adjust its parameters to the settings you
      want it to use to process your files.

8.   If you want to remove a plug-in from the chain, select it and click the Remove
      Selected Plug-In button.

9.   Plug-ins are applied to your audio data in the order that they appear in the
      chain. Because of this, you may want to move a plug-in to a different position in
      the chain. For example, if you apply EQ and reverb to a file, it's usually best to
      apply EQ first, so you want the EQ plug-in to come before the reverb plug-in in
      the chain. To move a plug-in to a different location in the chain, drag and drop it
      either left or right.

Audition a Plug-In Chain

After you've created your chain, you can listen to how it will affect your audio data by doing the
following:

1.   To listen to your new plug-in chain, click the Preview button.

2.   If you want to hear how your audio will sound when it's not being processed by
      the audio chain, click the Bypass button, and then click the Preview button.
      Click the Bypass button again, to turn the plug-in chain processing back on.

NOTE
Some plug-in effects not only change your audio data, but they also insert
additional data because of their nature. For example, when you apply reverb
to audio, the reverberation effect continues sounding even after the original
audio data has ceased to play. It does this because reverberation simulates the
echoing of audio environments. The reverberation doesn't just stop along with
the original audio, instead it slowly fades out. This extra data is known as an
effect tail.

3. You can deal with effect tails in three different ways. Click the Ignore Tail Data button to ignore the effect tail and have the audio stop playing as soon as it reaches the end of the original audio data selection. Click the Insert Tail Data button to insert the extra audio data at the end of the original data selection and have any existing data moved toward the end of the file. Click the Mix Tail Data button to mix the extra audio data into the file without moving any existing data. The Mix Tail Data option is the most natural sounding, so you want to keep this option activated most of the time.

Apply and Save a Plug-In Chain

After you've auditioned your new plug-in chain and heard how it affects your audio data, you can do two more things with it—apply it to your audio data and/or save it as a chain preset. To apply the chain to the currently selected audio data, click the Process Selection button. This means that the processing will be applied in a destructive manner, thus altering the original audio data. Of course, you can always use the Undo or Undo History functions to remove the changes.

Before you close the Audio Plug-In Chainer window, save your new chain as a preset. To do this, click the Save Chain Preset button to open the Save Plug-In Package dialog box (see Figure 9.31).

Figure 9.31
Use the Save Plug-In
Package dialog box to
save your chain as a
preset

Then, type in a name for the preset and click OK. Your new preset is now listed in the Preset drop-down list and in the DirectX Chains folder of the Plug-In Manager window. If you want to delete a preset, select the preset from the Preset drop-down list in the Audio Plug-In Chainer window and then click the Delete Chain Preset button.

The Audio Plug-In Chainer is an extremely powerful tool. As a matter of fact, I like to keep it open at all times when I'm working with Sound Forge. It allows me to quickly test out effects on my audio data without actually altering the data, and (because the Chainer runs in a window) I still have access to all the other features in Sound Forge at the same time.

10
Additional Audio Tools

Sound Forge provides so many tools and functions that it's difficult to categorize them all. Some are used for editing. Some are used for processing. And others are used to add effects. There are also a few other tools that don't fit in any of those categories. They give you the ability to fix, analyze, and synthesize audio data. In this chapter, you'll learn to:

► Repair your audio data with the Repair functions

► Analyze your audio data using spectrum analysis

► Create new sounds with simple synthesis

► Create new sounds with FM synthesis

In Need of Repair

In Chapter 7, I talk about the Pencil tool and how you can use it to fix glitches (such as pops and clicks) in your audio data. Sound Forge provides a few functions that make fixing glitches even easier.

Repair Stereo Audio

If you ever run across a situation in which one channel of your stereo audio file has a glitch but the other channel doesn't, you can use the Repair Channel function to fix the problem quickly and easily. Here is how it works:

1. If you don't know the location of the glitch, use the Find function as I described in Chapter 5. Otherwise, scroll and zoom the Data Window so that you can see the glitch in the audio waveform.

2. If the glitch is small (within 10 milliseconds in length), position the Current Position cursor at a point that is approximately at the center of the glitch. If you used the Find function, this is done automatically. Make sure only the channel containing the glitch has the Current Position cursor showing in it by pressing the Tab key on your computer keyboard (see Figure 10.1).

Figure 10.1
Press the Tab key on
your computer keyboard
so that only the glitched
channel is processed

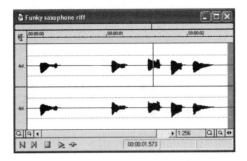

3. If the glitch is large, make a selection containing the glitched data. Make sure
    only the channel containing the glitch has the selection in it by pressing the Tab
    key on your computer keyboard (see Figure 10.2).

Figure 10.2
If the glitch is large,
make a selection instead
of just placing the
Current Position cursor

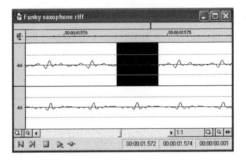

4. Choose Tools > Repair > Copy Other Channel. If you placed the Current Position
    cursor in the center of the glitch, Sound Forge copies 10 milliseconds of data
    (five milliseconds before and five milliseconds after the Current Position cursor)
    from the clean channel to the glitched channel. If you made a selection, Sound
    Forge copies the same amount of data as the selection (up to 0.5 seconds) from
    the clean channel to the glitched channel.

TIP
The Repair > Copy Other Channel function works best when the data in both
channels is similar. If the data is very different, the function may not work. In
this case, you may want to try one of the other Repair functions.

Repair with Replacement

If the data in the channels of your stereo audio is not similar at the point where a glitch occurs,
you can try replacing it with data from the same channel using the Repair Replace function.
This function also works if you have a mono audio file. The Repair Replace function works

almost exactly the same as the Repair > Copy Other Channel function, except that the clean data is taken from the audio immediately preceding the glitch in the waveform. Follow these steps to utilize the Repair Replace function:

1.   If you don't know the location of the glitch, use the Find function as I described in Chapter 5. Otherwise, scroll and zoom the Data Window so that you can see the glitch in the audio waveform.

2.   If the glitch is small (within 15 milliseconds in length), position the Current Position cursor at a point that is approximately at the center of the glitch. If you used the Find function, this is done automatically. If you're working on a stereo file, make sure only the channel containing the glitch has the Current Position cursor showing in it by pressing the Tab key on your computer keyboard.

3.   If the glitch is large, make a selection containing the glitched data. If you're working on a stereo file, make sure only the channel containing the glitch has the selection in it by pressing the Tab key on your computer keyboard.

4.   Choose Tools > Repair > Replace. If you placed the Current Position cursor in the center of the glitch, Sound Forge replaces 15 milliseconds of data surrounding the cursor with the 15 milliseconds of data that immediately preceded the glitch. If you made a selection, Sound Forge copies the same amount of data as the selection (up to 0.5 seconds) from the data that immediately preceded the glitch.

TIP

The Repair Replace function works best on large clicks or glitches. If too many replacements are made, however, you can sometimes get a strange echo effect. If that happens, try using the Repair Interpolate function instead.

Repair with Interpolation

The Repair Interpolate function is the most sophisticated of the Repair functions. This doesn't mean it always works better, though. You'll need to experiment. The Repair Interpolate function eliminates glitches by first making a logical guess at what the audio waveform is supposed to look like without the glitch, and then replacing the glitched data with the estimated data. Here is how the function works:

1.   If you don't know the location of the glitch, use the Find function as I described in Chapter 5. Otherwise, scroll and zoom the Data Window so that you can see the glitch in the audio waveform.

2.   The Repair Interpolate function works best on small glitches (5 milliseconds or less). For very small glitches, position the Current Position cursor at a point that is approximately at the center of the glitch. If you used the Find function, this is done automatically. For slightly larger glitches, make a selection containing the glitched data. If you're working on a stereo file, make sure only the channel

containing the glitch has the Current Position cursor or selection showing in it by pressing the Tab key on your computer keyboard.

3. Choose Tools > Repair > Interpolate.

Sound Forge analyzes the audio data and replaces the glitch with an estimate of what it thinks it should be. In some cases, this won't work and just introduces another glitch. If that happens, try using one of the other Repair functions. You'll need to test each one to see which works best on your damaged audio data.

TIP

Noise reduction and repairing audio data is a complicated topic. It can take a lot of time and patience to get good results. The more you know about the subject, the better your chances of success. To find out more, be sure to read my feature article in Issue 12 of DigiFreq titled, "Nix the Noise from Your Recordings." You can download the issue for free at:

http://www.digifreq.com/digifreq/issues.asp.

Spectrum Analysis

In Chapter 8, I talk about frequencies, the audio spectrum, and how different sounds are created via multiple, simultaneous vibrations at different frequencies. I also talk about how you can alter the tonal characteristics (or timbre) of a sound using equalization. But in order to know what frequencies should be boosted or cut to get the changes you want, you have to know what frequencies (and their amplitudes) are present within a sound. That's where *spectrum analysis* comes in.

If you happen to have a boom box or a stereo component that has an animated graph feature, which changes as music is being played, then you've had some experience with spectrum analysis. That animated graph shows the amplitudes of different frequencies within the music as it is being played. It can tell you if there is too much bass or too much treble and allow you to make the appropriate adjustments so that the music sounds better. Sound Forge's Spectrum Analysis function lets you do this, too, but with a much higher degree of accuracy.

You can use the Spectrum Analysis function to analyze the frequency content in your audio files and determine which frequencies are loud or soft. You can also use the function to find the fundamental pitch of a sound, or to track down strange noises in your audio (such as buzzes or hums). Then, you can use the equalization or pitch adjustment functions to make changes. Here is how the Spectrum Analysis function works:

1. Select the data in your audio file that you want to analyze. If you want to analyze the entire file, don't select any data or select it all by choosing Edit > Select All (or pressing Ctrl + A on your computer keyboard).

2. Choose Tools > Spectrum Analysis to open the Spectrum Analysis window (see Figure 10.3). The window displays a graph showing frequency values along the bottom and amplitude values along the left side. This lets you look at the graph, pick out a frequency, and find the amplitude of that frequency within your audio data. If you are analyzing a mono file, you'll see one graph. If you are analyzing a stereo file, you'll see two graphs (one for the left channel and one for the right channel).

Figure 10.3
Use the Spectrum Analysis function to analyze the frequency content in your audio files

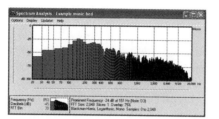

3. When you first open the window, the graph will be zoomed all the way out, making it difficult to pick out specific frequencies. To zoom in on a particular frequency or group of frequencies, click and drag your mouse within the graph to draw a box around the frequencies you want to view in more detail (see Figure 10.4).

TIP

Just like any other window, you can also change its size by clicking and dragging its corners (the window, not the graph). This gives you a larger graph (with more values displayed) to work with.

Figure 10.4
Click and drag within the graph to zoom in on specific frequencies

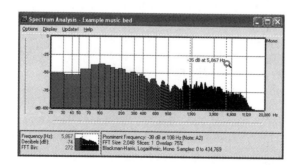

TIP

As you move your mouse within the graph, you'll see the mouse cursor display amplitude (in dB) and frequency (in Hz) values. By aligning the cursor to the top of a frequency bar in the graph, you can get a reading of the amplitude of that frequency. Also, by choosing Options > Show Position, you can turn this feature on or off. And by choosing Options > Show Notes, you can also have the cursor display note values for the frequencies you are inspecting.

4. When you zoom in on the graph, notice that the scroll bars on the left and bottom of the graph become active. These work like any other scroll bars in a window, and allow you to scroll through the different parts of the graph while zoomed in. You can also choose Display > Grab/Pan to turn the mouse into a scroll tool. In this mode, when you click and drag within the graph, the position of the graph moves. To go back to zoom mode, just choose Display > Grab/Pan again.

5. To zoom out all the way horizontally, choose Display > Zoom Out Full. To zoom out all the way vertically, choose Display > Normalize dB.

TIP

You can also zoom the graph to a specific range by choosing Display > Zoom To Range. To set the range for this function, choose Options > Settings to open the Spectrum Settings dialog box. In the Display Range section, set minimum and maximum values for the frequency (horizontal) range for the graph. Then, set maximum and minimum values for the amplitude (vertical) range of the graph using the Ceiling and Floor parameters, respectively.

6. To display the frequencies in the graph logarithmically rather than linearly, choose Display > Logarithmic. Basically, what this means is that the graph displays a wider range of low frequencies in this mode. So, if you are working with audio data with a lot of low frequency content (like a bass guitar part), you might want to display the graph logarithmically.

7. You can change the appearance of the graph in other ways, too. Initially, you see the Bar Graph mode. This is my favorite, because it shows individual bars for the frequencies displayed. But there are also Line Graph and Filled Graph modes. To use them, just choose Display > Line Graph or Display > Filled Graph.

8. Because the Spectrum Analysis function uses a window instead of a dialog box, you can keep it open as you edit your audio data. If you go back to the Data Window and select a different section of audio, you can switch to the already open Spectrum Analysis window to analyze the new data. The graph isn't updated automatically, though, so to update the graph, choose Update.

TIP

If you want the graph to be updated automatically with any data selections or edits that you make, choose Options > Auto Update in the Spectrum Analysis window.

TIP

You can also have the Spectrum Analysis function show graphs for different parts of your audio data simultaneously. Choose Options > Settings to open the Spectrum Settings dialog box. For the Slices Displayed parameter, choose how many graphs you want displayed (up to 64), and then choose whether you want them Forward or Backward according to the data in your file. Click OK. Depending on the number of graphs you choose, the Spectrum Analysis function splits your audio file into that many sections and shows a graph for each section. The graphs are shown beginning at the front of the file or at the back of the file, depending on if you choose the Forward or Backward options, respectively.

9. The Spectrum Analysis function can also be used in real time. If you choose Options > Monitor Playback, the graph changes as your data is played. Go ahead and try it. The display looks very cool. In addition to this, you can also use the function to analyze the audio that is coming into your sound card in real time. This means you can hook up a microphone to your sound card, speak or play something into it, and watch the graph show the frequency content of the audio. To activate this feature, choose Options > Monitor Input.

10. To set the accuracy of the Spectrum Analysis function, choose Options > Settings to open the Spectrum Settings dialog box (see Figure 10.5).

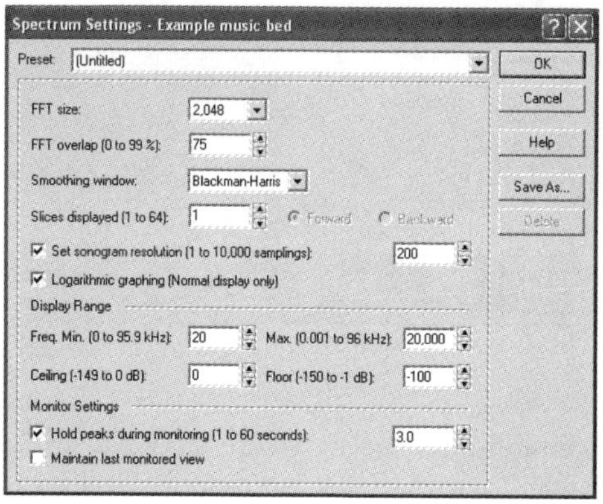

Figure 10.5
Adjust the accuracy of the Spectrum Analysis function with the Spectrum Settings dialog box

11. The Spectrum Analysis function uses an imaginary window as it analyzes your selected data, section by section. The size of this window (in samples) is determined by the FFT Size parameter. The bigger the window, the more accurate the analysis, but the slower the processing. A good number that provides a balance between accuracy and processing speed is 2,048.

12. The FFT Overlap parameter determines how much overlap there is from the window's last analysis position to its next position. Again, the more overlap, the more accurate the analysis, but the slower the processing. Usually, 75 percent is a good setting.

13. The Smoothing Window parameter determines what algorithm is used when analyzing your data. You can experiment with these to find the one that best fits the material you're analyzing, but most often, you'll probably want to use the Blackman-Harris setting, which is the most accurate.

14. There are also a number of presets available that set the graph parameters for you according to the type of data you want to analyze. Be sure to try them out. And after you've made your settings, click OK.

15. In addition to the Bar Graph, Line Graph, and Filled Graph modes, the Spectrum Analysis function provides a Sonogram mode. To activate it, choose Display > Sonogram (Color) and you'll see a very colorful graph, as shown in Figure 10.6. Instead of frequency and amplitude, this graph shows frequencies (on the left side of the graph) over time (on the bottom of the graph). This means that by reading the graph, you can see all the frequencies at a specific time in your selected data. Not only that, but the different colors represent the amplitudes of the frequencies. At the bottom of the window, you'll see a scale showing what colors represent what amplitudes in dB.

Figure 10.6

In addition to the Bar, Line, and Filled Graph modes, there is the Sonogram mode

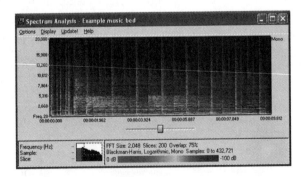

16. As in the other modes, you can move the mouse over the graph and read the amplitudes of specific frequencies in numerical values. The Sonogram doesn't allow you to zoom in or move around. And while using the Monitor Playback function, you see the Current Position cursor scroll within the graph rather than the graph itself changing.

17. If you want to change the intensity of the colors in the graph so you can get a better reading, just move the slider located just beneath the graph. Move it right for more intense colors, and move it left for less intense colors. Double-click the slider to move it back to its default position.

18. You can also view the Sonogram in black and white if you want. Just choose Display > Sonogram (B & W).

19. To adjust the accuracy of the Sonogram, choose Options > Settings to open the Spectrum Settings dialog box. Then, adjust the Set Sonogram Resolution parameter. The higher the setting, the more accurate the Sonogram but the more processing time it takes to create it. The default value of 200 usually works well. Click OK.

TIP

If you want a printout of your graph or Sonogram, just choose Options > Print Display.

20. When you're finished with the Spectrum Analysis function, choose Options > Close to close the window.

Spectrum Analysis Applications

Of course, knowing how to use the Spectrum Analysis function doesn't really give you any idea of why you might want to use it. So, let me take you through a couple of examples.

Prominent Pitch

Suppose you have a recording of an instrumental performance and you want to know what note the instrument is playing at a particular point in your audio file. This is how you can find out:

1. Select the data in your audio file that contains only the note being played for which you want to find the pitch.

2. Choose Tools > Spectrum Analysis.

3. If is isn't already, change the display mode to normal by choosing Display > Normal Display.

4. Now, look at the bottom right area of the Spectrum Analysis window. There you will see a bunch of text showing the various settings for the current graph. In addition, you'll see the text "Prominent Frequency." Next to that is shown the most prominent frequency in your selected data and the note (or pitch) represented by that frequency.

Find Glitches Manually

I talked about how to repair your audio data earlier in this chapter using the Repair functions. I also talked about how to use the Find function to locate glitches in your data, but sometimes even the Find function doesn't work and you need to look for the glitches manually. Most of the time, you can hear them easily, but you might not be able to quite zoom in on the exact spot at which they are located. The Spectrum Analysis function can help here.

1. Find the general area in your audio file where the glitch is located and select that data.

2. Choose Tools > Spectrum Analysis.

3. Choose Display > Sonogram (Color).

4. Look at the graph for thin spikes of color (see Figure 10.7). Those are glitches or clicks in your audio data.

Figure 10.7
Use the Sonogram mode
to find glitches in your
audio data

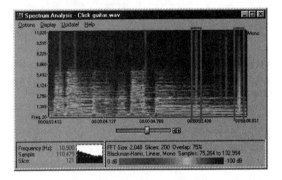

5. Make a note of the time at which the glitch occurs by reading the time values at the bottom of the graph.

6. Zoom in on that time in the Data Window to find the glitch in the audio waveform.

7. Refer to the earlier sections of this chapter for step-by-step instructions on how to fix the glitch.

Synthesis

In addition to all of the editing, processing, and effects functions I described in the previous chapters, Sound Forge allows you to create sounds from scratch with its trio of synthesis functions. These functions allow you to experiment with a number of different types of synthesis all from within Sound Forge. No other software or hardware components are required. You can do things like simulate telephone tones, try your hand at simple additive and subtractive synthesis, and create some really complex sounds with FM synthesis.

NOTE

I will not go into detail about the aspects of additive, subtractive, FM, or sound synthesis in general. This subject matter would fill many books in and of itself. However, you can find some good introductory information on the following Web sites: **http://tilt.largo.fl.us/faq/synthfaq.html** and **http://nmc.uoregon.edu/emi/emp_win/main.html**.

DTMF/MF Tones

The DTMF/MF function allows you to generate telephone tones. Why would you ever want or need to do this? I have no idea. But there have been some songs on the market that use telephone tones for effects, so maybe you'll get some use out of this function after all. Sonic Foundry tells me this function was added for the people who work in the telephone business so they can add special signals to their audio files to trigger events in the automated telephone systems. For whatever reason you may want to use it, here is how the function works:

1. Create a new empty audio file by choosing File > New (or pressing Ctrl + N on your computer keyboard) and setting the appropriate parameters in the New Window dialog box, or open an existing audio file. I talk about how to do this in Chapter 4. If you open an existing audio file, position the Current Position cursor to the location in the file at which you want to insert the telephone tones.

2. Choose Tools > Synthesis > DTMF/MF Tones to open the DTMF/MF Tones dialog box (see Figure 10.8).

Figure 10.8
Generate telephone tones with the DTMF/MF function

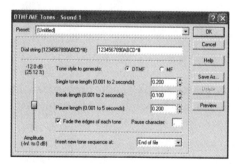

3. Set the Dial String parameter. This is where you enter the telephone number that you want to simulate. Just like on your touch-tone phone, you can enter numbers, letters, and even the asterisk or pound sign.

4. Choose an option for the Tone Style To Generate parameter. DTMF stands for Dual Tone Multi-Frequency. This is the name for the type of sound signals that are generated by standard touch-tone phones. MF stands for Multi-Frequency. This is the name for the type of sound signals that are used internally by the telephone companies to control the operation of the telephone networks.

5. Set the Single Tone Length parameter. This parameter determines the length (in

seconds) of each individual tone that is generated. To create an average length tone, use a setting of about 0.200.

6. Set the Break Length parameter. This parameter determines the amount of silence (in seconds) that occurs between each individual tone. To simulate normal dialing speed, use a setting of about 0.100.

7. In addition to the Break Length, you can also insert specific pauses between dialing tones. To do this, choose a setting for the Pause Character parameter (the default setting of a comma works well). Add commas to the Dial String parameter where you want the pauses to occur. Then, set the Pause Length parameter (in seconds) to specify how long of a pause there will be when the Pause Character is encountered in the Dial String when the tones are being generated.

8. Activate the Fade The Edges Of Each Tone option. This prevents glitching, so you almost always want to keep this option activated.

9. If you are inserting the tones into an existing audio file and you want them to be inserted at the Current Position cursor, choose the Cursor option for the Insert New Tone Sequence At parameter. You can also choose to insert the tones at the start or end of the file. If you are creating a new file, you don't need to set this parameter.

10. Set the Amplitude parameter to specify how loud you want the tones to be.

11. Click the Preview button to hear how your file will sound before you have Sound Forge make any actual changes to the data.

12. Click OK.

Sound Forge generates the telephone tones according to your parameter settings.

Simple Synthesis

The Simple Synthesis function allows you to generate very basic audio waves like the kind you might find on a synthesizer. You can use this function to experiment with different types of synthesis, and create your own unique synth sounds. Like its name implies, the Simple Synthesis function is very easy to use. Here is how it works:

1. Create a new empty audio file by choosing File > New (or pressing Ctrl + N on your computer keyboard) and setting the appropriate parameters in the New Window dialog box, or open an existing audio file. I talk about how to do this in Chapter 4. If you open an existing audio file, position the Current Position cursor to the location in the file at which you want to insert the synth tone.

2. Choose Tools > Synthesis > Simple to open the Simple Synthesis dialog box (see Figure 10.9).

Figure 10.9
Generate basic audio
waves with the Simple
Synthesis function

3.   Choose an option for the Waveform Shape parameter. This parameter determines
     the type of basic waveform that you want to generate. You can choose from Sine,
     Square, Saw, Triangle, Noise, and Absolute Sine. Try out each one to get an idea
     of what they sound like.

4.   Set the Length parameter. This parameter determines the length (in seconds) of
     the audio wave that is generated.

5.   Set the Frequency parameter. This parameter determines the frequency (or pitch)
     of the sound that is generated.

6.   If you are inserting the sound into an existing audio file and you want it to be
     inserted at the Current Position cursor, choose the Cursor option for the Insert
     New Waveform At parameter. You can also choose to insert the sound at the start
     or end of the file. If you are creating a new file, you don't need to set this
     parameter.

7.   Set the Amplitude parameter to specify how loud you want the sound to be.

8.   Click the Preview button to hear how your file will sound before you have
     Sound Forge make any actual changes to the data.

9.   Click OK.

Sound Forge generates the audio waveform according to your parameter settings.

Simple Synthesis Example

But what can you really do with the Simple Synthesis function other than just create basic synth
tones? Well, by combining the Simple Synthesis function with some of the other functions
available from within Sound Forge, you can create synthesized sounds from scratch. Here's an
example:

1.   Create a new empty audio file by choosing File > New and setting the
     appropriate parameters in the New Window dialog box.

2.   Choose Tools > Synthesis > Simple to open the Simple Synthesis dialog box.

3.   Set the Waveform Shape parameter to Square.

4.   Set the Length parameter to 3.

5.   Set the Frequency parameter to 261.6, which is the frequency of Middle C on the
     musical scale.

6.   Set the Amplitude parameter to –12 dB.

7.   Click OK. This gives us our first basic synth tone.

8. Create a new empty audio file by choosing File > New and setting the appropriate parameters in the New Window dialog box.

9. Choose Tools > Synthesis > Simple to open the Simple Synthesis dialog box.

10. Set the Waveform Shape parameter to Saw.

11. Set the Length parameter to 3.

12. Set the Frequency parameter to 466.2, which is the frequency of Bb above Middle C on the musical scale.

13. Set the Amplitude parameter to –12 dB.

14. Click OK. This gives us our second basic synth tone.

15. Select and copy all the data from the second synth tone.

16. Select all the data in the first synth tone.

17. Choose Edit > Paste Special > Mix (or press Ctrl + M on your computer keyboard) to open the Mix dialog box.

18. Choose the 50/50 Mix Preset and click OK. This gives us our mixed complex synth tone.

19. Choose Process > Fade > Graphic to open the Graphic Fade dialog box.

20. Choose the –6 dB Exponential Fade Out Preset and click OK.

21. Choose Effects > Flange/Wah-Wah to open the Flange/Wah-wah dialog box.

22. Choose the Fast Flange Preset and click OK.

23. Choose Effects > Reverb to open the Reverb dialog box.

24. Choose the Metal Tank Preset and click OK.

25. Play the audio file.

Isn't that cool? You just created a synthesizer sound from scratch, and this example only demonstrated a few of the Sound Forge functions that you can use when developing your own sounds. Feel free to experiment with all of the other processing and effects functions. You may stumble upon some really wild sounds. And if you find something you really like, save it as a WAV file and then import it into your digital audio sequencing application so you can use it in your next tune.

FM Synthesis

The FM Synthesis function allows you to create more complex synth sounds through the use of frequency modulation synthesis techniques. Many of the older Yamaha brand of synthesizers (such as the TX81Z) used this form of synthesis. By combining multiple simple waveforms in various configurations, frequency modulation synthesis allows you to create some very realistic and some not so realistic synth sounds. Here is how the FM Synthesis function works:

1. Create a new empty audio file by choosing File > New (or pressing Ctrl + N on your computer keyboard) and setting the appropriate parameters in the New Window dialog box, or open an existing audio file. I talk about how to do this in

Chapter 4. If you open an existing audio file, position the Current Position cursor to the location in the file at which you want to insert the synth tone.

2. Choose Tools > Synthesis > FM to open the FM Synthesis dialog box (see Figure 10.10).

Figure 10.10
Generate complex audio waves with the FM Synthesis function

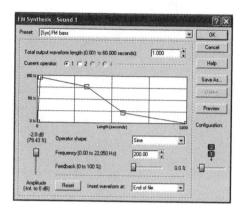

3. Set the Total Output Waveform Length parameter. This parameter determines the length (in seconds) of the audio wave that is generated.

4. Choose an option for the Configuration parameter. This parameter determines how many Operators you want to use to generate your sound and how they will be connected. You need to experiment to see how each option produces different types of sounds.

NOTE

In frequency modulation synthesis, an Operator is a basic waveform generator. You can think of an Operator as a single Simple Synthesis function with a couple of extra parameters. The FM Synthesis function allows you to use up to four Operators, so it's like having four Simple Synthesis functions combined in one. In addition, the Operators can be connected to one another in different ways. For example, for some options of the Configuration parameter, you'll notice that the output from one Operator is fed into another Operator. This means that the first Operator is being used to modulate the frequency of the second Operator, thus the phrase "frequency modulation synthesis." This technique can produce some very complex sounds.

5. The Current Operator parameter lets you choose which Operator you are going to work with. Each Operator has the same number and types of parameters, so I just go through the parameters for Operator 1.

6. Define an Amplitude Envelope for the current Operator using the Amplitude Graph. This graph works exactly the same as the graph in the Envelope function,

which I talk about in Chapter 9. The Amplitude Envelope controls the volume of the Operator over time.

7. Choose an option for the Operator Shape parameter. This parameter determines the type of basic waveform that you want to use for the current Operator. You can choose from Sine, Square, Saw, Triangle, Noise, and Absolute Sine, just like with the Simple Synthesis function.

8. Set the Frequency parameter. This parameter determines the frequency (or pitch) used for the current Operator.

9. Set the Feedback parameter. This parameter allows you to send the output from the current Operator back into itself, meaning you can have an Operator modulate (vibrate) its own frequency in addition to being modulated by another Operator. Experiment with this parameter to see how it affects the sound you're trying to create.

10. Set the Amplitude parameter to specify how loud you want the final output of the current Operator to be.

11. If you are using more than one Operator, go through Steps 5 through 10 for each additional Operator.

12. If you are inserting the sound into an existing audio file and you want it to be inserted at the Current Position cursor, choose the Cursor option for the Insert Waveform At parameter. You can also choose to insert the sound at the start or end of the file. If you are creating a new file, you don't need to set this parameter.

13. Click the Preview button to hear how your file will sound before you have Sound Forge make any actual changes to the data.

14. Click OK.

Sound Forge generates the audio waveform according to your parameter settings. For some examples of the sounds you can produce with the FM Synthesis function, be sure to check out the supplied presets.

TIP

Try saving some of the sounds that you create as WAV files and then use them as Impulses for the Acoustic Mirror function (which I talk about in Chapter 9). The only limit you have to abide by is to keep the length of the files at 12 seconds or less. You can get some very weird environmental simulations using this technique.

11

Producing for Multimedia and the Web

In addition to regular audio production, Sound Forge includes a number of features to help you create and edit audio for multimedia and the Internet. You can open a video file in Sound Forge and then add audio or edit existing audio. You can also save video files along with your edited audio. All of the editing and processing functions provided by Sound Forge make it easy for you to prepare your audio for distribution over the Web, including the ability to save files as RealAudio, MP3, or Windows Media. Sound Forge even allows you to read and write your audio data to and from CD. By providing these tools, Sound Forge gives you everything you need to deliver your audio to all available venues. In this chapter, you'll learn to:

▶ Work with video files

▶ Prepare your audio for Internet distribution

▶ Read audio from a CD

▶ Write audio to a CD

Work with Video Files

In Chapter 4, I cover all the steps needed for opening and saving video files in Sound Forge. But I don't actually cover how to work with the data after you load it into the program. The procedure is really not much different than working with audio files, except that video files contain both audio and video data.

The Video Strip

When you open a video file in Sound Forge, the first thing you notice is that the Data Window has a new section added to it (see Figure 11.1). This section is called the Video Strip. The Video Strip displays small frames of video data from the file. These frames show what is happening in the video at different points in time. They also allow you to see how the video and audio data are synchronized.

Figure 11.1
The Video Strip in the
Data Window lets you
view your video data

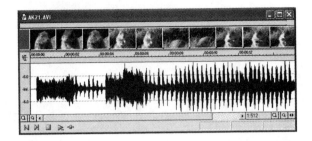

If you play the file, you notice that the Video Strip becomes animated and plays the video data along with the audio data as the Current Position cursor moves within the Data Window. Give it a try and you'll see what I mean. If you do not want the Video Strip animated, you can turn the option off by right-clicking within the Video Strip and choosing Animate from the shortcut menu to remove the check mark (see Figure 11.2).

Figure 11.2
Turn the Video Strip
animation on or off with
the Animate option

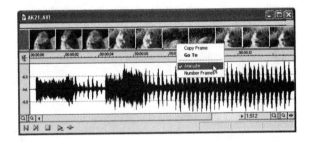

The Video Strip also provides a few other options that might be helpful to you.

Number Frames

By right-clicking in the Video Strip and choosing the Number Frames option from the shortcut menu, you can specify whether Sound Forge displays video frame numbers inside the Video Strip (see Figure 11.3). Using frame numbers can sometimes help you when you're trying to specify when a sound or other piece of audio should occur at a certain place within the video.

Figure 11.3
Use the Number Frames
option to show frame
numbers in the Video
Strip

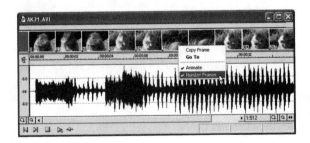

TIP
By choosing Options > Preferences > Video and using the Frame Numbering On Thumbnails drop-down list, you can choose whether frames are numbered using frame numbers or media time code.

Go To

You can also use the Video Strip to navigate through your file. Just right-click within one of the sections shown in the Video Strip and choose Go To from the shortcut menu. The Current Position cursor then jumps to the beginning of that section within the file. This gives you a quick way to audition different sections in your video file.

Copy

By right-clicking in the Video Strip and choosing the Copy option from the shortcut menu, Sound Forge copies the current video frame to the Windows clipboard. Because you can't edit video data within Sound Forge, however, I don't know why you would ever need this option.

Video Editing?

Sound Forge doesn't allow you to alter the video of your file in any way. For that, you need a dedicated video editing application. You can, however, edit the audio data in a video file just like you do in a plain audio file, and as such, change the length of the file.

Cutting

If you cut some audio data from your video file, this removes the audio data but leaves the video data intact. As shown in Figure 11.4, notice that the audio data is cut short while the video data remains. When you play a file like this, the video data at the end of the file plays, but there is no sound.

Figure 11.4
Cutting audio data from a video file doesn't affect the video data

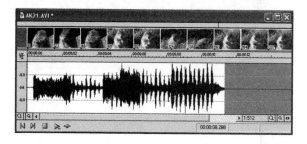

Pasting

By pasting data to a video file, however, you can actually lengthen the file. What happens here is if you have more audio data in the file than video data, the end of the file is padded with blank video (see Figure 11.5). This means that when you play the file, you hear the audio data at the end, but there is no video displayed. So, in a sense, you can add video data to a file, although it is just blank.

Figure 11.5
Pasting audio data to a video file adds blank video data to the end of the file

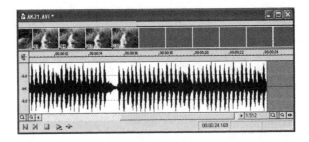

TIP

If you find working with the Video Strip difficult because of its size, just position your mouse over the small gray bar underneath the Video Strip. Then, click and drag downward to change the size of the Video Strip (see Figure 11.6).

Figure 11.6
Change the size of the Video Strip by clicking and dragging the gray bar beneath it

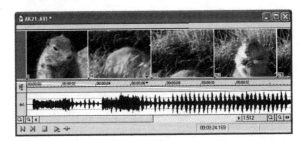

The Video Preview Window

In addition to the Video Strip, Sound Forge lets you view your video data in a more convenient way via the Video Preview Window (see Figure 11.7). To open the Video Preview Window, choose View > Video Preview (or press Alt + 4 on your computer keyboard).

Figure 11.7
Use the Video Preview
Window for a more
convenient way to view
your video data

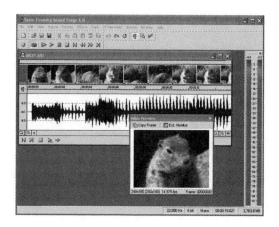

The main difference between the Video Strip and the Video Preview Window is that the Video Preview Window option provides a dedicated viewing area for video data only. In addition, it lets you view the video at any size (within the limitations of your computer monitor). Just like with any other window in Windows, you can change the size of the Video Preview Window by clicking and dragging on its corners and sides. Depending on the mode of operation, this also changes the viewing size of your video. Initially, the Video Preview Window displays video in the Integral Stretch mode (see Figure 11.8). In this mode, the size of the video only changes when the size of the Video Preview Window is big enough to display the video at the larger size without distorting it vertically or horizontally (i.e., keeping its aspect ratio).

Figure 11.8
Initially, the Video
Preview Window
displays video in the
Integral Stretch mode

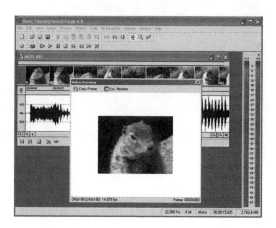

CHAPTER 11

TIP

When using the Integral Stretch mode, notice that the background of the Video Preview Window may not match the video background. To change the color of the window background, right-click in the window and choose White Background, Black Background, or Default Background from the shortcut menu.

If you want the video to fill the entire Video Preview Window, right-click in the window and choose Integral Stretch from the shortcut menu. This disables the Integral Stretch mode and stretches the viewing size of the video to match the size and shape of the window, but by doing so, it can also sometimes distort the video, making it more difficult to view (see Figure 11.9).

Figure 11.9
Disable the Integral Stretch mode to stretch the viewing size of video

TIP

If you have a slow computer system, stretching the video in the Video Preview Window can sometimes bog your system down. If that happens, right-click in the window and choose Passive Update from the shortcut menu. This tells Sound Forge to update the video data only when your computer processor is idle.

TIP

You can also save computer processing power while using the Video Preview Window by making the window smaller. First, double-click on the title bar of the window to automatically resize the window to fit the size of the video. Double-click the title bar again to display the video at half of its original size.

External Monitor

If you have an additional external monitor hooked up to your computer system, you can tell Sound Forge to send the video display from the Video Preview Window to that external monitor. First, you need to set up the monitor by doing the following:

1. Choose Options > Preferences > Video to open the Preferences > Video dialog box (see Figure 11.10).

Figure 11.10
Use the Preferences >
Video dialog box to set
up an external monitor

2. Use the External Monitor Device drop-down list to choose the monitor you want to use.

3. Click OK.

After you've set up your monitor, right-click in the Video Preview Window and choose External Monitor from the shortcut menu.

Prepare Audio for the Internet

In addition to video files, I also talk about how to save audio files in the RealAudio, MP3, and Window Media formats in Chapter 4. But I don't actually talk about how to process your files before saving them to these formats. Because the RealAudio, MP3, and Windows Media formats all use compression to reduce the size of audio data so that it's easier to download over the Internet, they can sometimes affect the sound of your audio. You can compensate for these unwanted changes in quality, though, by following a few simple processing procedures before you convert your files.

Remove DC Offset

As I mention in Chapter 8, it's always a good idea to remove any DC offset that may be present in your audio data before doing any processing. Otherwise, you can sometimes add unwanted anomalies. To remove DC offset:

1. Select all the data in your audio file by choosing Edit > Select All (or pressing Ctrl + A on your computer keyboard).

2. Choose Process > DC Offset to open the DC Offset dialog box.

3. Choose the Remove DC Offset (Scan Entire Sound File) Preset.

4. Click OK.

Apply Equalization

Equalize your file while keeping in mind that most of the high-end and extreme low-end content might be lost when you save the file to one of the compressed file formats. It may take some experimentation, but cutting the low frequencies (below 60 Hz) and the high frequencies (above 10 kHz) is a good place to start. This helps in reducing any of the anomalies that can occur during the file format compression. To compensate for the frequencies being cut, you can boost some of the low frequencies that are still intact around 200 Hz. You can also boost the mid-range frequencies around 2.5 kHz. This emphasizes the more important content in your audio, such as vocals, if there are any. What's great about Sound Forge is that it allows you to accomplish all of this equalization with one process. Here's how it's done:

1. Select all the data in your audio file by choosing Edit > Select All (or pressing Ctrl + A on your computer keyboard).

2. Choose Process > EQ > Paragraphic to open the Paragraphic EQ dialog box.

3. Activate the Enable Low-Shelf option. Set its frequency to 60 Hz. Then, set its gain to –Inf. Doing this cuts out any frequencies below 60 Hz, as I mentioned earlier.

4. Activate the Enable High-Shelf option. Set its frequency to 10,000 Hz. Then, set its gain to –Inf. Doing this cuts out any frequencies above 10 kHz, as I mentioned earlier.

5. Set the gain on the first parametric band to +3.0 dB. Then, set its Center Frequency to 200 Hz. This boosts the low frequencies around 200 Hz. You can experiment with how much the frequencies are boosted, but I wouldn't go any higher than +6.0 dB.

6. Set the gain on the second parametric band to +3.0 dB. Then, set its Center Frequency to 2,500 Hz. This boosts the mid-range frequencies around 2,500 Hz. You can experiment with how much the frequencies are boosted, but I wouldn't go any higher than +6.0 dB.

7. Leave all the other parameters set to their defaults. When you're finished, the Paragraphic EQ dialog box should look similar to Figure 11.11.

Figure 11.11
Use the Paragraphic EQ
function to equalize
your file in a single
process

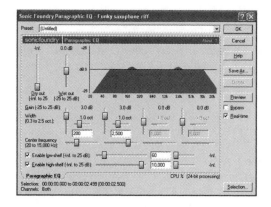

8. Click the Preview button to audition your file before making any changes. If you hear any clipping or distortion, try lowering the gain on one or both of the parametric bands.

9. Click OK.

Apply Dynamic Processing

In addition to altering the frequency content of your audio, converting to RealAudio, MP3, or Windows Media can reduce the dynamic (amplitude) range, making your audio sound flat or dull. Adding a bit of dynamic processing before conversion gives you some control over your final signal levels, rather than leaving them to chance. To accomplish this, you need to use Sound Forge's Graphic Dynamics function:

1. Select all the data in your audio file by choosing Edit > Select All (or pressing Ctrl + A on your computer keyboard).

2. Choose Effects > Dynamics > Graphic to open the Graphic Dynamics dialog box.

3. Choose the 2:1 Compression Starting At –18 dB Preset. You can experiment with the Ratio parameter if you want. A good ratio range is between 2:1 and 4:1, but it may vary with some audio material, so you have to use your own judgment. But be careful, because too much dynamic processing can sometimes add unwanted artifacts and make your audio sound dull and lifeless.

4. Click the Preview button to audition your file before making any changes. If you hear any clipping or distortion, try lowering the Output Gain parameter.

5. Click OK.

Normalize

The last step is to normalize your audio. As I talk about in Chapter 8, normalization raises the amplitude of an audio signal as high as it can go without causing clipping or distortion. This guarantees that your file uses the maximum amount of digital resolution and amplitude available. It also ensures that you use the highest possible volume when converting your file for the Internet, which helps in masking low-level noise and possible compression artifacts. To accomplish this, use Sound Forge's Normalize function:

CHAPTER 11

1. Select all the data in your audio file by choosing Edit > Select All (or pressing Ctrl + A on your computer keyboard).

2. Choose Process > Normalize to open the Normalize dialog box.

3. Choose the Maximize Peak Value Preset.

4. Click the Scan Levels button to find the highest amplitude level in your audio data.

5. Set the Normalize To parameter to anywhere between –0.50 dB and –1 dB. In this case, you don't want to normalize to 0 dB (or 100 percent) because the RealAudio, MP3, and Windows Media conversion processes don't always handle 0 dB signals very well. They can sometimes "choke" on such a high amplitude signal, so it's best to leave a small amount of dynamic room for the conversion process to work its magic.

6. Click the Preview button to audition your file before making any changes. If you hear any clipping or distortion, try lowering the Normalize To parameter.

7. Click OK.

Now, your file is ready to be converted to RealAudio, MP3, or Windows Media (see Chapter 4 for more information).

Sound Forge CD Functions

Of course, the Internet is not the only way you'll want to distribute your audio. You'll probably need to burn your audio to CD just as often, if not more. Sound Forge provides two CD functions that allow you to write and read your audio to and from CD.

Burn CD

The Burn CD function lets you burn (write) your audio files to CD one track at a time. It is a very simple function and doesn't provide any elaborate features like many other CD burning applications. Here is how the Burn CD function works:

1. Make sure that your audio file is using a 16-bit bit depth and a 44.1 kHz sampling rate. This is the standard rate for audio data on an audio CD. If your file is not using these settings, use the Dither and Resample functions as explained in Chapter 8.

2. Place a blank CD-R disc into your computer's CD-R drive.

3. Choose Tools > Burn CD to open the Burn CD dialog box (see Figure 11.12). In the dialog box, Sound Forge shows you how much space is needed on the disc for your audio data, and how much time is left available on the disc.

Figure 11.12
Use the Burn CD
function to burn an
audio file to CD

4. Click the Add Audio button. Sound Forge burns your audio to the disc.

5. If you want to burn another file to the disc, click Cancel. Open another audio file, and then follow Steps 1 through 3 again.

6. When you are finished burning all your files to the disc, click Close Disc. This permanently "seals" the disc and allows it to be played in any audio CD player.

NOTE

If you want to burn files to your disc in the future, you don't have to close it right away. Just leave the disc open and come back to it during another CD-burning session. As long as the disc is open, however, it cannot be played in a standard audio CD player. You must close the disc before it can be played in an audio CD player. When you close the disc, however, you can no longer add files to it.

Extract Audio From CD

In addition to burning audio to a CD, Sound Forge allows you to rip (read) audio from an existing audio CD. This can come in handy if you have an old disc with some of your original material that you might like to remaster, or if you have a disc full of sound effects in audio format that you want to use in a project. To rip audio from a CD, use the Extract Audio From CD function:

1. Place an audio CD into your computer's CD-ROM drive.

2. Choose File > Extract Audio From CD to open the Extract Audio From CD dialog box (see Figure 11.13).

Figure 11.13
Use the Extract Audio
From CD function to rip
audio from an existing
audio CD

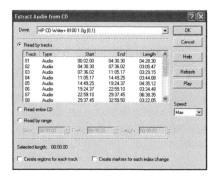

3. The Drive parameter drop-down list shows all the CD drives connected to your computer system. Choose a drive from the list.

4. If you want to extract specific tracks from the audio CD, choose the Read By Tracks option. You will see a list of tracks that are on the disc, along with their start/end times and lengths. Select the tracks (by highlighting them) in the list that you want to extract from the disc.

5. If you want to extract all the audio from the CD, choose the Read Entire CD option.

6. If you want to extract a certain time range from the CD, choose the Read By Range option. Then, set the start and end times for the range of audio you want to extract. You can adjust the length of the range by setting the Length parameter.

7. If you want Sound Forge to automatically create Regions (see Chapter 5 for more information about Regions) for each track on the disc, activate the Create Regions For Each Track option.

8. If you want Sound Forge to automatically create Markers (see Chapter 5 for more information about Markers) to indicate the beginning of each track on the disc, activate the Create Markers For Each Index Change option.

9. Set the Speed parameter to specify the speed at which you want your CD drive to read the disc. You should usually leave this set to Max.

10. Click the Play button to audition the audio you have chosen to extract from the disc.

11. Click OK.

If you choose the Read By Tracks option, Sound Forge extracts the tracks you selected and puts them each in a separate Data Window. If you choose the Read Entire CD option, Sound Forge extracts all the audio from the disc and puts it into a single Data Window. If you choose the Read By Range option, Sound Forge extracts only that specific range of audio from the disc and puts it into a single Data Window.

12

Using Sound Forge with MIDI

Although Sound Forge is a digital audio editing application, the program provides some MIDI features that can come in handy in certain situations. For example, you can synchronize your MIDI sequencing application to Sound Forge for synchronized audio and MIDI data playback while both programs are running on the same computer system. You can also set up Sound Forge to act as a digital audio playback device, which plays your audio data when triggered via MIDI notes from a keyboard or sequencer. These additional features expand Sound Forge's usefulness beyond digital audio editing. In this chapter, you'll learn to:

▶ Use the Virtual MIDI Keyboard

▶ Use the Virtual MIDI Router

▶ Sync your MIDI sequencer to Sound Forge

▶ Trigger Sound Forge from your MIDI sequencer

The Virtual MIDI Keyboard

If you don't have a real MIDI instrument, or you just need a quick way to play MIDI sounds, you can use the Virtual MIDI Keyboard. The Keyboard is a utility that lets you use your computer mouse to send MIDI Note On messages. Some convenient uses include being able to test your MIDI interface or audition the sounds on your computer sound card. You can also use it to trigger sounds on your sample-playback device after creating the sample loops in Sound Forge (I talk more about sampling in Chapter 13). The Keyboard works just like a real MIDI keyboard, except that it is a software program rather than a piece of hardware. To access the Keyboard, choose View > Keyboard or press Alt + 3 on your computer keyboard (see Figure 12.1).

Figure 12.1
Use the Virtual MIDI
Keyboard to play MIDI
sounds with your
computer mouse

Configure the Keyboard

Before you can use it, you need to adjust a number of parameters, just like on a real MIDI keyboard. These include the MIDI output port, MIDI channel, and MIDI velocity (volume) that you want the Keyboard to use when you play it.

Set the Output Port

First, you need to set the MIDI output port to specify where the Keyboard should send MIDI data. To do this, click the MIDI Out button and select a MIDI output port from the drop-down list (see Figure 12.2).

Figure 12.2
Click the MIDI Out button to set the MIDI output port

Set the MIDI Channel

You also need to specify the MIDI channel you want to use. The Keyboard only sends MIDI data to the MIDI channel that you choose. Initially, the Keyboard is set to MIDI channel 1. If you want to change the channel, click the up/down arrows next to the MIDI Channel Display (see Figure 12.3). Click the up arrow to increase the MIDI channel and click the down arrow to decrease the MIDI channel.

Figure 12.3
Change the MIDI channel using the up/down arrows next to the MIDI Channel Display

Set the Volume

The Volume parameter controls the MIDI velocity of each note that is sent from the Keyboard. Initially, the Volume parameter is set to 127 (the highest value). You probably won't need to adjust it, but if you do, simply drag the Volume parameter slider up or down (see Figure 12.4). Drag the slider up to increase the volume; drag the slider down to decrease the volume.

Figure 12.4
Change the volume using the Volume parameter slider

Turn On the Keyboard

Finally, you need to turn the Keyboard on using the On/Off button (see Figure 12.5). This parameter might seem strange, because the Keyboard is a software program, but the On/Off button is useful for disabling the Keyboard during those times when you don't want any MIDI data to be sent accidentally.

Figure 12.5
Use the On/Off button
to turn the Keyboard on
or off

Play the Keyboard

To play the Keyboard, click any of the piano keys (see Figure 12.6) with your mouse. When you click a key, the Keyboard sends a MIDI Note On message to the MIDI port and channel that you chose earlier using the volume that you set. To keep the note sounding, hold down your mouse button rather than letting it go immediately when you click.

Figure 12.6
Click the piano keys to
play the Keyboard

TIP

If you want to play a succession of notes on the Keyboard, hold down your left mouse button, and then move your mouse along the keys. The Keyboard automatically plays each note as you move your mouse and continue to hold down your mouse button.

Resize the Keyboard

If you find the keys on the Keyboard to be a bit small, you can easily make them larger. To change the size of the Keyboard, just click and drag the corners or sides of its window, just like any other window in Windows (see Figure 12.7).

Figure 12.7
Resize the Keyboard by
clicking and dragging
the sides or corners of
its window

Change the Keyboard Position

As you play the Keyboard, you'll notice that only three octaves are shown, rather than the full 88 keys as on a real piano keyboard. If you want to play some of the lower or higher octave notes, you can change the position of the keys by clicking the Octave buttons (see Figure 12.8). Click the left arrow Octave button to move the keys down an octave. Click the right arrow Octave button to move the keys up an octave. As you move the keys up or down each octave, notice the octave numbers are shown on the bottom of each C key on the piano keyboard.

Figure 12.8
Change the octave range
of the piano keys by
clicking on the Octave
buttons

Change the Sound

In addition to sending MIDI Note On messages, the Keyboard lets you send Program Change messages so that you can change the sound of the synth to which you are sending MIDI data. To do this, first make sure the Keyboard is configured to send program changes by clicking the MIDI Out button and activating the Send Program Changes option shown at the bottom of the pop-up menu (see Figure 12.9).

Figure 12.9
Activate the Send
Program Changes option
using the MIDI Out
button

To change the patch (sound) of your synth, use the Instrument drop-down list (see Figure 12.10). This list is organized to display all 127 General MIDI patch names. If your synth doesn't support General MIDI, you can simply choose a patch using the standard MIDI program change numbers (0 to 127) shown next to the names. When you choose a patch from the list, the Keyboard sends a program change message to your synth. Then, when you play the keys with your mouse, you should hear that new patch being played.

Figure 12.10
Use the Instrument
drop-down list to
change the sound of
your synth

Play Chords

Because the Keyboard can only be played with your computer mouse, normally you can play only one note at a time. The Keyboard, however, provides some special play modes that let you play chords and octaves with your mouse. To activate these special play modes, use the Note drop-down list (see Figure 12.11).

Figure 12.11
Use the Note drop-down list to use the Keyboard's special play modes

From the list, choose the type of chord you want to play. There is also an option to play octaves. After you've made your choice, click the piano keys. Now, instead of a single note being played, the Keyboard plays the type of chord you chose from the list. The chord is based upon the key that you click with your mouse. For instance, if you choose the Major option from the Note drop-down list, and then click a C key, the Keyboard plays a C major chord. Isn't that cool? Try some of the other options and have a little fun with the Keyboard before reading the next section of this chapter.

The Virtual MIDI Router

NOTE

Beginning with Sound Forge 6, Sonic Foundry is no longer updating or supporting the Virtual MIDI Router. In addition, the VMR is no longer included on the Sound Forge CD-ROM. This was done because there are now other alternatives on the market, so Sonic Foundry felt it was no longer necessary for them to continue developing this type of product.

The VMR, however, is still available for download from the Sonic Foundry Web site, so I feel that it is a good idea to include some information about it. You can download the VMR at:

http://www.sonicfoundry.com/download/step2.asp?DID=317.

Normally, when you run a MIDI program on a computer, you run that one program and nothing else. You use the program to compose your music by connecting your computer to a synthesizer via a hardware-based MIDI interface. Your MIDI program sends MIDI data to the MIDI interface, which in turn sends the data to your synth. The synth then plays the sounds that you specify. But these days, computers have become so powerful, they can easily run multiple programs at once. Some of those programs can now replace hardware-based synthesizers so that you can have both your MIDI program and MIDI synth residing inside your computer. In this case, there's no need for a hardware-based MIDI interface. Instead, you need a software-based MIDI interface. That's where the Sonic Foundry Virtual MIDI Router (VMR) comes in. The VMR acts like a software-based MIDI interface and it allows you to send MIDI data from one program to another while both programs are running on the same computer system.

Why do you need the VMR? Well, I already covered one situation: to drive a software-based synth from your MIDI sequencing application. But in regard to Sound Forge, a couple of useful scenarios come to mind. One is the ability to synchronize your MIDI sequencer to Sound Forge so that you can play an audio file in Sound Forge and play MIDI data in your MIDI sequencer simultaneously in sync with one another. Another scenario is the ability to use Sound Forge as a sample-playback device, in which you could use your MIDI sequencer to trigger the playback of audio files in Sound Forge. I explain these scenarios in more detail later. First, let me explain how to install and set up the VMR.

Install and Configure the VMR

As I mentioned earlier, the VMR is no longer included with Sound Forge. So you need to download and install the VMR manually. To do so, follow these steps:

NOTE

The following instructions cover installing the VMR within Windows 98. The VMR also runs within Windows NT and Windows XP, but the installation procedure may be slightly different. Please read the additional instructions included with the VMR download.

1. Download and save the VMR file from the Sonic Foundry Web site into a new folder on your hard drive. Then, double-click the downloaded file to extract the VMR files for installation.

2. In Windows, click the Start button and choose Settings > Control Panel to open the Windows Control Panel (see Figure 12.12).

Figure 12.12
Open the Windows Control Panel to begin the VMR installation

3. Double-click the Add New Hardware option in the Control Panel to open the Add New Hardware Wizard (see Figure 12.13).

Figure 12.13
Open the Add New Hardware Wizard

4. Click Next.

5. Click Next again to show the Devices list (see Figure 12.14).

Figure 12.14
Look at the Devices list and choose an option

6. Choose the No, The Device Isn't In The List option.

7. Click Next.

8. On the next page, the Wizard asks, "Do you want Windows to search for your new hardware?" Choose the No, I Want To Select The Hardware From A List option. Then, click Next to display the Hardware Types list (see Figure 12.15).

Figure 12.15
Choose an option from the Hardware Types list

9. Choose the Sound, Video And Game Controllers option in the Hardware Types list. Then, click Next.

10. On the next page, click the Have Disk button to open the Install From Disk dialog box (see Figure 12.16).

Figure 12.16
Use the Install From
Disk dialog box to
specify the location of
the VMR

11. In the Copy Manufacturer's Files From parameter, type the location of the new folder you created that holds the extracted VMR files. Then, click OK to open the Select Device dialog box (see Figure 12.17).

Figure 12.17
Use the Select Device
dialog box to choose the
VMR for installation

12. Choose the Sonic Foundry Virtual MIDI Router option from the Models list. Then, click OK.

13. On the last page of the Add New Hardware Wizard, click Finish.

14. Windows installs the VMR and then displays the Configure Sonic Foundry VMR dialog box (see Figure 12.18).

Figure 12.18
Use the Configure Sonic
Foundry VMR dialog
box to specify a number
of virtual MIDI ports

15. The VMR allows you to use up to four virtual MIDI ports. Specify how many virtual MIDI ports you want to use by choosing an option from the Virtual MIDI Routing Ports drop-down list. Then, click OK.

CAUTION

Windows 98 or NT may crash on startup if you have more than 11 MIDI devices installed. This can happen if you have a multiport MIDI interface or have multiple MIDI interfaces connected to your computer. If you have system errors after installing the VMR, try reducing the number of ports used by the VMR (see the following section), or remove the VMR from your system.

16. Restart Windows.

After Windows is restarted, the VMR is ready to be used.

Reconfigure the VMR

In case you ever need to change the number of virtual MIDI ports provided by the VMR, follow these steps:

1. In Windows, click the Start button and choose Settings > Control Panel to open the Windows Control Panel.

2. Double-click the Multimedia option in the Control Panel to open the Multimedia Properties dialog box (see Figure 12.19).

Figure 12.19
Use the Multimedia
Properties dialog box to
reconfigure the VMR

3. Click the Devices tab and click the plus sign next to the MIDI Devices And Instruments option. Then, choose the Sonic Foundry MIDI Router option from the list. If there is more than one, choose any one of them (see Figure 12.20).

Figure 12.20
Access the VMR under
the Devices tab

4. Click the Properties button to open the Sonic Foundry MIDI Router Properties dialog box (see Figure 12.21).

Figure 12.21
Change the VMR
settings in the Sonic
Foundry MIDI Router
Properties dialog box

5. Click the Settings button to open the Configure Sonic Foundry VMR dialog box (shown earlier).

6. Choose a new number of virtual MIDI ports using the Virtual MIDI Routing Ports drop-down list.

7. Click OK.

8. Click OK in the Sonic Foundry MIDI Router Properties dialog box.

9. Click OK in the Multimedia Properties dialog box.

10. Restart Windows.

After Windows restarts, the VMR will be configured to use the number of virtual MIDI ports that you specified.

Sync Your Sequencer to Sound Forge

Earlier, I mentioned one of the ways in which you might utilize the VMR: synchronizing your MIDI sequencing application to Sound Forge. By doing this, you can play an audio file in Sound Forge and have the MIDI data in your sequencer play along in time with the audio. And, simultaneously, both applications can be running on the same computer system. To demonstrate this scenario, I will use the SONAR MIDI sequencing application from Cakewalk Music Software, but this procedure can be done using any sequencing program that provides synchronization features. I explain synchronization in Chapter 6, so I don't cover it in detail here. Instead, I just walk you through the steps you need to accomplish this task:

1. Start SONAR (I assume you know how to use your MIDI sequencing software).

2. Open a Project file containing the MIDI data you want to sync to Sound Forge.

3. Choose Options > Project to open the Project Options dialog box, and click the Clock tab (see Figure 12.22).

Figure 12.22
Use the Project Options
dialog box to set the
synchronization options
for SONAR

4. In the Source section, choose the SMPTE/MTC option.

5. In the SMPTE/MTC Format section, choose the 30 Frame Non-Drop option.

6. Click OK.

7. Choose Options > MIDI Devices to open the MIDI Ports dialog box (see Figure 12.23).

Figure 12.23
Use the MIDI Ports
dialog box to set the
MIDI ports that SONAR
will use

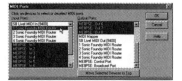

8. In the Input Ports list, select the Sonic Foundry MIDI Router option. If there is more than one, chose the option that begins with the number 1, as in "1 Sonic Foundry MIDI Router."

9. Click OK.

10. Start Sound Forge.

11. Choose Options > Preferences to open the Preferences dialog box, and click the MIDI/Sync tab (see Figure 12.24).

Figure 12.24
Use the Preferences
dialog box to set the
synchronization options
for Sound Forge

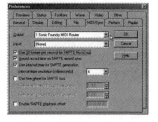

12. In the Output parameter drop-down list, choose the Sonic Foundry MIDI Router option. If there is more than one, chose the option that begins with the number 1, as in "1 Sonic Foundry MIDI Router."

13. Click OK.

14. To change the Time Ruler measurements in the Data Window, choose Options > Status Format > SMPTE 30 (30 fps, Audio).

15. Turn synchronization output on by choosing Options > MIDI In/Out > Generate MIDI Timecode (or press F7 on your computer keyboard).

16. Switch to SONAR, and start playback. When you activate playback, SONAR won't respond right away. Instead, it displays a message saying "Waiting for 30 Frame (Non-Drop)."

17. Switch to Sound Forge and start playback of the audio file. Sound Forge then sends sync code to SONAR through the VMR, and both Sound Forge and SONAR play their data in sync with one another.

18. To stop playback, don't use the commands in SONAR; instead, stop playback from within Sound Forge. Or, wait until the end of the audio file and both programs stop playing automatically.

You can use this procedure in many situations. For example, you may be editing a vocal part in Sound Forge, but you want to hear how it sounds along with the music you've composed in your MIDI sequencer while you are editing. Experiment with it and I'm sure you'll find some good uses for the information.

Trigger Sound Forge From Your MIDI Sequencer

Another creative use for the VMR is to trigger the playback of audio data within Sound Forge from your MIDI sequencer. This scenario uses the VMR to link your sequencer and Sound Forge together, but not via synchronization. This time, Regions and MIDI Triggers are utilized. As in the previous example, I will use the SONAR MIDI sequencing application from Cakewalk Music Software, but this procedure can be done using any sequencing program.

Build a Sound File

The first thing you need to do is use Sound Forge to create an audio file containing all the sounds that you want to trigger via your MIDI sequencer. This file can contain anything from instruments sounds or sound effects, to vocal phrases or any other kind of short audio recordings. To build a file, follow these steps:

1. Start Sound Forge and choose File > New (or press Ctrl + N on your computer keyboard) to create a new audio file. Be sure to choose the same format settings (bit depth, sample rate, and number of channels) as the audio data you will be adding to the file.

2. Open the audio file you want to add to your new audio file.

TIP

If you have some audio snippets on a CD, you can use the File > Extract Audio From CD function to rip the audio from the CD into Sound Forge. In addition, you can use the Simple Synthesis and FM Synthesis functions to create your own sound effects for use in your new audio file.

3. Select the data from the opened audio file and paste it into the new audio file.

TIP

When selecting data from the opened audio file, be sure there isn't any silence at the beginning or end of the selection. This ensures that the audio data will play as soon as you trigger it via MIDI.

4. Select the data you just pasted in the new audio file.

5. Choose Special > Regions List > Insert (or press R on your computer keyboard) to open the Insert Marker/Region dialog box (see Figure 12.25).

Figure 12.25
Use the Insert
Marker/Region dialog
box to create a Region
for the data in your new
audio file

6. All of the parameters (except the Trigger) in the dialog box are set for you automatically because you selected the data beforehand. But, if you want to change the name of the Region for identification purposes, type a new name into the Name parameter.

7. Assign a MIDI Trigger to the Region by first choosing MIDI: Note On – Play option in the Trigger drop-down list. Then, choose a channel and note to use for this Region. Later, you will need to use the same MIDI channel and note to trigger playback of this Region.

8. Click OK.

9. Choose Special > Transport > Go To End (or press Ctrl + End on your computer keyboard) to move the Current Position cursor to the end of the new audio file. You will paste your next piece of audio here.

10. Close the other opened audio file.

11. Go through Steps 2 to 10 for each new piece of audio you want to add to your new audio file. When assigning the MIDI channel and note for the MIDI Trigger for each Region, you probably want to use the same channel for each Region, but be sure to use a different MIDI note.

12. Save your new audio file as a WAV file and be sure to activate the Save Metadata With File option in the Save As dialog box.

Now, you're ready to start triggering sounds in Sound Forge via MIDI through the VMR.

Trigger Your Sounds

After you have created a sound file complete with Regions that have MIDI Triggers assigned to them, you can set up Sound Forge and your MIDI sequencer (in this case, SONAR) to start triggering the sounds. Here's how:

1. Start SONAR (I assume you know how to use your MIDI sequencing software).

2. Create a new project or open an existing one, and create a new MIDI track containing the notes to trigger the Regions in the Sound Forge audio file. Be sure to use the same MIDI notes that you assigned to the Regions in your audio file. Also, assign the same MIDI channel to this track that you assigned to the Regions in your audio file.

3. Choose Options > MIDI Devices to open the MIDI Ports dialog box.

4. In the Output Ports list, select the Sonic Foundry MIDI Router option. If there is more than one, chose the option that begins with the number 1, as in "1 Sonic Foundry MIDI Router."

5. Click OK.

6. Start Sound Forge.

7. Open the audio file containing the sounds to be triggered.

8. Choose Options > Preferences to open the Preferences dialog box, and click the MIDI/Sync tab.

9. In the Input parameter drop-down list, choose the Sonic Foundry MIDI Router option. If there is more than one, chose the option that begins with the number 1, as in "1 Sonic Foundry MIDI Router."

10. Click OK.

11. Choose Options > MIDI In/Out > Trigger From MIDI/MTC (or press Ctrl + F7 on your computer keyboard) to activate MIDI Triggers in Sound Forge.

12. Switch to SONAR and start the playback of your project.

SONAR will now send MIDI note data on the MIDI channel you chose through the VMR into Sound Forge and trigger the Regions in the opened audio file.

TIP

You can also use the Virtual MIDI Keyboard to trigger Regions. Just assign the output of the Keyboard to the VMR port you are using in Sound Forge. In the previous example, it would be "1 Sonic Foundry MIDI Router." When you click the appropriate keys corresponding to the MIDI Trigger notes of the Regions in your audio file, the Regions are played.

13

Sound Forge and Sampling

Congratulations! You've made it to the final chapter of the book. You've learned how to record, edit, process, and even share your audio files with the rest of the world. But there is still one area of Sound Forge that I haven't told you about: the unique functions and tools provided by the program that allow you to create your own samples. So, in this chapter, you'll learn to:

▶ Define samples

▶ Create and edit samples

▶ Use the Loop Tuner

▶ Save and transmit samples

What are Samples?

As you've seen with the Simple Synthesis and FM Synthesis functions (which I talk about in Chapter 10), creating sounds via basic synthesis methods involves using basic audio waveforms. These methods don't allow you to create very realistic sounds, though. Because of this, many modern MIDI instruments and sound cards use sample-playback to produce sounds. Sample-playback can produce some very realistic sounds. The reason for this realism lies in the fact that a sample-playback device plays samples, which are actually audio recordings of real-life instruments and sounds. When the sample-playback device receives a MIDI Note On message, instead of creating a sound electronically from scratch, it plays a digital sample, which can be anything from the sound of a piano note to the sound of a coyote howling.

What makes samples different from regular audio recordings is that they are usually short in length (though not always), and they are usually looped (played over and over again). In addition, there are actually three kinds of samples: One-Shot samples (which are usually used for sound effects or single percussion sounds because they are only played once from beginning to end, rather than being looped), Loop samples (also called sample loops, which are used to replicate entire instrumental performances, such as a four-bar drum kit performance), and Sustaining samples (which are usually used to replicate real acoustic instrument sounds meant to be performed using MIDI Note messages).

Create and Edit Samples

Samples can be used in many different ways, and Sound Forge gives you the tools to create and manipulate your own samples. To show you how to utilize these tools, I walk you through a number of examples that explain how to create/edit all of the different types of samples mentioned earlier.

One-Shot Samples

The One-Shot is the easiest type of sample to create, basically because it is just an audio recording with a few sample-specific parameters. There isn't any looping involved. To create a One-Shot sample, follow this example:

1. Choose File > New (or press Ctrl + N on your computer keyboard) to open the New Window dialog box. For this example, set the Sample Rate, Bit Depth, and Channels parameters to 44,100 Hz, 16-bit, and Mono, respectively. Then, click OK to create a new audio file.

2. Choose Tools > Synthesis > FM to open the FM Synthesis dialog box. Choose the Another One preset, and click OK (see Figure 13.1). For this example, we are using the FM Synthesis function to provide the audio data for our sample, but you can use anything you want: percussion instrument sound, vocal phrase, sound effect; anything that is only played once rather than looped when triggered.

Figure 13.1
Use the FM Synthesis function to create a sound effect One-Shot sample

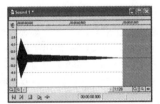

3. Choose Edit > Select All (or press Ctrl + A on your computer keyboard) to select all the data in your audio file.

4. Choose Special > Insert Sample Loop (or press L on your computer keyboard) to open the Edit Sample dialog box (see Figure 13.2).

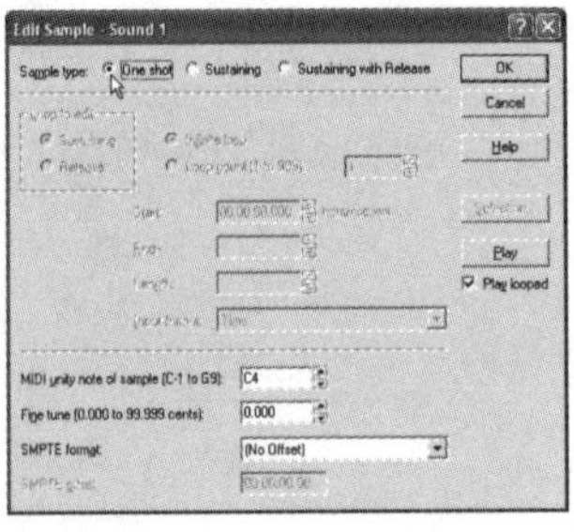

Figure 13.2
Use the Edit Sample dialog box to turn your audio file into a sample

5. To create a One-Shot sample, choose the One-Shot option for the Sample Type parameter.

6. Enter a musical note value for the MIDI Unity Note Of Sample parameter. This MIDI unity note is the original pitch at which your sample was recorded. This means that if you play the sample via your sample-playback device using the MIDI unity note, the sample sounds the same as it does now inside of Sound Forge. But if you use a different note, the pitch of the sample is changed, making it sound higher or lower depending on if you use notes that are higher or lower than the MIDI unity note. For One-Shot samples, you can set the MIDI unity note to anything you want.

7. Enter a value for the Fine Tune parameter. You don't really need to use this parameter. It is just an informational parameter telling your sample-playback device to adjust the pitch of your sample during playback. If you need your sample to be fine-tuned, however, you have the option.

8. Enter a value for the SMPTE Format and SMPTE Offset parameters. Again, these parameters are not really needed. You can leave these alone most of the time. But some sample-playback devices allow you to set an SMPTE offset for SMPTE synchronization purposes; so again, if you need it, you have the option available.

9. Click OK.

That's all there is to creating a One-Shot sample. From here, you either save the file for use in sample-playback software or transfer the file electronically to your external sample-playback device. I talk more about these topics later.

Loop Samples

Loop samples (or sample loops) are the second-easiest type of samples to create. They are also the most popular type of samples in use today because of the prevalence of sample-playback software, such as Sonic Foundry's ACID. Sample-playback applications allow you to create entire musical performances by piecing together sample loops, with nothing else needed. You can even buy sample loops on CD, which have been recorded in a professional studio. A number of companies sell these types of discs. Just open a current issue of Electronic Musician magazine or Keyboard magazine, and you'll find tons of ads for sample loop discs. Of course, buying sample loops isn't as much fun as creating your own. To create a Loop sample, follow this example:

1. Choose File > New (or press Ctrl + N on your computer keyboard) to open the New Window dialog box. For this example, set the Sample Rate, Bit Depth, and Channels parameters to 44,100 Hz, 16-bit, and Mono, respectively. Then, click OK to create a new audio file.

2. Choose Tools > Synthesis > FM to open the FM Synthesis dialog box. Choose the Something Else preset, and click OK (see Figure 13.3). For this example, we are using the FM Synthesis function to provide the audio data for our sample, but you can use anything you want: drum kit performance, guitar riff, keyboard riff; anything that can be used to loop over and over when triggered.

Figure 13.3
Use the FM Synthesis
function to create the
data for a Loop sample

3. Choose Edit > Select All (or press Ctrl + A on your computer keyboard) to select
    all the data in your audio file.

4. Choose Special > Insert Sample Loop (or press L on your computer keyboard) to
    open the Edit Sample dialog box (see Figure 13.4).

Figure 13.4
Use the Edit Sample
dialog box to turn your
audio file into a Loop
sample

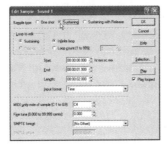

5. To create a Loop sample, choose the Sustaining option for the Sample Type
    parameter.

6. If you want the sample to loop forever (which is usually the case), choose the
    Infinite Loop option. If you only want the sample to loop a specified number of
    times, choose the Loop Count option and enter a number for the amount of loops
    to be performed. This option may or may not work with your sample-playback
    device. Most often, looping is controlled via MIDI. However long the MIDI
    trigger note for the sample is held is how long the sample loops.

7. You can adjust the loop start and end points within the sample by choosing an
    option for the Input Format and then adjusting the Start, End, and Length
    parameters. Because you made a selection of data beforehand, you shouldn't
    need to touch these parameters.

8. Enter a musical note value for the MIDI Unity Note Of Sample parameter.

9. Enter a value for the Fine Tune parameter, if needed.

10. Enter a value for the SMPTE Format and SMPTE Offset parameters, if needed.

11. Click OK. Your audio file now has loop points inserted at the beginning and end
    of the file (see Figure 13.5). These points tell your sample-playback device how
    to loop the sample. In this case, the sample is played and then loops from the
    end back to the beginning, and so on.

Figure 13.5
Start and end loop
points are inserted into
your audio file, turning
it into a sample loop

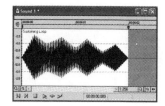

Sustaining Samples

Similar to Loop samples, Sustaining samples can also be looped infinitely, but instead of the entire sample being looped, only a portion of the sample is looped. Creating this loop within the sample is what makes Sustaining samples the most difficult to create. Not to worry, though. The procedure isn't really that difficult. It sometimes just takes a lot of trial and error. To create a Sustaining sample, follow this example:

1. Choose File > New (or press Ctrl + N on your computer keyboard) to open the New Window dialog box. For this example, set the Sample Rate, Bit Depth, and Channels parameters to 44,100 Hz, 16-bit, and Mono, respectively. Then, click OK to create a new audio file.

2. Choose Tools > Synthesis > FM to open the FM Synthesis dialog box. Choose the FM Horn preset, set the Configuration parameter so that only one Operator is used (move the slider all the way to the left), and click OK (see Figure 13.6). For this example, we are using the FM Synthesis function to provide the audio data for our sample, but you can use anything you want: the note played on a piano, guitar, synth pad; anything that can be used to replicate the sound of a playable instrument that can be sustained.

Figure 13.6
Use the FM Synthesis
function to create the
data for a Sustaining
sample

3. This time, instead of selecting all the data in the file, you want to select only a section of data that will be used as the sustaining loop. This is the part of the sample that will be looped over and over again as you hold a note on your MIDI keyboard. Because of this, you want to find a part of the file that doesn't change, so that the loop sounds seamless. It takes a little trial and error, but if you listen to the file, you should be able to pick out a good section to select. For this example, just click and drag your mouse to make a selection that looks similar to the one shown in Figure 13.7.

Figure 13.7
Click and drag your
mouse to make a quick
data selection

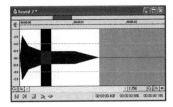

4. Press Q on your computer keyboard to activate looped playback, and then press
    the space bar on your computer keyboard to hear how your data selection will
    sound when looped. Press the space bar again to stop playback. The data
    selection sounds good, but not quite perfect, right? We'll fix that in a minute.

5. Choose Special > Insert Sample Loop (or press L on your computer keyboard) to
    open the Edit Sample dialog box (see Figure 13.8).

Figure 13.8
Use the Edit Sample
dialog box to turn
your data selection
into a loop

6. For the Sample Type parameter, choose the Sustaining option.

7. Choose the Infinite Loop option. Because we previously made a data selection,
    the Start, End, and Length parameters are already set.

8. Enter a musical note value for the MIDI Unity Note Of Sample parameter.

9. Enter a value for the Fine Tune parameter, if needed.

10. Enter a value for the SMPTE Format and SMPTE Offset parameters, if needed.

11. Click OK. There are now loop points at the beginning and end of your data
    selection (see Figure 13.9).

Figure 13.9
Close the Edit Sample
dialog box to create loop
points around your data
selection

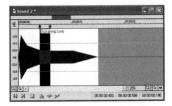

If you created a perfect data selection, you wouldn't need to take any more steps to create a Sustaining sample. Most of the time, however, you won't get the loop settings right on the first try. When listening to the data selection in the previous example, you probably noticed a "clicking" or "thumping" sound every time the data was looped. This is because the data selection wasn't fine-tuned. Sound Forge provides a special tool for fine-tuning samples called the Loop Tuner.

The Loop Tuner

When you create a loop, you want to make it sound as seamless as possible—you want the audio waveform at the end of the loop to line up just about perfectly with the beginning of the loop so that you can't actually hear that the data is being looped. Doing this via simple data selection is nearly impossible, but the Loop Tuner makes the process much easier. To use the Loop Tuner to fix the sample from the previous example, do the following:

1. Assuming you have the sample from the previous example already open, choose View > Loop Tuner (or press Ctrl + L on your computer keyboard) to open the Loop Tuner (see Figure 13.10). You'll notice a new section open beneath the audio in the Data Window. This is the Loop Tuner, which is actually a part of the Data Window. This means that you can have a separate Loop Tuner open for each Data Window that you have open.

Figure 13.10
The Loop Tuner is actually a part of the Data Window

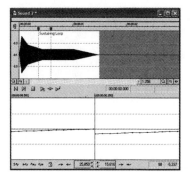

2. Take a look at the Loop Tuner. Like the Data Window, it also displays the waveform of your audio, but in a special way. The vertical line in the center of the Loop Tuner marks the point at which the end (left side of the vertical line) and beginning (right side of the vertical line) loop points meet when the data is looped. At this point, the audio waveform should be at a zero crossing to avoid "clicks" when looping. In this example, you can see that both loop points are not at the zero axis, which is why you can hear "clicking" when the data is looped (see Figure 13.11).

Figure 13.11
If the audio waveform
isn't smoothly
connected, "clicking"
can occur

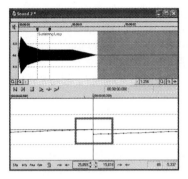

3. To fix this, you need to adjust the end and beginning loop points. To adjust the points with precision, the Loop Tuner provides controls at the bottom of its window that let you move the end loop point left or right to the next zero crossing in the audio waveform. You can also move the end loop point one point at a time along the audio waveform with the Tune Position controls. The start loop point can be manipulated in this manner as well (see Figure 13.12). For this example, move the end loop point so that it is at the position 31,271, and move the start loop position so that it is at the position 18,242.

Figure 13.12
Use the Tune Position
controls to fine-tune
the start and end
loop points

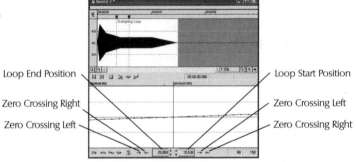

Loop End Position

Zero Crossing Right

Zero Crossing Left

Loop Start Position

Zero Crossing Left

Zero Crossing Right

4. Use the playback controls at the bottom of the Loop Tuner window to test your new settings. Click the Play Pre-Loop button to play the section of the sample before the loop. Click the Play Post-Loop button to play the section of the sample after the loop. Click the Play Loop button to play the loop section of the sample. Click the Play Loop button again to stop playback (see Figure 13.13).

Figure 13.13
Use the playback
controls to test your
adjusted loop points

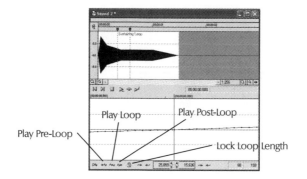

Play Pre-Loop

Play Loop

Play Post-Loop

Lock Loop Length

5. The loop should now sound seamless. To lock the loop points in place, click the Lock Loop Length button.

Now, you have a Sustaining sample with a great sounding loop.

Sustaining with Release Samples

Earlier, I mentioned that there are three different types of samples. Although that's true, there is also a special type of Sustaining sample. This sample allows you to set up two different loops inside of it: a sustaining loop and a release loop. The procedure for creating this type of loop is basically the same as a standard Sustaining sample, but with a few extra steps:

1. Open an existing audio file or create a new one.

2. Select the section of data that you want to loop within the file.

3. Choose Special > Insert Sample Loop (or press L on your computer keyboard) to open the Edit Sample dialog box (see Figure 13.14).

Figure 13.14
Use the Edit Sample
dialog box to create a
special Sustaining With
Release sample

4. For the Sample Type parameter, choose the Sustaining With Release option.

5. For the Loop To Edit parameter, choose the Sustaining option.

6. Choose the Loop Count option and enter the number of times you want the first selection to loop.

7. Set the MIDI Unity Note Of Sample, Fine Tune, and SMPTE Format/Offset parameters accordingly.

8. Click OK.

9. Select another section of data that occurs in the audio file after the first selection (see Figure 13.15).

Figure 13.15
Make another data selection to define the second loop

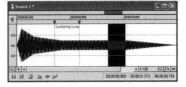

10. Choose Special > Edit Sample to open the Edit Sample dialog box.

11. For the Loop To Edit parameter, choose the Release option.

12. Choose the Loop Count option and enter the number of times you want the second selection to loop.

13. Click the Selection button to open the Set Selection dialog box. Then, choose the Current Selection preset, and click OK.

14. Click OK in the Edit Sample dialog box.

Now, you have a sample containing two loops. When the sample is played, the data before the first loop plays. Then, the first loop repeats itself the number of times you specified. After that, the data between the first and second loops plays, then the second loop repeats itself the number of times you specified. And finally, the last part of the sample plays.

Save and Transmit Samples

When you're finished creating and editing your sample, you should save it. Be sure to activate the Save Metadata With File option in the Save As dialog box. If you don't do this, your loop points will be lost.

Send Your Sample

In addition, if you have an external sample-playback device, you can send your new sample to the device for playback using Sound Forge's Sampler function. To send your sample to the device, follow these steps:

1. Make sure your sample audio file is open, then choose Tools > Sampler to open the Sampler dialog box (see Figure 13.16).

Figure 13.16
Use the Sampler function to send your sample to an external sample-playback device

2. Set the Logical Send/Receive Sample Number parameter. This is the number your sample-playback device uses as its location reference for samples. Refer to the documentation that came with your device for more information.

3. Click the Configure button to open the Sampler Configuration dialog box (see Figure 13.17).

Figure 13.17
Use the Sampler Configuration dialog box to tell Sound Forge the type of sample-playback device you are using

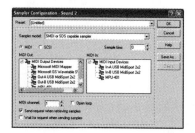

4. Choose an option from the Sampler Model drop-down list. If your device is shown in the list, choose it and skip to Step 13. Otherwise, choose the SMDI Or SDS Capable Sampler option from the list.

5. If your device is connected to your computer via MIDI, choose the MIDI option. Otherwise, skip to Step 11.

6. In the MIDI Out list, choose the MIDI output port to which your device is connected.

7. In the MIDI In list, choose the MIDI input port to which your device is connected.

8. Set the MIDI Channel parameter to the channel at which your device is set.

9. Activate the Open Loop option if your device does not use "handshaking." Refer to the documentation that came with your device for more information.

10. If your device sends a request before samples can be sent to it, activate the Wait For Request When Sending Samples option. Refer to the documentation that came with your device for more information.

11. If your device is connected to your computer via SCSI, choose the SCSI option.

12. Choose the SCSI connection to which your device is connected in the Sampler list.

13. Click OK.

14. Click Send Sample.

15. Click Close.

CHAPTER 13

Retrieve a Sample

In addition to sending samples to an external device, you can also retrieve samples from an external device. The procedure is pretty much the same as when sending a sample, except for a couple things. If you choose the MIDI option in the Sampler Configuration dialog box, and your device needs to receive a request when you want to retrieve a sample from it, be sure to activate the Send Request When Retrieving Samples option. And in the Sampler dialog box, click Get Sample rather than Send Sample. After the sample is retrieved, it overwrites any data in the currently active Data Window.

TIP

For more information about creating samples, and how to create samples specifically for Sonic Foundry's ACID software, read Appendix A.

Appendix A
Using Sound Forge with ACID

Back in Chapter 13, I explained how you can create and edit your own sample loops, as well as transfer them to an external hardware sampling device. I also mentioned how sample loops can be used within software applications for the purposes of composing music. One such software application is Sonic Foundry's ACID. ACID is a loop-based composing tool that allows you to arrange individual sample loops into complete compositions. What is so special about ACID is that it automatically takes care of the sometimes tedious chore of matching the playback tempo and pitch of each loop you use in a song.

Although ACID is perfectly capable of working with any sample loops in the WAV file format (see Chapter 4 for more information about WAV files), the program provides better results if you prepare your loops beforehand using a special process. Preparing a sample loop for use with ACID involves adding extra information to the audio file that lets ACID know the basic tempo, pitch, and playback properties of the file. ACID can then more accurately shift the tempo and pitch of the loop.

If you already own ACID, you can easily prepare your files from within the program itself. Just in case, however, Sound Forge provides a number of special tools so that you can prepare your files even if you don't have the ACID application on hand. Plus, it can be more convenient to prepare your files within Sound Forge if you are creating a lot of original loops.

ACID Looping Tools

The first set of special tools that Sound Forge provides is called the ACID Looping tools, although this is a bit of a misnomer, because these tools really don't have anything to do with preparing your files for ACID. These tools can be used for creating any kind of sample loops, not just loops for ACID. The tools are especially useful when working with loops that contain many beat or measure divisions.

The Halve Selection Tool

The Halve Selection tool allows you to reduce your current data selection to half its size. This means that if you have two seconds of audio data selected (see Figure A.1), using the Halve Selection tool, you can reduce the selection to one second of audio data (see Figure A.2).

Figure A.1
Shown here is two seconds of selected audio data before the Halve Selection tool has been used

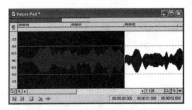

Figure A.2
Shown here is one second of selected audio data after the Halve Selection tool was used on the example from Figure A.1

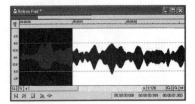

This procedure doesn't do anything to the audio data itself; it simply changes the amount of data that is currently selected. This tool can be very useful, for example, if you have a two-measure bass riff selected but you want to quickly and easily apply an effect to only one measure of the data. To use the Halve Selection tool, simply choose Special > ACID Looping Tools > Halve Selection (or press ; on your computer keyboard). If you don't have any data currently selected, activating the tool doesn't do anything.

The Double Selection Tool

The Double Selection tool is the exact opposite of the Halve Selection tool. Instead of reducing the current selection to half its size, it doubles the current selection. This means that if you have two seconds of audio data selected (see Figure A.3), by using the Double Selection tool, you can increase the selection to four seconds of audio data (see Figure A.4).

Figure A.3
Shown here is two seconds of selected audio data before the Double Selection tool has been used

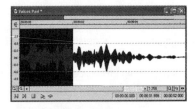

Figure A.4
Shown here is four seconds of selected audio data after the Double Selection tool was used on the example from Figure A.3

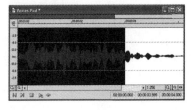

Again, this procedure doesn't do anything to the audio data itself; it simply changes the amount of data that is currently selected. This tool can be very useful, for example, if you have one beat of a percussion riff selected, but you need to quickly and easily select and cut out two of the beats from the loop. To use the Double Selection tool, simply choose Special > ACID Looping Tools > Double Selection (or press ' on your computer keyboard). If you don't have any data currently selected, activating the tool doesn't do anything.

Shift Selection Left and Right

Instead of reducing or increasing the amount of currently selected data, the Shift Selection Left and Shift Selection Right tools simply move the current selection to the left or right within the file by the same amount of the current selection. In other words, if you have a sample that is three measures long and you have selected the second measure in the loop (see Figure A.5), choosing the Shift Selection Left Tool deselects the second measure and selects the first measure (see Figure A.6), because the selection is moved one measure to the left. If you choose the Shift Selection Right Tool, again, the second measure is deselected, but this time the third measure is selected because the selection is moved one measure to the right (see Figure A.7). To use the Shift Selection Left or Shift Selection Right tools, simply choose Special > ACID Looping Tools > Shift Selection Left (or press < on your computer keyboard) or Special > ACID Looping Tools > Shift Selection Right (or press > on your computer keyboard), respectively.

Figure A.5
Shown here is a three-measure sample loop with the second measure selected

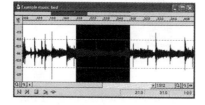

Figure A.6
Shown here is the same three-measure sample loop with the first measure selected after the Shift Selection Left Tool is applied

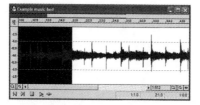

Figure A.7
Shown here is the same three-measure sample loop with the third measure selected after the Shift Selection Right Tool is applied

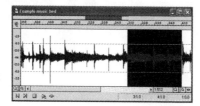

Rotate Audio

The last of the ACID Looping tools is called the Rotate Audio tool. Unlike the previously mentioned tools, this tool actually alters the audio data in your file. The Rotate Audio tool "rotates" audio data from one end of your file to the other, depending on your current data selection. For example, suppose you have a small portion of the beginning of your audio file selected (see Figure A.8).

Figure A.8
Shown here is a small data selection at the beginning of an audio file

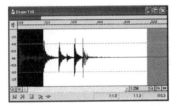

If you choose Special > ACID Looping Tools > Rotate Audio (or press : on your computer keyboard), the currently selected data is cut and then pasted to the end of the file (see Figure A.9).

Figure A.9
Shown here is the same small data selection moved to the end of the audio file after the Rotate Audio Tool has been chosen

Now, if you had initially selected a portion of data at the end of the file, the Rotate Audio tool would instead cut and paste that data from the end of the file to the beginning of the file. See how it works? This tool is very useful if you want to quickly and easily move the first or last beat or measure of a loop to the opposite end, or vice versa.

NOTE
There are also two exceptions to using the Rotate Audio tool. One is that if you don't have any data selected, the first quarter of the file is cut from the beginning and then pasted on to the end. The other exception is that if you have some data selected in the middle of the file, the Rotate Audio tool simply does nothing.

Editing ACID Loop Properties

As I mentioned earlier, to prepare your sample loop for use within ACID, you need to use a special process. This process involves adding extra information to the audio file. To do this, you must use the Edit ACID Properties dialog box (see Figure A.10) by choosing Special > Edit ACID Properties.

Figure A.10
The Edit ACID Properties dialog box allows you to ACIDize your sample loops

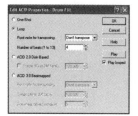

In the dialog box, you'll notice a number of different options and parameters. By choosing the appropriate settings, ACID can determine the correct way to handle your sample loop when your loop is loaded into an ACID project.

One-Shot

The first available option in the Edit ACID Properties dialog box is called One-Shot. If your sample loop is meant to be played once rather than looping over and over again, this is the option you want to choose. A One-Shot sample does not get time-stretched along with the tempo changes of an ACID project, and the sample's pitch does not change along with key changes in an ACID project. A good example of a One-Shot sample is a drum set cymbal crash.

Loop

The second available option in the Edit ACID Properties dialog box is called Loop. This is the option you want if your sample loop is meant to be played over and over again, such as a looping bass guitar riff. Sample loops that are designated as loops in ACID are time-stretched and have their pitch changed along with the tempo and key changes of an ACID project. In order for ACID to change the loop appropriately, it needs to know the initial tempo and pitch of the loop.

Number Of Beats

To specify the tempo of your loop, you simply enter the number of musical beats the loop contains into the Number Of Beats parameter. You can figure out how many beats are in your loop by counting off while you listen to it play. I'll give you an example later on in this appendix. One thing to note is that if you enter the wrong number of beats, ACID does not play your loop at the proper speed. For instance, if your loop contains 16 beats but you enter 8 for the Number Of Beats, ACID plays your loop back twice as fast as the loop should be played.

Root Note For Transposing

To specify the pitch of your loop, you simply enter a note value into the Root Note For Transposing parameter. This root note is the original pitch at which your sample loop was recorded. You need to know this beforehand, or you'll have to figure it out manually using a tuner.

TIP

By using the Spectrum Analysis feature (described in Chapter 10), you can sometimes find the root note of a sample loop. Just select all the data in your loop, and choose Tools > Spectrum Analysis to analyze the data. At the bottom of the Spectrum Analysis window, Sound Forge shows the most prominent frequency (pitch) within the data. More often than not, that is the root note.

One other thing to consider is that if you want your sample loop to be time-stretched but not transposed (such as would probably be the case with most percussion-based loops), you can choose the Don't Transpose option for the Root Note For Transposing parameter.

ACID 2.0 Disk-Based

Most of the sample loops that are used in an ACID project are played from your computer's memory, but if you have some really long samples (such as an entire vocal track), you might not have enough memory in your computer to use those samples. In this case, you can specify that ACID play your sample by reading it directly off of your hard disk drive. To do that, you simply select the ACID 2.0 Disk-Based option in the Edit ACID Properties dialog box. Disk-based samples cannot have their pitch transposed, but if you specify a tempo, you can make it so ACID time-stretches the samples. To do so, just type in a tempo (in beats per minute) for the sample into the Tempo parameter. You need to know the tempo at which the sample was originally recorded.

ACID 3.0 Beatmapped

If you are using ACID 3.0, then you have an additional option at your disposal. The ACID 3.0 Beatmapped option is similar to the ACID 2.0 Disk-Based option, meaning it is used mainly with really long samples. The difference is that in addition to time-stretching, you can have ACID 3.0 Beatmapped samples transposed according to the ACID project pitch. Simply set the Root Note For Transposing option (as explained earlier for the Loop option). And of course, set the Tempo option for time-stretching. One additional option lets you specify where the downbeat (or first beat in the first measure) for the sample occurs. Most often, you'll probably leave this set to zero.

Preparing an ACID File – A Step-by-Step Example

Now that you know about all of the special ACID tools that Sound Forge provides, let's go through a step-by-step example on how to actually use them to prepare a file.

1. Choose File > Open (or press Ctrl + O on your computer keyboard) to display the Open dialog box. Select your file. For this example, let's use one of the files that is included with Sound Forge. Select the file called FILL.PCA. Click Open.

2. Press the space bar on your computer keyboard to play the file. It's a drum fill sample loop. Because it's not a single instrument sample that might just play once, we can rule out it being a One-Shot sample. And because it's easily small enough to be played from within your computer's memory, we can rule out it being an ACID 2.0 Disk-Based or ACID 3.0 Beatmapped sample. That means we'll be designating this file as a Loop for ACID. Before we edit the ACID properties for the loop, we need to figure out how many beats it contains. Play the file a few more times and see if you can count out the beats.

3. Select Special > Edit ACID Properties to open the Edit ACID Properties dialog box.

4. Choose the Loop option.

5. For the Number Of Beats parameter, type in 4. Did you guess it correctly?

6. Because this is a percussion loop, there's really no pitch involved and we don't want ACID to transpose the loop by mistake. So, for the Root Note For Transposing parameter, select Don't Transpose.

7. Click OK.

8. Save your file in the WAV file format.

CAUTION

When you save your newly ACID-compatible file, be sure to activate the Save Metadata With File option in the Save As dialog box. If you don't do this, the special ACID information that you entered in the Edit ACID Properties dialog box is not saved along with the file.

Appendix B
Batch Processing Your Files

After using Sound Forge on a regular basis, you'll more than likely build up a large collection of audio files including sound effects, sample loops, and more. What happens when you come upon a particular project that requires you to process a number of files using identical procedures? For example, you may want to remove the DC offset, add effects, or convert the format of a large group of files. Normally, you have to do this all manually, one file at a time. However, Sound Forge provides an extremely useful utility called the Batch Converter, which can handle these types of chores with ease.

The Batch Converter comes as a separate program on the Sound Forge CD and you need to install it manually. It is not automatically installed with Sound Forge. To install the Batch Converter, just put the Sound Forge CD into your CD-ROM drive, wait for the Setup screen, click Install Batch Converter 5.0, and follow the instructions. After the Batch Converter is installed, you can access it in Windows by clicking Start > All Programs > Sonic Foundry > Batch Converter 5.0 > Batch Converter 5.0.

Because this is an appendix and not an entire chapter, I'm not going to go into every single detail of the Batch Converter application. However, I do walk you through a step-by-step example to show you how it can be used to process your own files. Back in Chapter 11, I talked about preparing audio files for the Internet. For this example, I walk you through how to set up a Batch Converter script that processes your files and converts them to the Ogg Vorbis format, making them ready to be posted on the Internet.

Create a Batch Converter Script

Upon launching the Batch Converter, you will see the script interface, which is accessed by clicking the Script tab at the bottom of the screen (see Figure B.1). You use this interface to set up how your files will be processed by the Batch Converter. First, you need to start a new script and assign the effects you want to apply to the files in the Audio Processing section.

Figure B.1
Use the script interface
to define a processing
procedure that will be
applied to your files by
the Batch Converter

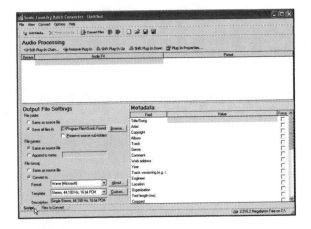

Audio Processing

To start a new script and set up the effects in the Audio Processing section for this example, do
the following:

1. Choose File > New Script (or press Ctrl + N on your computer keyboard) to start
    a new script.

2. In the Audio Processing section, click the Edit Plug-In Chain button to open the
    Plug-In Chooser dialog box (see Figure B.2). This window displays all the
    DirectX effects and Sound Forge effects that are installed on your computer.

Figure B.2
Use the Plug-In Chooser
dialog box to add effects
to the Audio Processing
section of your script

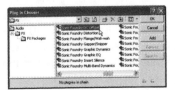

3. Select the Sonic Foundry DC Offset effect and click OK. The effect is then added
    to the Audio Processing section of the script. If you ever want to remove an
    effect from the Audio Processing section, just select the effect and click the
    Remove Plug-In button.

4. Select the Sonic Foundry DC Offset effect and click the Plug-In Properties button
    to open the Properties dialog box (see Figure B.3). This box allows you to edit
    the settings for the selected effect.

Figure B.3
Use the Properties
dialog box to edit the
effect settings

5. Choose the Automatically Detect and Remove option and click OK.

6. Click the Edit Plug-In Chain button and add the Sonic Foundry Paragraphic EQ effect to the Audio Processing section. This time instead of clicking OK in the Plug-In Chooser dialog box, select the effect and click the Add button. This allows you to add a number of effects at once without having to close the Plug-In Chooser dialog box.

7. Select the Sonic Foundry Normalize effect and click Add.

8. Select the Sonic Foundry Graphic Dynamics effect and click Add. Then click OK to close the dialog box. You should now have four effects listed in the Audio Processing section of the script (see Figure B.4).

Figure B.4
All effects added
to the Audio Processing
section are shown
as a list

9. We need to change the order of the last two effects because the effects are applied in the same order they are listed, and we want the files to be normalized last. To change the order of the effects, use the Shift Plug-In Up and Shift Plug-In Down buttons. For this example, select the Sonic Foundry Normalize effect and click the Shift Plug-In Down button.

10. Select the Sonic Foundry Paragraphic EQ effect and click the Plug-In Properties button to open the Properties dialog box (see Figure B.5).

Figure B.5
Use the Properties
dialog box to set the
parameters for the
Paragraphic EQ effect

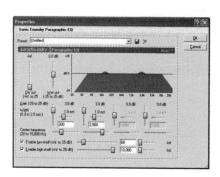

11. Activate the Enable Low-Shelf and Enable High-Shelf options. Set the low-shelf frequency to 60 Hz and the high-shelf frequency to 10,000 Hz. Set the gain for both to –Inf.

12. Set the gain for both the first and second parametric bands to +3.0 dB. Set the Center Frequency for the first band to 200 Hz and the Center Frequency for the second band to 2,500 Hz. Then click OK.

13. Select the Sonic Foundry Graphic Dynamics effect and click the Plug-In Properties button to open the Properties dialog box (see Figure B.6).

Figure B.6
Use the Properties dialog box to set the parameters for the Graphic Dynamics effect

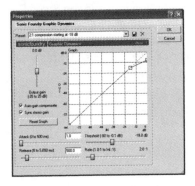

14. Choose the 2:1 Compression Starting At –18 dB preset from the Preset drop-down list and click OK.

15. Select the Sonic Foundry Normalize effect and click the Plug-In Properties button to open the Properties dialog box (see Figure B.7).

Figure B.7
Use the Properties dialog box to set the parameters for the Normalize effect

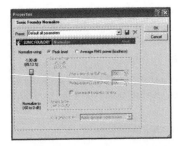

16. Activate the Peak Level option and set the Normalize To parameter to –1.00 dB. Click OK.

Output File Settings

Now that we have set up how each file will be processed, we need to set up how each file will be saved, named, and converted. For these tasks, we need to set some parameters in the Output File Settings section of the script interface as follows:

1. In the File Folder area, you can choose where the converted files will be stored. If you choose the Same As Source File option, the converted files will be saved in the same location as the original files. The Save All File In option lets you choose a specific disk location using the Browse button. For this example, choose the Same As Source File option (see Figure B.8).

Figure B.8
The File Folder area lets you choose where the converted files will be stored

2. In the File Names area, you can specify how the converted files will be named. If you choose the Same As Source File option, the converted files will have the same name as the original files except with a different file extension. The Append To Name option lets you add additional text to the original file name. For this example, choose the Append To Name option and type "-BatchConverted" without the quotes into the text box (see Figure B.9).

Figure B.9
The File Names area lets you specify how the converted files will be named

3. In the File Format area, you can choose whether the converted files will be changed to a different file format. If you choose the Same As Source File option, the converted files will use the same file format as the original files. The Convert To option lets you specify the format to which the converted files will be

changed using the Format and Template drop-down list. For more information about file formats and the Format and Template drop-down lists, see Chapter 4. For this example, choose the Convert To option. Then choose OggVorbis in the Format drop-down list and choose 128 Kbps, CD Quality in the Template drop-down list (see Figure B.10).

Figure B.10
The File Format area lets you choose whether the converted files will be changed to a different file format

Metadata

When you choose a format in the File Format area of the Output File Settings section, the Batch Converter displays the text fields associated with that format in the Metadata area. These text fields can be used to add information to each converted file. The name of each field is shown in the Field column and the value of each field is shown in the Value column (see Figure B.11).

Figure B.11
The Metadata section can be used to add textual information to the converted files

For this example, we're going to leave this section blank, but if you want to add a text field in the Metadata section, just put a check mark in the Force column next to the text field you want to add. Then click in the Value column for that field and type in the information you want to include. Do this for each text field you want to add.

Save the Script

With all the parameters set for the script, all that's left to do in the script interface is to save the script. To save a script, do the following:

1.   Choose File > Save Script As to open the Save As dialog box (see Figure B.12).

Figure B.12
Use the Save As dialog box to save your script before moving on to the next part of the Batch Converter set up process

2.   Use the Save In drop-down list to choose a folder location in which to save the script file.

3.   Type a name for the script in the File Name field. For this example, type in Internet Audio.

4.   Click Save.

5.   To later open the script, choose File > Open Script (or press Ctrl + O on your computer keyboard) to display the Open dialog box. Select the file you want to open. It will have a .BCS file extension. Then click Open.

Define Files to Convert

After you've created and saved a script, the only thing left to do is specify what files are to be converted. To do so, follow these steps:

1.   Click the Files To Convert tab at the bottom of the Batch Converter window to access the Files To Convert interface. Shown is a blank list with descriptive labels along the top (see Figure B.13). These labels designate different columns in the list and describe different characteristics of the files that will be listed here.

Figure B.13
The Files To Convert interface is a large list showing many different types of information for each of the files to be converted

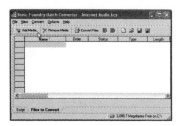

2. To add a file to the list, click the Add Media button to open the Add Media dialog box (see Figure B.14).

Figure B.14
Use the Add Media
dialog box to add files
to the list

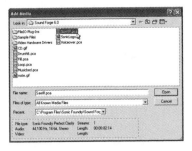

3. Use the Look In drop-down list to choose a folder location in which to find your files.

4. Select a file to be added. Information about the file is displayed in the bottom section of the box.

TIP

You can select more than one file to be added at once. To do so, just hold down the Ctrl key on your computer keyboard while selecting files with your mouse.

5. Click Open. The file is added to the list in the Files To Convert interface (see Figure B.15).

Figure B.15
Closing the Add Media
dialog box adds the
selected file to the list

6. If you need to delete a file from the list, select the file and click the Remove Media button.

TIP

For an even quicker way to add files to the list, you can drag files or folders from Windows Explorer into the Files To Convert interface. All selected files and files inside of folders are added to the list automatically.

Convert the Files

With the script ready and the files listed, simply choose Convert > Convert Files (or press Ctrl + Space on your computer keyboard) to start the conversion process. The Batch Converter goes through the list one file at a time and runs each file through the script that you created. When the conversion process is finished, each file in the list has its Status changed to Complete (see Figure B.16).

Figure B.16

You know your files have been processed when the Status column displays the word Complete

Appendix C
Backing Up Your Files

At the end of every audio editing session, I back up my files. It doesn't matter whether I'm running late or whether I'm so tired that I can barely keep my eyes open. I always back up my files. Why? Because there once was a time I didn't really think much of making backups. I did it occasionally—just to be safe—but I never thought I'd run into any trouble. Then, one day I tried to boot up my PC, and *poof*! My hard drive crashed, taking a lot of important files with it, including a project that I spent weeks working on. Believe me, after that experience, I never took file backups for granted again, and you shouldn't either.

Backing up your files really isn't difficult, and it doesn't take up very much extra time. Because of their large size, most audio files do not fit on something as small as a floppy disk, but if you have an Iomega Zip disk drive (or similar "super floppy" drive), you might be able to make a quick backup copy that way.

Back Up with Easy CD Creator

If you have a bunch of files to back up, you need a much larger storage format such as a CD-recordable drive. To back up your files to CD, you need CD-recording software, and when it comes to software, almost 90 percent of the drives on the market include a "lite" version of Easy CD Creator from Roxio. Because of its popularity, I'll discuss how to use Easy CD Creator along with your CD-R drive to back up data files. The procedure is similar to creating an audio CD, and you can use the Easy CD Creator Wizard to step through the process like this:

1. Start Easy CD Creator.
2. Choose File > New CD Project > Data CD to create an untitled data CD project.
3. In the Select Source Files drop-down list, choose the drive containing the file(s) you want to burn to CD.
4. In the file list below the Select Source Files drop-down list, select the file(s) you want to burn to CD.
5. Click the Add button to add the selected file(s) to your data CD project. The file(s) are added to the data CD project list in the bottom half of the Easy CD Creator window (see Figure C.1).

Figure C.1

When you're creating a data CD, you can select any file or files from any of the storage drives connected to your computer system

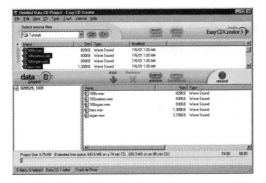

6. To remove a file from the project list, select it and click the Remove button.

7. Repeat Steps 3 through 6 until you've finished adding all your files to the project.

8. Click the Record button to open the Record CD Setup dialog box. Click the Options button to reveal the entire dialog box.

9. Choose your CD-R drive using the Select CD-R Drive drop-down list.

10. Choose the write speed for your drive using the Write Speed drop-down list.

11. Choose the number of copies you want to make by typing a number into the Number Of Copies parameter.

12. Decide whether you want to add more files to the CD later. If you want to add more files later, choose the Track-At-Once and Don't Finalize Session options in the Record Method section. If you don't want to add more files later, choose the Track-At-Once and Finalize CD options.

13. When you're creating a CD, it helps to first have your system do a test. Testing ensures the best quality and improves your chances for a successful burn. Although testing nearly doubles the time required to create a CD, Roxio recommends testing at least the first few times you use the program. After that, you can probably skip it. Choose the Test and Record CD option in the Record Options section.

14. To burn your CD, click the Start Recording button.

Back Up with Windows XP

Those of you who are running Sound Forge under Windows XP don't have to worry about extra CD-burning software because Windows XP provides built-in CD-burning capabilities—not just for audio CDs, but for data CDs as well. If you are using Windows XP, you can back up your audio files to CD using the following procedure:

1. Insert a blank CD-R or CD-RW disc into your CD recording drive. If Windows XP opens a CD Drive window, just click Cancel.

2. In Windows XP, choose Start > My Computer to open My Computer (see Figure C.2).

Figure C.2
Use My Computer in Windows XP to select your audio files

3. Double-click on the hard disk drive icon and navigate to the location of your audio file(s). Then select the file(s) that you want to back up.

4. On the left side of the window, you'll see a section called File and Folder Tasks (see Figure C.3). Click on the option called Copy This File (for single files) or Copy The Selected Items (for multiple files).

Figure C.3
Choose the appropriate option in the File and Folder Tasks section

5. In the Copy Items dialog box, select your CD-recording drive and click the Copy button.

6. A balloon message pops up in the Windows XP Taskbar saying, "You have files waiting to be written to the CD." Click the balloon to open a new window for your CD-recording drive (see Figure C.4). The right side of the window lists the files to be burned.

Figure C.4
The CD Drive window lists the files to be burned

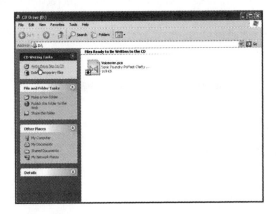

7. On the left side of the window, you'll see a section called CD Writing Tasks. Click on the option called Write These Files To CD to open the CD Writing Wizard (see Figure C.5).

Figure C.5
Use the CD Writing Wizard to burn your files to CD

8. Enter a name for the CD in the CD Name field, and click Next. Windows XP then burns your file to the CD.

9. Follow the remaining prompts and click Finish when you are done.

TIP

Sometimes, you may find that you have an audio file that is actually too big to fit on a single CD. Audio files can get quite large, especially if you are using a high bit depth (such as 24-bit) or a high sampling rate (such as 96 kHz). In this case, it would seem that you have no way of storing your file on a data CD. Well, if you use a file-splitting utility, you can get around this limitation.

A file-splitting utility takes your file and divides it into smaller files that can then be burned to multiple CDs. These smaller files represent different sections of your one large file. If you ever need to access the file again, you can copy the smaller files from the CDs to your hard drive, and then use the utility to combine them into the large file.

Take a look at the following Internet site for a list of some of the available file-splitting utilities:

http://download.cnet.com/downloads/1,10150,0-10001-103-0-1-7,00.html?tag=srch&qt=file+split&cn=&ca=10001.

Now, don't you feel better already? You can rest easy knowing that all your hard recording work won't be lost even if your computer does decide to give up on you one of these days. Believe me, it's not a fun experience.

Appendix D
Sound Forge Resources on the Web

Although I've made every effort to include as much information as possible about Sound Forge within this book, someone always has that one question that goes unanswered. However, I'm not going to leave you out in the cold with nowhere to turn.

I spent some time searching the Internet and found that it provides a number of resources you can use to locate any additional information you might need. I've tried to list all the quality sites that are available, but I may have missed a few. If you know of a great Sound Forge-related Web site that's not on this list, please drop me a note at **www.garrigus.com** so that I can be sure to include the site in the next edition of this book.

DigiFreq

http://www.digifreq.com/digifreq/
This is one of the first sites you should visit. I have created a site called DigiFreq that provides free news, reviews, tips, and techniques for music technology users. There is a Discussion area, where you can post your questions and get them answered directly by me. There is also a Live Chat area, where I hold scheduled chat sessions. You can also get a free subscription to the DigiFreq monthly music technology newsletter, which includes articles, tips, and all kinds of information about music technology, including Sound Forge. Plus, as a subscriber, you are eligible to win free music products each month, and you also have access to all the newsletter back issues. Be sure to stop by to sign up for the free newsletter and to meet all of the other *Sound Forge 6 Power!* readers out there!

Sonic Foundry Support Homepage

http://www.sonicfoundry.com/support/
The Sonic Foundry Support Homepage is also one of the first places you should look for answers. Sonic Foundry provides a large selection of materials, including product updates, a knowledge base, and more. You can also find tutorials and helpful publications and resources. And, of course, you can get in touch with Sonic Foundry's Tech Support people if you need to.

Official Sonic Foundry Forums

http://www.sonicfoundry.com/forums/

Another place you can look for help is the Official Sonic Foundry Forums. The Sonic Foundry Forums not only provide you with direct access to Sonic Foundry Technical Support, but also to other users. You can find specific topics geared toward many of the different products available from Sonic Foundry, including Sound Forge.

AudioForums.com

http://www.audioforums.com/

AudioForums.com is yet another Web site where you can find discussions about Sonic Foundry products. You won't find anything overly special about this site, but you can find some good information here, so I thought I should include it. This site also includes discussion areas for audio-related topics, such as PC Audio Hardware, Mac Audio Hardware, Studio Gear, and more.

Sound Forge Users Mailing List

http://www.viagram.no/privat/sfusers/

This site provides an e-mail-based discussion list specifically for Sound Forge users.

Synth Zone

http://www.synthzone.com/

Although not a dedicated Sound Forge site, the Synth Zone is an excellent MIDI, synthesizer, and electronic music production resource guide. You can find links to a ton of information, such as patches and associated software, for just about any synthesizer product from just about any manufacturer. You can also find links to discussion groups, classifieds ads and auctions, music and audio software downloads, and more.

Harmony Central

http://www.harmony-central.com/

Another excellent nondedicated Sound Forge site, Harmony Central is one of the best Internet resources for musicians. Updated on a daily basis, the site provides industry news and separate "departments" for Guitar, Bass, Effects, Software, Recording, MIDI, Keyboard and Synths, Drums and Percussion, Computers and Music, and a Bands Page. Sifting through all the information on this site takes awhile, but it's definitely worth the time and effort.

ProRec

http://www.prorec.com/

An additional nondedicated Sound Forge site, ProRec is one of the best audio recording resources for musicians. Updated regularly, the site provides industry news, articles, and reviews. Like Harmony Central, sifting through all the information on this site takes a while, but it's definitely worth the time and effort.

Index

Index

Index

W

Z

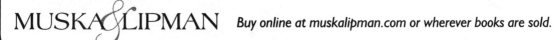

Electronic Musician

Mail in the attached card today to receive your

3 free issues
of **Electronic Musician**!

Courtesy of **Muska & Lipman** and **Electronic Musician**.